Jesus
in Ancient Palestine

by Karyn Henley

Child Sensitive Communication, LLC

Copyright © 2010, 2013 by Karyn Henley. All rights reserved.

Exclusively administered by Child Sensitive Communication, LLC.
www.KarynHenley.com

No part of this publication may be reproduced, stored in a retrieval system, or transmitted in any form or by any means (electronic, mechanical, photocopying, recording, or otherwise) without prior written permission.

Cover photo © Jupiter.com. All rights reserved. Used by permission.

Interior illustrations by Marlene Ekman. Interior illustrations © 1998 Karyn Henley. All rights reserved. Exclusively administered by Child Sensitive Communication, LLC.

Bible story excerpts are taken from the *Day By Day Kid's Bible*, © 1998 Karyn Henley. All rights reserved. Exclusively administered by Child Sensitive Communication, LLC.

Dandelion logo is a trademark of Karyn Henley.

ISBN 978-1-933803-51-7

CONTENTS

The Writers	12
Ancient Palestine	14
Priests	16
An Angel at the Altar – Luke 1:5-25	
Girls in Ancient Palestine	18
A Message for Mary – Luke 1:26-56	
Biblical Names	20
Naming the Baby – Luke 1:57-80	
Houses and Guests	22
A Trip to Bethlehem – Matthew 1:18-25; Luke 2:1-7	
The Promised One	24
Shepherds Hear the News – Luke 2:8-20	
The Firstborn	26
No More Waiting – Luke 2:21-38	
Magi	28
Wise Men from the East – Matthew 2:1-8; Luke 2:39-40	
Rich Gifts and a Dangerous King	30
A Child In Danger – Matthew 2: 9-23	
Boys' Lives and Education	32
In the Big City – Luke 2:41-52	
Clothes	34
The Man Who Wore Camel's Hair – Matthew 3:1-6; Mark 1:2-6; Luke 3:1-6	
Snakes	36
What Should We Do? – Matthew 3:7-10; Luke 3: 7-14	
Washing and Baptism	38
Jesus at the River – Matthew 3:11-17; Mark 1:7-11; Luke 3:15-18, 21-23	
Angels	40
Trying to Make Jesus Do Wrong – Matthew 4:1-11; Mark 1:12-13; Luke 4:1-13	
Men of the Desert	42
Who Is John? – John 1:19-27	
Sin and the "Lamb of God"	44
The Lamb of God – John 1:29-51	
A Wedding Party	46
A Wedding Party – John 2:1-11	
Ropes and Temple Courtyard	48
The Money Tables – John 2:13-25	
Lights at Night	50
A Night Visit – John 3:1-21	
The Jordan River	52
The Groom – John 3:22–4:3	
Wells and Water	54
Water from a Well – John 4:3-26	
Samaritans	56
Bringing In Crops – John 4:27-42	

Measuring Time 58 *A Sick Son – John 4:43-54*	**The Sabbath** 78 *On the Worship Day – Matthew 12:1-8;* *Mark 2:23-28; Luke 6:1-5*
Synagogues 60 *Jesus' Home Town – Matthew 4:12-17;* *Mark 1:14-15; Luke 3:19-20; 4:14-30*	**Pharisees** 80 *Watching Jesus – Matthew 12:9-14;* *Mark 3:1-6; Luke 6:6-11*
Nazareth 62 *Pushed by the Crowd – Luke 4:22-30*	**Galilee** 82 *Crowds – Matthew 12:15-21; Mark 3:7-12*
Fishing 64 *Nets Full of Fish – Matthew 4:18-22;* *Mark 1:16-20; Luke 5:1-11*	**Jesus' Twelve Friends** 84 *Friends and Helpers – Mark 3:13-19;* *Luke 6:12-19*
How News Spread 66 *Many Sick People – Matthew 8:14-17;* *Mark 1:21-34; Luke 4:31-41*	**How Rabbis Taught** 86 *Up the Mountain – Matthew 5:1-12;* *Luke 6:20-23*
Leper Laws 68 *People from Everywhere – Matthew 4:23-25;* *8:1-4; Mark 1:35-45; Luke 4:42-44; 5:12-15*	**Salt and the Table "Barrel"** 88 *Salt and Light – Matthew 5:13-16;* *Luke 6:24-26*
Roofs 70 *A Hole in the Roof – Matthew 9:1-8;* *Mark 2:1-12; Luke 5:18-26*	**Law and Prophets** 90 *You have Heard – Matthew 5:17-28*
Matthew and the Tax Collectors 72 *A Party at Matthew's – Matthew 9:9-15;* *Mark 2:13-20; Luke 5:27-35*	**Rabbis' Sayings** 92 *An Eye for an Eye – Matthew 5:29-42;* *Luke 6:27-31*
Pools in Jerusalem 74 *At the Pool – John 5:1-15*	**Roman Numerals** 94 *Loving and Lending – Matthew 5:43-48;* *Luke 6:32-36*
Fathers and Sons 76 *Father and Son – John 5:16-47*	**Rabbis' Prayers** 96 *Your Secret – Matthew 6:1-8*

Common Prayers 98 *This is How – Matthew 6:9-21*	**A Sin that Can't be Forgiven** 118 *A Pack of Snakes – Matthew 12:31-37; Mark 3:28-30*
Birds and Flowers 100 *Birds' Food and Flowers' Clothes – Matthew 6:22-34; Luke 6:37-38*	**Signs and Wonders** 120 *Wanting a Sign – Matthew 12:38-45; Mark 3:38-45; Luke 11:24-26*
Humor and Word Pictures 102 *The Dust and the Log – Matthew 7:1-14; Luke 6:39-42*	**Families** 122 *Family – Matthew 12:46-50; Mark 3:31-35; Luke 11:27-28*
Fruits of Ancient Palestine 104 *Good Fruit and Bad Fruit – Matthew 7:15-29; Luke 6:43-49*	**Unmarked Graves** 124 *The Cup and the Dish – Luke 11:37-46, 52*
Rains 106 *Standing in the Rain – Matthew 7:21-29; Luke 6:46-49*	**Rooftop Teaching** 126 *From the Roof Tops – Luke 11:53–12:12*
Centurions 108 *The Captain's Servant – Matthew 8:5-13; Luke 7:1-10*	**Storing Treasure** 128 *The Rich Man's Barns – Luke 12:13-21*
Funeral Processions 110 *Getting a Son Back – Luke 7:11-17*	**Servants and Slaves** 130 *The Wise Servant – Luke 12:35-48*
Prophets? 112 *What Did You Come to See? – Matthew 11:1-19; Luke 7:18-35*	**A Time of Peace and Trouble** 132 *Clouds from the West – Luke 12:51-56; 13:6-9*
Poor Meals, Rich Meals 114 *Perfume – Luke 7:36-50*	**Oxen and Donkeys** 134 *The Woman Who Couldn't Stand Up Tall – Luke 13:10-17*
Women Followers 116 *Town to Town – Matthew 12:22-30; Mark 3:20-27; Luke 8:1-3*	**Farming** 136 *Seeds and Dirt – Matthew 13:1-23; Mark 4:1-20; Luke 8:4-15*

Farming by the Months 138
  The One Who Hears – Matthew 13:16-23;
  Mark 4: 13-20; Luke 8:11-15

A Farmer's Year 140
  Weeds – Matthew 13:24-30, 36-43;
  Mark 4:26-29

Parables 142
  Seeds, Yeast, Pearls, and Nets –
  Matthew 13:31-35, 44-52; Mark 4:30-34;
  Luke 13:18-21

Beds and Sleeping 144
  Foxes Have Dens – Matthew 8:19-22;
  Luke 9:57-62

Storms on Lake Galilee 146
  The Storm – Matthew 8:23-27; Mark
  4:35-41; Luke 8:22-25

Demons 148
  The Man Who Lived by Graves –
  Matthew 8:28-34; Mark 5:1-20;
  Luke 8:26-39

Doctors 150
  Touching Jesus' Coat – Matthew
  9:1, 18-22; Mark 5:21-34; Luke
  8:40-48

Medicines 152
  The Sick Little Girl – Matthew 9:23-
  26; Mark 5:35-43; Luke 8:49-56

Sickness and Blindness 154
  Two Men Who Could Not See –
  Matthew 9:27-33

Carpenters 156
  Sheep with No Shepherd – Matthew 9:35-38;
  13:53-58; Mark 6:1-6

Transportation 158
  Like Sheep Going Where Wolves Are –
  Matthew 10:1-16, 40-42; Mark 6:7-11;
  Luke 9:1-5

Fortress of Machaerus 160
  John in Trouble – Matthew 14:1-12;
  Mark 6:14-29; Luke 9:7-9

Marketplaces 162
  From All the Towns – Matthew 14:13-15;
  Mark 6:30-36; Luke 9:10-12; John 6:1-3

Barley Bread 164
  Bread for Everyone – Matthew 14:16-21;
  Mark 6:37-44; Luke 9:13-17; John 6:4-14

Boats 166
  On Top of the Water – Matthew 14:22-36;
  Mark 6:45-56; John 6:15-21

Bread 168
  Bread from Heaven – John 6:22-40

Ways of Baking 170
  Who Will Leave? – John 6:41-71

The Pharisees' Way of Washing 172
  The Leaders' Rules – Matthew 15:1-9;
  Mark 7:1-13

Roads 174
  Angry Leaders – Matthew 15:10-20;
  Mark 7:14-23; John 7:1

Pets 176
Making People Well – Matthew 15:21-31; Mark 7:24-37

Meat and Fish 178
Seven Rolls – Matthew 15:32; Mark 8:1-7

Superstitions 180
The Evening Sky – Matthew 15:39-16:4; Mark 8:8-12

Baskets 182
Yeast – Matthew 16:5-12; Mark 8:13-21

Keys in Ancient Palestine 184
Keys – Matthew 16:13-20; Mark 8:22-30; Luke 9:18-21

Getting Behind Jesus 186
What's Coming – Matthew 16:21-28; Mark 8:31-9:1; Luke 9:22-27

Fullers, the Law, and the Prophets 188
As White As Light – Matthew 17:1-13; Mark 9:2-13; Luke 9:28-36

Mustard Seeds and Mountain Movers 190
Everything Is Possible – Matthew 17:14-21; Mark 9:14-29; Luke 9:37-43

Taxes 192
Fishing for Money – Matthew 17:22-27; Mark 9:30-32; Luke 9:44-45

Rulers and Leaders 194
Who Is the Greatest? – Matthew 18:1; Mark 9:33-35; Luke 9:46; 17:7-10

Games 196
A Little Child and a Little Sheep – Matthew 18:2-14; Mark 9:36-37; Luke 9:47-48

Value of a Name 198
In Jesus' Name – Matthew 18:15-20; Mark 9:38-41; Luke 9:49-50; 17:1-2

Lending and Debts 200
The Servant Who Would Not Forgive – Matthew 18:21-35; Luke 17:3-4

Holidays 202
Whispering about Jesus – John 7:2-31

Rebels 204
Is He the One? – John 7:14-31

"Living Water" 206
Streams of Living Water – John 7:32-8:1

Writing 208
Writing on the Ground – John 8:2-11

Lights and Lamps 210
The World's Light – John 8:12-59

The "Fathers" 212
Whose Children – John 8:38-59

Spit 214
Seeing for the First Time – John 9:1-7

Sabbath Rules 216	**Measuring** 240
How Could This Happen? – John 9:8-17	*Building and Going to War – Luke 14:25-33*
Kicked Out 218	**Coins** 242
The Men Who Could Not Believe – John 9:18-38	*Lost and Found – Luke 15:1-10*
Shepherds 220	**Costs** 244
The Shepherd's Voice – John 10:1-12	*Pig Food – Luke 15:11-32*
More About Shepherds 222	**Unclean Jobs** 246
Dying for the Sheep – John 10:13-21	*A Little and a Lot – Luke 16:1-12*
Proving Someone Was Healed 224	**Beliefs About the Afterlife** 248
Ten Men and One Thank-You – Luke 17:11-19	*Lazarus and the Rich Man – Luke 16:14-15, 19-31*
Yokes 226	**Scavenger Birds** 250
Seventy-Two Men – Matthew 11:25-30; Luke 10:1-11, 16-21	*Like Lightning – Luke 17:20-37*
Thieves and Bandits 228	**Judges** 252
The Neighbor – Luke 10:25-37	*The Judge – Luke 18:1-8*
Women Disciples 230	**Fasting and Prayer** 254
All This Work – Luke 10:38-42	*The Proud Prayer – Luke 18:9-14*
Winter at Solomon's Walk 232	**Workers and Jobs** 256
Throwing Rocks – John 10:22-33, 39-42	*Workers Who Fussed – Matthew 20:1-16*
Doors and Gates 234	**Burial in Ancient Palestine** 258
Like a Hen Gathering Chicks – Luke 13:22-35	*A Trip to Bethany – John 11:1-17*
A Dinner Party 236	**More About Burial** 260
The Best Places at the Table – Luke 14:1, 7-14	*Deep Sadness – John 11:18-41*
Feasting 238	**The Dead** 262
A Dinner Party in Heaven – Luke 14:15-24	*Out of the Grave – John 11:41-54*

Parents and Children 264
Like a Child – Matthew 19:13-26;
Mark 10:13-27; Luke 18:15-27

Expecting a Messiah 266
To Sit at Your Right Hand – Matthew 20:
17- 28; Mark 10:32-45; Luke 18:31-34

Tax Collectors 268
Up in a Tree – Luke 19:1-10

The Poor 270
By the Side of the Road – Matthew
20:29-34; Mark 10:46-52; Luke 18:35-43

Bankers and Merchants 272
The Servants and the Money – Luke 19:11-15

True to Herod's Story 274
The King – Luke 19:16-27

Perfume 276
A Jar of Perfume – Matthew 26:6-13; Mark
14:1-11; Luke 19:28; John 11:55–12:11

A King on a Donkey 278
A Colt – Matthew 21:1-9; Mark 11:1-10;
Luke 19:29-40; John 12:12-16

A Fig Tree 280
A Fig Tree – Matthew 21:10-11, 18-22;
Mark 11:11-14; John 12:17-19

Kinds of Priests 282
A Hiding Place for Robbers – Matthew
21:12-16; Mark 11:15-18; Luke 19:45-48

Making Sense of a Strange Answer 284
A Seed – John 12:20-36

A Word Picture 286
Two Sons and a Grape Garden –
Matthew 21:20-32; Luke 20:1-8

Landlords and Stewards 288
The Farmers and the Grape Garden –
Matthew 21:33-46; Mark 12:1-12;
Luke 20:9-19

Sadducees 290
Tricks – Matthew 22:15-22; Mark 12:13-25;
Luke 20:20-40

Jewish Laws 292
What's More Important? – Matthew 22:34-46;
Mark 12:28-37; Luke 20:41-44

Temple Giving 294
The Most Money – Mark 12:41-44;
Luke 21:1-4

Herod's Temple 296
When Will This Happen? – Matthew
24:1-14; Mark 13:1-13; Luke 21:5-19

The Destruction of Jerusalem 298
Days to Come – Matthew 24:15-27;
Mark 13:14-23; Luke 21:5-19

Pictures of the Future 300
No One Knows – Matthew 24:29-36;
Mark 13: 24-37; Luke 21:25-36

Weddings 302 *Ten Lamps – Matthew 25:1-13*	Trouble in the Ancient World 320 *The Rule – John 15:12-16; 16:7-8, 20-33*
Sheep vs. Goats 304 *Sheep and Goats – Matthew 25:31-45*	More Trouble 322 *Out of the World – John 17*
Thirty Coins 306 *Thirty Silver Coins – Matthew 26:3-5, 14-16; Mark 14:1-2, 10-11; Luke 21:37–22:6; John 12:37-47*	The Gethsemane 324 *Praying in the Garden – Matthew 26:36-46; Mark 14:32-42; Luke 22:39-46; John 18:1*
Passover 308 *The Room Upstairs – Matthew 26:17-20, 26-29; Mark 14:12-17, 22-25; Luke 22:7-20; John 13:1*	Greetings 326 *Judas and the Guards – Matthew 26:47-49; Mark 14:43-46; Luke 22:47-48; John 18:2-8*
Foot Washing 310 *Clean Feet – John 13:3-17*	Temple Guards 328 *Swinging a Sword – Matthew 26:50-56; Mark 14:47-52; Luke 22:49-53; John 18:9-11*
Dipping Into a Dish 312 *Lord, Who Is It? – Matthew 26:21-25; Mark 14:18-21; Luke 22:21-23; John 13:18-30*	A Trial 330 *Before the High Priest – Matthew 26:57-63; Mark 14:53-61; Luke 22:54-57; John 18:12-23*
"My Father's House" 314 *Where Are You Going? – Matthew 26:34-35; Mark 14:29-31; Luke 22:31-34; John 13:31–14:14*	Cockcrow 332 *The Rooster Crows – Matthew 26:63-75; Mark 14:61-72; Luke 22:58-65; John 18:25-27*
The Holy Spirit 316 *Never Alone – Luke 22:35-38; John 14:15-21, 26-31*	Blood Money 334 *The Son of God – Matthew 27:1, 3-10; Mark 15:1; Luke 22:66-71*
	Pilate 336 *Not Allowed to Kill – Matthew 27:2, 11-14; Mark 15:1-5; Luke 23:1-7; John 18:28-38*
Gardens and Vines 318 *The Vine – Matthew 26:30; Mark 14:26; Luke 22:39; John 15:1-11*	Dreams 338 *A Dream – Matthew 27:15-23; Mark 15:6-14; Luke 23:13-23; John 18:39-40*

A Strange Game 340
*The King of the Jews – Matthew 27:27-30;
Mark 15:15-19; John 19:1-12*

Pilate's Downfall 342
*On The Judge's Seat – Matthew 27: 24-26;
Luke 23:24-25; John 19:13-16*

Crucifixion 344
*Skull Hill – Matthew 27:31-34; Mark
15:20-23; Luke 23:26-34; John 19:17-18*

Three Languages 346
*A Sign in Three Languages – Matthew 27:35-
37; Mark 15:24-27; Luke 23:34; John 19:19-24*

Crosses 348
*Close to the Cross – Matthew 27:39-44;
Mark 15:29-32; Luke 23:35-37, 39-43;
John 19:25-27*

The Temple Veil 350
*Open Graves – Matthew 27:45-54;
Mark 15:33-39; Luke 23:44-48; John 19:28-30*

Preparing for Burial 352
*The Grave – Matthew 27:57-61; Mark
15:42-47; Luke 23:50-56; John 19:31-42*

Sealing Tombs 354
*Angels – Matthew 27:62-28:8; Mark 16:1-8;
Luke 24:1-3; John 20:1*

Witness of a Woman 356
Running to the Grave – John 20:2-18

False Stories About
the Empty Tomb 358
The Guards' Story – Matthew 28:11-15

More Sense and Nonsense 362

Night Travel 364
*Two Friends on the Road –
Mark 16:12-13; Luke 24:13-33*

Doubt 366
*In a Locked Room – Mark 16:14;
Luke 24:33-44; John 20:19-29*

Back to Fishing 368
Going Fishing – John 21:1-12

Three Questions 370
Do You Love Me? – John 21:13-24

The "Whole World" 372
*Going into the Clouds – Matthew 28:18-20;
Mark 16:15, 19; Luke 24:45-53; Acts 1:6-11*

What Tradition Says About 374
Jesus' Closest Friends

Sources 376

WEEK 1

 Monday

The Writers

As the people who had seen and heard Jesus in person grew old, some began writing about Him. They wanted people who had never met Jesus to have an account of His life. The writings we can trust the most come from the pens of Matthew, Mark, Luke, and John. Each of these writers tells what he saw for himself or what he heard from eyewitnesses. But because they have different personalities and write for different kinds of readers, each of their books comes from a different point of view.

Traditional symbols show how each writer portrays Jesus:
Matthew: a lion – symbol of Jesus' strength and authority
Mark: a bull – symbol of Jesus' servant nature
Luke: a man – symbol of Jesus' wisdom
John: an eagle – symbol of Jesus being above all, the Most High God

All four of these writers agree that Jesus is God's Son. Here are some of the ways they are different:

Matthew

- a Jewish tax collector
- saw Jesus himself
- wrote to Jews
- shows Jesus as the promised King of Jews
- writes about "kingdom of heaven"
- lots of teachings and miracles
- says "it came true"
- longest book

Mark

- a Jew, son of a rich woman
- wrote that he heard from Peter
- wrote to Romans
- shows Jesus as a servant
- likes to say "suddenly"
- lots of miracles
- tells people's feelings (afraid, amazed)
- shortest book

Luke

- a doctor; not a Jew
- interviewed eyewitnesses
- wrote to thinkers
- shows Jesus as perfect man
- likes to tell about people
- lots of parables
- tells geography
- tells Jewish customs

John

- a Jewish fisherman
- saw Jesus himself
- wrote to all people
- shows Jesus as Son of God
- talks about believing
- tells different miracles
- tells Jesus' sayings, "I am..." (Light, Way)
- miracles are called signs"

Ancient Palestine

You can see what people of Jesus' time considered to be "the whole world" by tracing it on a globe or map. Keep Israel at the center. Start north of there in Turkey. Run your finger northwest to England, then south past Spain, down into the top part of Africa and east toward Egypt. Go past Egypt, east to India, then north a bit to circle around and end up where you started. That was the world they knew.

In Jesus' time, the land we now call Israel was called "Palestine," a word that came from "Philistine." The Philistines were people who once lived in that area. You can read about the Philistines in the Old Testament. Samson and King David fought them.

Palestine was always a very important land bridge. If you wanted to go from the west of the "world" to the east, or from east to west, you would cross Palestine. If you wanted to go by land from north to south, or south to north, you would travel through Palestine. Traders and caravans journeyed across. Armies marched across. People from all over the known world passed through. Some stayed to make it their home. They brought their languages and religions and customs with them. So if you lived in Palestine in Jesus' time, you could hear all kinds of languages and learn about all kinds of beliefs.

Because it was such a well-traveled land bridge, Palestine was a place where many battles happened. Kings and rulers fought for control of this land. They wanted to be in charge of the going and coming of people and the buying and selling of the products they carried. The Egyptians had owned Palestine, the Persians had owned it, the Greeks had owned it, and in Jesus' time, the empire of Rome owned it.

Roman soldiers were a common sight in Palestine. They were the policemen of that time, not in the sense of fighting crime, but in the sense of keeping peace in towns and along roads. They also fought battles when necessary. Roman soldiers were known for forming a battle line by standing side by side holding shields made of wood and leather. Then they walked forward together. The shields made a wall in front of them. So their enemies faced a walking wall.

The eagle was the symbol of Rome and its power. People living in Palestine saw the eagle in sculptures and on buildings and shields. Of course, to the Jews, the eagle and the presence of Roman soldiers were reminders that they did not rule themselves. Most Jews tried to keep peace with the Romans, but they did not like them. The Jewish people longed to be free to run their own nation and not be ruled by a foreign army with foreign laws and taxes.

 Wednesday

Priests

In Jesus' time, the temple in Jerusalem was the one main worship place. The priests who worked there did not all live in Jerusalem. Many of them lived in different towns. They came to Jerusalem when it was their turn to serve at the temple. A priest was considered to be an important man, of course, but some were considered more important than others.

Zechariah was an ordinary priest, not one of the more important ones. He was at the altar burning incense, a mix of dry spices. He sprinkled these spices onto a flame to make a strong smell. All priestly duties had been done for hundreds of years, day in and day out. So Zechariah had served at the temple many times.

An Angel at the Altar
Luke 1:5-25

Herod was the king of Judea. At that time, there was a priest named Zechariah. He had a wife named Elizabeth. They both obeyed God's laws. God saw that they were good people. But they had no children, and they were growing old.

One day Zechariah was at the worship house. It was his turn to help with the worship. He left the people worshiping and praying outside, and he went inside. What Zechariah saw surprised and scared him. An angel was standing at the right side of the altar.

"Don't be afraid, Zechariah," said the angel. "God heard your prayer. Your wife, Elizabeth, will have a baby boy. You'll name him John. Your son will make you happy. In fact, many people will be happy when he is born. God will call him great. But he must never drink wine. He will be filled with the Holy Spirit as soon as he is born. John will help many people turn back to God. He will have the spirit and power of Elijah. He will help fathers show love to their children. Because of John, many people who disobey will want to obey. Then people will be ready for the Lord."

"How can I be sure that what you say is true?" asked Zechariah. "After all, my wife and I are old."

"My name is Gabriel," said the angel. "I come from God. He sent me to tell you this good news. But you did not believe me. So you won't be able to talk until the day this happens."

All this time, the people were waiting for Zechariah to come out. They began to wonder what was taking so long. At last, Zechariah came out, but he couldn't talk. All he could do was make sign language to tell the people that he'd seen something special from God.

Soon it was time for Zechariah to go home. So he went back to Elizabeth.

It wasn't long before the angel's words came true. Elizabeth was going to have a baby. "God has done this for me," Elizabeth said. "God has been kind. I'm not sad anymore about not having children."

Thursday

Girls in Ancient Palestine

Mary probably spent her days the way most girls did: learning from her mother how to keep house, bake, and weave. Some chores had to be done every day. One was baking the daily bread. The other was going to the well to get water for the day. Mary would have learned to carry the family's water jar on her shoulder or on her head.

Most girls did not go to school. They learned whatever their mothers or fathers taught them. We think Mary learned a lot from her mother and father because of the words she used to praise God when she went to see Elizabeth.

Girls married young. Mary was probably thirteen when the angel Gabriel came to her. The word "angel" means "messenger." Most people describe angels as having wings, and that's the way we often see them in pictures. But the Bible never shows or tells of angels with wings. In fact, angels are often mistaken for ordinary people, though sometimes they seem to glow or shine, or they wear white clothes.

A Message for Mary
Luke 1:26-56

God sent the angel Gabriel with a message again, this time to the town of Nazareth. Gabriel went to a young woman named Mary. She had never slept with a man the way a wife would. But she was planning to marry a man named Joseph.

"Hello!" Gabriel said to Mary. "You are very special. God is with you!"

Mary was afraid. She wondered what the angel meant.

"Don't be afraid," said Gabriel. "God is happy with you. You will have a baby boy. You are to name him Jesus. He will be great and will be called Son of the Most High. He will rule over God's people. His kingdom will last forever."

"How can this happen?" asked Mary. "I'm not even married yet."

"The Holy Spirit will come to you," said Gabriel. "God's power will come over you like a shadow. So the baby will be holy. He will be God's Son. Elizabeth, who is in your family, is going to have a baby too. You know how old she is. People thought she couldn't have a baby. But the baby has been growing inside her for six months. There is nothing God can't do."

"I'm God's servant," said Mary. "Let it happen just the way you said it would."

Not long after that, Mary went to Elizabeth's house. Elizabeth lived in the hill country.

Mary went in to say hello. Right away the baby growing inside Elizabeth jumped.

Then the Holy Spirit filled Elizabeth. "God has been very good to you, Mary!" she said. "God will bring what's good to your child! But what's so special about me? Why should my Lord's mother come to visit me? Yet when I heard your voice, the baby inside me jumped for joy. You have God's riches, because you believe God will do what he says."

"How great God is!" said Mary. "My spirit is happy with God. He saves me! He can tell that I know I'm not important. Now everyone will say God has been good to me. He has done wonderful, great things for me. His name is holy and good. He is kind to everyone who looks up to him. He has done powerful things for many years. He sends proud people away and brings down rulers. But he lifts up people who know he is the great one."

Mary stayed with Elizabeth for three months. Then she went back home.

 Friday

Biblical Names

In the ancient world, a name was supposed to express a person's character, nature, and personality. People thought if you knew someone's name, you knew what they were like.

A person usually had only a first name. To keep from getting people with the same name mixed up, if you were a boy, you could add to your name the word "Bar" plus your father's name. "Bar" means "son of." Simon Barjonah means Simon son of Jonah. Or you might add your birthplace or hometown to your name. Like " Mary Magdalene," which means Mary from Magdala. Or like "Jesus of Nazareth."

In Jesus' time, you might hear your name spoken in Greek, Aramaic (which all Jews spoke), or Roman (Latin). "Jesus" is Greek for the Aramaic name Joshua or Yeshua. It means "God saves."

Zechariah could not speak, so he wrote the name of his son, probably in Aramaic, which is a form of Hebrew. There are no vowels in Hebrew. Plus, Hebrew is written and read right to left, not left to right like our language. The name *John* means "God has been gracious."

Naming the Baby
Luke 1:57-80

Elizabeth's friends and family were happy. They heard what God had done for her. They got together after the baby was born to give him his father's name, Zechariah.

But Elizabeth said, "No! We will call him John!"

"John?" they said. "None of your family has the name John." They used sign language for Zechariah and asked him what he wanted to name the baby.

Zechariah asked for something to write on. Everyone was surprised when he wrote, "His name will be John." Right then, Zechariah could talk again. He cheered for God. Friends and family were amazed.

Then Zechariah was filled with the Holy Spirit. "Cheer for God the Lord!" he said. "The Lord has come to save his people. He is saving us through the family of David. It's just what he promised through the prophets long ago. My child, you will be called God's prophet. You'll see God's plans and tell about them. You'll go ahead of the Lord and make a way ready for him. You'll let his people know how to be saved and have their sins forgiven."

The news went all over the hill country. People talked about what had happened. Everybody who heard about it wondered, "What will this child be? God is with him in a special way."

As time went by, John grew. He turned out to be strong in spirit. After he grew up, he went to live in the desert.

WEEK 2

 Monday

Houses and Guests

Except for inns in big cities, most inns in Jesus' time were called "caravanseries," because that's where caravans stopped. A caravan is a group of people traveling together. In Jesus' time, they traveled with their camels, donkeys, packs, and carts. Because Bethlehem was on the caravan road between Jerusalem and Egypt, there had been a caravansery there since David the shepherd boy lived there. That was probably the inn Mary and Joseph tried to stay in.

A caravansery was like a fort, open to the sky in the middle. A well usually stood in the center of the yard. Stables lined the walls around the sides. Above the stables were rooms. Some people stayed on the upstairs level. They slept on mats or on their cloaks. Other people stayed on the lower level with their animals. It was not the safest place to stay; some travelers were thieves and might rob you or even kill you while you slept. Travelers might get rowdy and noisy. It was not a comfortable place.

It would have taken Mary and Joseph about five days of walking to get from Nazareth to Bethlehem, even if Mary rode a donkey. Maybe by the time they got to the caravansery, there were no rooms left on the upper floor and they had to stay with the animals below. Or maybe Joseph saw how crowded the inn was and said, "This is no place for my pregnant wife." They may have gone to a cave in the hills where the town's farmers and shepherds kept their animals.

Or they may have stayed in an ordinary house. People often housed guests who were traveling through, whether they knew them or not. Also, most homes were one big room. There was a low loft or platform at one end where the people slept, while their animals spent the night in the other part of the room. The Bible does not say Jesus was born in a stable, only that He was laid in a manger. It may have been in a house. Wherever it was, it was near animals.

A Trip to Bethlehem
Matthew 1:18-25; Luke 2:1-7

Here's what happened when it was almost time for Jesus to be born. First, his mother, Mary, was supposed to marry Joseph. Then she found out she was going to have a baby, God's Son. Joseph didn't know the baby would be God's Son. He just knew this didn't seem right. Mary should not have a baby before she married. So he planned to say he wouldn't marry her.

But God sent an angel to Joseph in a dream. "Joseph," said the angel, "don't be afraid to let Mary be your wife. She will have a baby boy by the power of the Holy Spirit. You will name him Jesus. He will save his people from sin."

Everything happened just as Isaiah the prophet had said many years before: "There will be a young woman. She will never have slept with a man like a wife would. But she will have a baby. She will call him Immanuel, which means 'God with us.'"

Joseph woke up from his dream. He married Mary. But he did not sleep with her the way a husband would until her baby boy was born.

At that time, Caesar Augustus was the highest ruler. He made a law that said it was time to count all the people. So everyone had to go back to the towns where their families from long ago had been born. Joseph had to go to Bethlehem in the hill country, because he was from the family of King David. Joseph took Mary with him.

While they were in Bethlehem, the baby was born. It was a boy. Mary wrapped him in warm cloth. She had to lay him in a feed box for animals, because there was no place to stay at the inn. The rooms were full.

 Tuesday

The Promised One

People of other religions had been settling in ancient Palestine for years. Egyptians, Greeks, and Romans had ruled over the land, and people from those nations had moved in to live. Caravans brought people and their ideas across the trade roads that ran through Palestine. Some of those people stayed too. All these people brought their ideas and religions. But most religions looked back in time to honor and celebrate special people or special events.

Jews were different. They looked forward to a time when God would send a man who would be a war leader and save their nation from its outside rulers like the Romans. They called this war leader the same word God had used to talk about leaders in the past – certain kings and priests and even foreign rulers like Cyrus. The word meant "the Lord's anointed (chosen)." In Jesus' language, Aramaic, the word was "Messiah." In Greek, it was "Christos" ("Christ" in English). Promised One, the Anointed, the Messiah, the Christ – all these words mean the same thing. Even so, no one ever thought this Promised One would be born to a poor family or that His first crib would be a feed box.

Shepherds Hear the News
Luke 2:8-20

That night, shepherds were out in the fields near Bethlehem, taking care of their sheep. God sent an angel to them with God's greatness shining all around. They were afraid.

"Don't be afraid," said the angel. "I bringing good news, great joy for all people. Today, in the town of Bethlehem, a baby was born. He is Jesus Christ the Lord, and he has come to save you. Here's how you'll know it's him. You'll find the baby lying in a feed box."

All of a sudden many, many angels came. They all cheered for God. "God in highest heaven gets the praise for this!" they said. "Peace is coming to earth! God's goodness is coming to people." Then the angels went back to heaven.

"Let's go see what happened in Bethlehem," said the shepherds.

They hurried into town. There they found Mary and Joseph with the baby in a feed box for animals.

Then the shepherds left to tell everyone what the angels said. People who heard it were surprised. The shepherds went back to their fields, cheering for God. They thanked him for what they had heard and seen. It was just the way the angel said it would be.

Mary thought deeply about everything that happened. She kept it all in her heart like a special gift.

 Wednesday

The Firstborn

According to Jewish law and custom, the first of everything belonged to God. You actually brought the first of your animals and crops to the temple as a gift to sacrifice to God. The first of everything included your first son. Of course, you didn't actually give your firstborn son away. Instead, you offered an animal as a sign that your firstborn was dedicated to God.

The firstborn son was seen as a sign of the father's strength. When new parents went to the temple, the father would claim that his firstborn son belonged to God. That was his way of saying that, as a father, his strength came from God.

Jesus was the sign of God's strength, because God was His Father. As God's own Son, Jesus belonged to God in a very special way.

Mary and Joseph traveled only five miles to get to Jerusalem from Bethlehem. At the temple, Joseph bought the two pigeons or doves that were supposed to be sacrificed. Richer people could afford to buy a sheep to sacrifice, but Joseph could not afford a sheep. Besides the money for birds, Joseph would have to pay five shekels at the temple as part of bringing the baby as the firstborn.

No More Waiting
Luke 2:21-38

Eight days later, Mary and Joseph named the baby Jesus, the name the angel gave him. Then they had to do what God's law said: "Every first-born boy must be God's." So after a few days, they took the baby to Jerusalem. God's law said to offer a gift of two doves or pigeons. So Mary and Joseph offered their gift. They promised God that the baby would belong to him.

A man named Simeon lived in Jerusalem. He loved and obeyed God, and the Holy Spirit was with him. Simeon had been waiting for the Promised One who would save God's people. The Holy Spirit had told him that he would see this special person before he died. That day, the Spirit told Simeon to go to the worship house. That's when Joseph and Mary brought Jesus in.

Simeon held baby Jesus and praised God. "God, you promised this," he said. "I can now die in peace. I have seen the one who will save. All people will see him. He will be like a light. He will show God to people who are not Jews. He will show Israel how great God is."

Mary and Joseph were surprised to hear this. Simeon prayed for good things for them, too. Then he said, "Many people in Israel will fall and rise because of this child. He will be a sign. Some people will speak against him. He will make it easy to see what people think. But your heart, Mary, will feel like it has been cut open."

A woman prophet named Anna was also at the worship house. She had been married when she was very young. But her husband had died after seven years. After that, she had no husband. Now she was 84 years old. Anna stayed at the worship house. She worshiped night and day. She prayed. Sometimes she even went without food to worship God.

Anna came up to Mary, Joseph, and baby Jesus. She thanked God. She talked about Jesus to everyone who was waiting to be saved.

Thursday

Magi

The men we call "wise men" were also called "magi." They were from the East, probably Persia, although they may have been from Babylon or the Arabian desert. Magi were thought to be seekers and teachers of truth, good at telling the meaning of dreams. In their country, they taught kings and princes. People honored them as holy men, gifted in astrology and expert in medicine and the science of nature.

In ancient times, most people believed in astrology, even many Jews. One Jewish rabbi said, "Wisdom and wealth is determined by the planet under which one is born." Another rabbi said, "The stars have no influence whatever upon the fate of the Israelites." So the rabbis disagreed. What common Jewish people believed depended on which rabbi they followed.

But the magis were not Jews. In their country, it was their job to study the night sky. So when they saw a star that signaled the birth of a king, they were so certain it was true that they loaded their caravan with gifts and went to see this King for themselves.

Wise Men from the East
Matthew 2:1-8; Luke 2:39-40

Some time after Jesus had been born, wise men from the East came to Jerusalem. They began asking about Jesus. "Where is the child who was born to be King of the Jews? We saw his star in the east. We have come to worship this baby king."

King Herod was upset when he heard about their questions. All Jerusalem was upset. So King Herod called the worship leaders and Jewish teachers together. He asked them where the Promised One was to be born.

They said he was to be born in Bethlehem. They told King Herod what the prophet Micah had said: "Bethlehem, you are a small town in Judah. But a ruler for my people will come from you. He will lead my people like a shepherd."

King Herod called a secret meeting with the wise men. He found out when they first saw the star. Then he told them to go to Bethlehem. "Look carefully for this baby," he said. "When you find him, report back to me. Then I can go worship him too."

 Friday

Rich Gifts and a Dangerous King

Gold is a gift for a king. The wise men knew that. But they may not have understood the deeper meaning of their other gifts. Frankincense was the sign of a priest who offered incense at the temple. The Latin word for priest is *pontifex*, which means "bridge-builder." That's exactly what Jesus did. He became a bridge to connect humans with God. Myrrh is a spice used to prepare a body to be buried. It was a sign that Jesus was born to die for us.

Because three kinds of gifts are named, many people think there were three wise men. But the Bible does not say how many wise men made the journey to see baby Jesus. We do know that they went to the exact person they should have stayed away from: King Herod. He was a dangerous man.

The emperor in Rome was the highest ruler, but he appointed Herod to be king of Palestine. Herod killed anyone he thought might be against him, even if they were in his own family. He had 10 wives. When he became ruler, he killed many of the rich Jewish leaders. Later, he killed one of his wives and her mother. He killed three of his own sons. If he thought anyone might be a threat to his power, he got rid of them.

A Child in Danger
Matthew 2:9-23

The wise men left the king and followed the star. It went ahead of them, then stopped over a house. They were full of joy. They went in and saw the child Jesus with his mother, Mary. The wise men bowed down and worshiped Jesus. Then they took out their rich gifts. They gave him gold, sweet-smelling incense, and myrrh.

Now God talked to the wise men in a dream. He told them not to go back to King Herod. So they took another road back to their own land.

Then an angel of God came to Joseph in a dream. "Get up," said the angel. "King Herod will look for the child. He will try to kill him. So take the child and his mother. Leave for Egypt. Stay there until I tell you to come back."

So Joseph got up. That night he took Mary and Jesus and left for Egypt. There they stayed until King Herod died. That made the prophet Hosea's words come true: "He was my son. I took him out of Egypt."

When King Herod saw that the wise men had fooled him, he was angry. He gave orders to kill all the baby boys in Bethlehem who were two years old or younger. That made the prophet Jeremiah's words come true: "A crying voice comes from Ramah. It sounds like Rachel crying for her children. She won't let anyone cheer her up. Her children have died."

In time, Herod died. Then God sent an angel again in a dream to Joseph. "You can take Jesus and Mary back home," said the angel. "The people who tried to kill Jesus are dead."

So Joseph took Jesus and Mary back to Israel. But Joseph heard that Herod's son was now the king. He was afraid to go back to Bethlehem. Besides, he was told in a dream to stay away from Bethlehem. So Joseph took his family to Galilee. They lived there in a town called Nazareth. That made the words of the prophets come true: Jesus would be called a Nazarene.

Jesus grew up in Nazareth. He grew strong and wise, and God's kind love was with him.

WEEK 3

 Monday

Boys' Lives and Education

In Jesus' time, only boys went to school. If you were a Jewish boy back then, you would learn your letters, practice writing, and recite what the rabbi read from a scroll. The only thing you studied was God's laws and what we call the Old Testament scriptures. Most learning was done by memorizing. Your teacher, called a rabbi, would read a verse slowly in a rhythm, and you would say each verse after him. The rhythm helped you remember it.

You would learn to write by first using a stylus on wax. The stylus was a stick of bone, bronze, or wood, pointed on one end, blunt on the other. The wax was in the form of a tablet. You wrote on wax, because you could erase it by rubbing across it with the blunt end of the stylus. When you could write fairly well, you were allowed to write with a reed pen dipped in black ink. With ink, you would write on parchment, which was a thin layer of sheepskin or goatskin. You would write the Hebrew way, right to left, using only consonants, because there were no vowels in Hebrew.

You started school when you were about six. Classes were six days a week at the town's worship house, a synagogue, the same place your father went for worship services. The teacher was always a man. You brought lunch from home: bread and wine (mixed with water). When you were 13 years old, there was no more school, unless you wanted to study more religion. In that case, you would go to Jerusalem to study with the "doctors of the law."

In the Big City
Luke 2:41-52

Once a year, Joseph and Mary went to Jerusalem for the Passover holiday. When Jesus was 12 years old, he went too. After the special holiday for God, Joseph and Mary began the trip home. But Jesus stayed in Jerusalem.

Joseph and Mary didn't know that Jesus had stayed behind. They thought he was with their friends or family. So they traveled for a whole day without him. Then they began to look for Jesus. They looked to see if he was with their family. They looked to see if he was with their friends. But they couldn't find him. So they went back to Jerusalem.

For three days, they looked through the city. At last they found Jesus. He was in the worship house, sitting with the teachers, listening to them. He was also asking them questions. Everyone was surprised by how much he understood. They were surprised at his answers.

Joseph and Mary were surprised too. Mary said, "Son, why have you done this to us? We've been worried. We've been looking for you."

"Why did you have to look for me?" Jesus asked. "Didn't you know I would be in my Father's house?"

They didn't understand what Jesus was talking about. But Mary thought about it. She kept these things as rich gifts in her heart.

Jesus went back to Nazareth with Joseph and Mary. Jesus obeyed them. He grew taller. He grew wiser. He grew as a friend to God and people.

Clothes

In Jesus' time, men, women, and children all wore tunics, although men's tunics were usually shorter than women's. Most people wore a cloak over their tunic. Women might fold their cloaks so they could carry a baby in it. People might also use their folded cloak as a cushion for a special guest to sit on. Lots of people used their cloaks as blankets at night. That's probably what Jesus did when He went into the desert.

People also wore belts made from a wide strip of cloth or leather. A dagger could be slipped between the belt and tunic. Workmen pulled the bottom back edge of their tunics between their legs and tucked it into the front of their belts to leave their legs free for working. That was called "girding your loins." Belts were also used as pockets, because they were folded in half lengthwise and worn with the fold down, the open side up. That made a space in which to carry small items like coins.

People also wore head cloths. These were large squares of cloth folded from corner to corner to make a triangle. It was placed on your head with the folded edge at your forehead and the point hanging down your back. A cord was tied around your head to keep it on.

Some men dressed differently. These were men who spent a lot of time outdoors in all kinds of weather. They might wear cloaks of animal skins or coats of woven animal hair. John the Baptist wore clothes woven out of camel hair. His belt was leather.

The Man Who Wore Camel's Hair
Matthew 3:1-6; Mark 1:2-6; Luke 3:1-6

Another Caesar was now the highest ruler of the land. He had ruled for 15 years when God sent word to Zechariah's son, John.

John was in the desert. He wore clothes made of camel's hair. He wore a leather belt. He ate honey and locusts.

Many people went to hear John teach near the Jordan River. He told them to be sorry for their sins and to be baptized. That made the prophet Isaiah's words come true: "There's a voice calling in the desert. Make the way ready for the Lord. Make a flat road for him. Valleys will get higher. Hills will get lower. Bumpy ground will get smooth. God will show who he is. He will show all the world how he saves."

Crowds of people came to hear John and to be baptized in the river. Many of them said they had sinned and were sorry. So John dipped them under the water. He baptized them, and God forgave them.

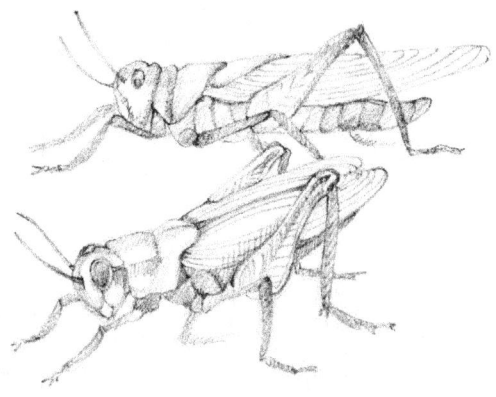

 Wednesday

Snakes

There were two kinds of snakes in ancient Palestine: 1) Colubrine snakes, which were very common, but harmless. People protected them, because they ate bugs and other pests. 2) Vipers, which were venomous and dangerous. Vipers lived mainly in forests around the Jordan River. John used the word "vipers" when he called the Jewish leaders "snakes." Maybe he meant that their teachings were poisonous and that people should stay away from them.

What Should We Do?
Matthew 3:7-10; Luke 3:7-14

John told some of the Jewish leaders, "You're a pack of snakes! Who told you to get away from God's anger? Do things that will show you are sorry for your sins. Don't say you're good enough because you're from Abraham's family. God can turn rocks into children for Abraham. What happens if a tree doesn't grow good fruit? It's cut down and tossed into the fire. So stop doing wrong and do good, or you'll be in trouble."

"What should we do?" asked the people.

"Let's say you have two coats," said John. "Share one with someone who doesn't have a coat. Let's say you have food. Share it with someone who needs food."

Men who gathered tax money came to be baptized. They asked, "What should we do, Teacher?"

"Don't take more money than you should," he said.

Men from the army asked, "What should we do?"

"Don't make people give you money," John said. "Don't lie to get people in trouble. Be happy with the money you're paid."

 Thursday

Washing and Baptism

If you lived in Jesus' time, you would not have a toothbrush. To make your breath smell better, you would chew "scented pepper," probably a kind of anise. It tastes like licorice.

You would not wash your whole body often, because there was not much water, and it was hard to carry it from the well. So you mostly just washed your hands, face, and feet. Rich people's houses sometimes had pools for bathing. In cities, there were public pools where you could go to wash. But there was no deodorant. To smell good, you might scrub yourself with strong-smelling herbs like rosemary or marjoram.

One group of Jews regularly dipped their whole bodies in water as a sign of becoming pure in heart. They were called Essenes, and they lived out in the desert. That's where John the Baptist lived. Because his father was a priest, he was a priest by birth. He could have grown up to serve at the temple. Instead, he lived in the desert. "Desert" doesn't mean it was all sand. It means the area was deserted. No one else lived there. John may have lived in one of the Essenes' communities for awhile. But by the time Jesus came to him at the river, John was on his own. His baptism was meant to prepare people's hearts to hear Jesus.

Jesus at the River
Matthew 3:11-17; Mark 1:7-11; Luke 3:15-18, 21-23

People wondered if John was the one God had promised to send. John told them, "I just dip you into water. But someone else is going to come who has more power than I have. I'm not even good enough to untie his shoes. He will soak you with the Holy Spirit. He will bring fire. He will gather what's good the way wheat is gathered into a barn. But he will burn up everything that's not good."

One day Jesus came to the Jordan River. He asked John to dip him under the water.

John tried to stop him. "You should baptize me in water," said John. "Instead, you want me to baptize you?"

"Yes," said Jesus. "Go ahead. It's the right thing to do, and we should do everything that's right."

So John dipped Jesus into the water.

When Jesus came up out of the water, he saw heaven opened. God's Spirit came down like a dove and landed on him.

"This is my Son," said a voice from heaven. "I love him. I am very happy with him."

Jesus was about 30 years old.

 Friday

Angels

Many years before Jesus' time, God's people had been taken captive into Babylon. When they returned home to Palestine, they brought a strong belief in angels with them. During the years between our Old Testament and New Testament, there was a great deal of discussion and wondering about angels. One group of Jews, priests and rich people known as Sadducees, did not believe in angels. But almost everyone else did. Most people said God had given a guardian angel charge over each person who obeyed the religious rules.

People had names for many of the angels. People gave each of them different characteristics and jobs. Among the named angels were Michael, Gabriel, Raphael, Raguel, Phanuel, and Saraquiel. Notice the "el" on the end of each name. "El" means "God." These were good angels.

People also believed there were bad angels, led by Satan. Satan means "the accuser," the one working against God's good purposes.

Trying to Make Jesus Do Wrong
Matthew 4:1-11; Mark 1:12-13; Luke 4:1-13

The Spirit led Jesus into the desert. He went without food for 40 days and 40 nights. He was hungry.

Satan came to him. "Are you really God's Son?" he asked. "Then why don't you turn the rocks into bread?"

"God's Word says that people don't live just by eating bread," said Jesus. "They live by believing every word God says."

Satan took Jesus to Jerusalem. They stood on the tallest part of the worship house. "If you really are God's Son, jump off," said Satan. "God's Word says that his angels will keep you safe. God will tell them to lift you up in their hands. You won't even hit your foot on a rock."

"God's Word also says not to test the Lord your God," said Jesus.

Satan took Jesus to a high mountain. He showed Jesus the riches of all the world's kingdoms. "I'll give all this to you," Satan said. "Just bow down and worship me."

"Get away from me, Satan," said Jesus. "God's Word says to worship only the Lord your God. Serve only him."

Then Satan left. Angels came and took care of Jesus.

WEEK 4

 Monday

Men of the Desert

It was not unusual for Jewish men to take time off and go into the desert to visit one of the communities of holy men, the Essenes who lived in the desert. Some men went there simply to be alone for awhile. Others went to try to come closer to God. Still others went to ask one of the desert-dwellers to be their teacher or give them wise counsel.

John the Baptist was not part of the Essene community, at least not by the time Jesus came along. Instead, John was a desert wanderer with people coming to him to be taught. But his call, "the voice of one crying in the wilderness," was a common expression among the holy men of the desert.

We have read that John ate locusts and wild honey. In those days, honey was a common food in Jesus' time. It was one thing used as a sweetener instead of sugar, which they didn't have. Locusts were common food as well. Locusts looked a bit like shrimp and were the same color. To prepare locusts to eat, you usually (but not always) took off the head and legs, then dried their bodies in the sun. When they were dry, you mixed them with honey or vinegar to preserve them until you were ready to eat them. Or you ground them into a powder, which was bitter. Then you mixed locust powder with wheat flour to make bread (kind of like Chinese "shrimp-bread.")

Who Is John?
John 1:19-27

The Jews in Jerusalem sent some men to find out who John was.

"I'm not the Promised One," said John.

"Then who are you?" they asked. "Are you Elijah?"

"No," he said.

"Are you the Prophet?" they asked.

"No," he said.

At last they asked, "Who are you? What should we tell the men who sent us?"

John answered with the prophet Isaiah's words. "I am a voice calling in the desert, 'Make a flat road for God!'"

"You say you are not the Promised One or Elijah or the Prophet," said some Jewish leaders. "Why, then, do you dip people in water?"

"It's true that I baptize people," said John. "But someone is here who will come after me. I'm not even good enough to untie his shoes."

 Tuesday

Sin and the "Lamb of God"

The word "sin" means "missing the mark." It's like aiming an arrow at the bull's eye of a target and missing it. To make up for their sin or to show they were sorry, Jews usually went to the temple and offered an animal. The kind of animal they offered depended on whether they were rich or poor. If you were a high priest, you offered a bull. If you were a king, you offered a ram. If you were a land owner, a storekeeper, or a trader, you offered a goat or lamb. If you were poor, you offered a pair of birds. If you were very poor, you might offer only some flour. So what John the Baptist said about Jesus being the Lamb who could take away the sin of the whole world must have sounded amazing.

The Lamb of God
John 1:29-51

The next day, John saw Jesus coming. "Look!" said John. "It's the Lamb of God. He takes away the sin of the world. This is the man I was talking about when I said a man would come after me. He is greater than I am. He lived before I did. I didn't know him myself. But I came to dip people in water to show God's people who he is."

Then John told what happened. "God sent me to dip people in water. He said I would see his Holy Spirit come down and stay on a man. Then I would know he was the one. He will baptize with the Holy Spirit. I saw God's Spirit come and stay on this man. So I know he is God's Son."

The next day John was at the same place with two of his followers. One of them was Andrew. When John saw Jesus going by, he said, "Look! It's the Lamb of God!"

Andrew and his friend heard what John said. So they followed Jesus.

Jesus turned around and saw them. "What do you want?" he asked.

"Teacher, we want to know where you're staying," they said.

"Come and see," said Jesus.

So Andrew and his friend went with Jesus. They saw where Jesus was staying. It was already four o'clock in the afternoon, but they spent the rest of the day with Jesus.

At the end of the day, they left. Right away, Andrew went to get his brother. "We met the Promised One!" Andrew said. Then he took his brother to meet Jesus too.

Jesus took a good look at Andrew's brother. He said, "Your name is Simon. But I'm going to call you Peter, the rock."

The next day Jesus wanted to go to Galilee. He saw Philip and said, "Come with me."

Now Philip was from the same town as Andrew and Peter. He went to find Nathanael. "We found the man Moses wrote about," said Philip. "The prophets wrote about him too. His name is Jesus. He's from Nazareth."

"Nazareth?" said Nathanael. "Can anything good come from Nazareth?"

"Come and find out," said Philip. So Nathanael went with Philip.

Jesus saw Nathanael coming. "Here is a man who tells the truth," said Jesus. "There are no lies in him!"

"How could you know me?" asked Nathanael.

"I saw you before," said Jesus. "You were under the fig tree. That was before Philip came and got you."

"Teacher!" said Nathanael. "You are God's Son! You are the King of God's people!"

"Do you believe because I saw you under the tree?" asked Jesus. "You'll see greater things than that. You'll see heaven open and God's angels going up and down with me."

A Wedding Party

A Jewish wedding party lasted for several days. Guests would eat the fanciest foods the host could afford. Usually that included honey cakes or pastries drizzled in honey.

The bride and groom were treated like a king and queen. The bride wore a headband that often had coins on it. The groom might wear a crown. In our time, on holidays you might go out and throw a football or shoot baskets or toss a softball. The young men in Jesus' time might go out during one of the days of the wedding and play games of skill.

At a Jewish feast or wedding, the host had to serve wine. The rabbis (teachers) said, "Without wine, there is no joy." The wine they drank was mixed with water. In fact, it was more water than wine, and it was a disgrace to get drunk. Even so, it would be terribly embarrassing to the bride and groom if they ran out of wine.

A Wedding Party
John 2:1-11

Two days later, there was a wedding in Galilee in a town called Cana. Jesus and his friends went. His mother went too.

But the people having the party ran out of wine. So Jesus' mother went to him. "They're out of wine!" she said.

"Why do you want me to take care of things like this?" said Jesus. "It's not time yet."

Jesus' mother talked to the servants. "Do whatever he asks you to do," she said.

There were six big stone jars close by. The jars were there to hold water. Each jar could hold about 20 to 30 gallons. The Jews used the water to wash their hands in a special way.

"Fill those jars with water," Jesus told the servants.

The servants filled the jars all the way to the top.

"Now," said Jesus, "dip some out. Take it to the man in charge of the party."

The servants did what Jesus said.

The man in charge took a drink. He didn't know it had been water. That's because it had turned into wine. But the servants knew. The man in charge talked to the man who just got married. "Most people give everyone the best wine first," he said. "After awhile, everyone has had too much to drink. So they bring out wine that's not as good. But you saved the best wine for now."

This was the first wonder Jesus did. It showed how great he was. Then Jesus' followers believed in him.

Thursday

Ropes and the Temple Courtyard

Only priests could go into the tall temple itself, which means Jesus never went inside the temple building. But He did go as far as any Jewish man could: into the yard in front of the building where the altar was. That yard was the men's yard. It was surrounded by a wall, Women were not allowed in. Jewish women had to stay outside the walls of the men's yard in what was known as the courtyard of the women. But it was only for Jewish women. Both men and women who were not Jews had to stay outside the wall around the women's courtyard. Even if they believed in God and had come to worship. The yard where they had to stay was called the courtyard of the Gentiles (non-Jews). It was huge. That's where people sold animals to sacrifice or changed money into coins the temple would accept.

Jesus had seen these money-changers and sellers many times before. But this time, it seems He finally got fed up with it. He made a rope whip. When he was a boy, he probably learned, like all boys, how to tie several kinds of knots. Some knots worked best for leading a cow or ox, other knots held wood together when you were building. Other knots were good for hauling things. Still others were used on boats and nets. Jesus probably knew just what kind of knot he needed for the kind of whip he wanted. Then he used the whip to chase the sellers and moneychangers out of the temple.

Jesus said the temple was supposed to be a place where all people – even non-Jews – could go and pray. But this courtyard for non-Jews was as busy and noisy as a market. The sellers were not respecting non-Jews, who had no choice as to where to pray. They were not allowed any closer to the Temple.

The Money Tables
John 2:13-25

It was almost time for the Passover holiday. So Jesus went to the worship house in Jerusalem. In the closed-in yards around the worship house, men were selling cows and sheep and doves. Other men sat at money tables. They were changing money so people from different places could buy things.

Jesus got some rope and made a whip. Then he chased out the sheep and cows. He tossed the money here and there. He turned the money tables over. "Get these out of here!" he told the people selling doves. "How dare you turn my Father's house into a store!"

Jesus' followers remembered a psalm: "I care so much for your house! I just have to do something about it."

But the Jews said, "Prove that you have the right to do this. Show us a wonder."

"Tear down this worship house," said Jesus. "I will bring it back in three days."

"Three days?" said the Jews. "It took 46 years to build this worship house."

But Jesus was really talking about his body. His followers remembered this after he died and came back to life again. Then they believed the words Jesus said.

Many people saw Jesus at the Passover holiday. They saw the wonders he was doing. So they believed in him. But Jesus didn't trust the people. He knew what was in their hearts.

 # Lights at Night

There were no street lights in Jesus' time, and there were no candles. So if you wanted to go somewhere at night you would have to see by moonlight, lamp, lantern, or torch. Torches were long poles with cloth wrapped around one end. The cloth was dipped in oil and set on fire. Lamps were shaped like bowls with lids on them. The lids usually had two holes. One held a thick wick, and the other was for pouring olive oil into. Olive oil was the fuel. The wick would soak up the oil, then you would light the wick. Nicodemus used one of these ways to see as he made his way through town to visit Jesus.

Nicodemus was a leader of a group of Jews called Pharisees. They had studied God's laws and had tried to apply them to every situation they could think of. So they had lots of little rules that they thought would help them please God. They tried to make sure all Jews knew and followed these rules. They also accused and blamed people who didn't keep all the rules.

A Night Visit
John 3:1-21

There was once a man named Nicodemus. He was one of the Jewish leaders. One night he came to see Jesus. "We know you are a teacher from God," he said. "Nobody can do the wonders you do unless God is with him."

Jesus answered, "Nobody can even see God's kingdom without being born again."

"Born again?" asked Nicodemus. "How can a person be born when he is old? I'm sure he can't go back inside his mother."

"To get into God's kingdom, you must be born of water and God's Spirit," said Jesus. "A body is born from a body. A spirit is born from God's Spirit. Don't be surprised, but you have to be born again. The wind blows where it wants to. You hear it, but you can't see where it's coming from. You can't see where it's going. It's the same with people born of the Spirit."

"How can that be true?" asked Nicodemus.

"You are a teacher of God's people," said Jesus. "Don't you understand? The truth is, we talk about things we know about. We tell what we've seen. But you people don't believe us.

"I told you about things of the earth, and you don't believe me. Will you believe if I tell you about heaven? Nobody has gone into heaven but the one who came from heaven. I came from heaven."

Then Jesus told about the time God's people were in the desert. Moses put a metal snake high on a pole. People who had snake bites could look at it. Then they would live. Jesus said, "The Son of Man has to be lifted up too. Then everyone who believes in him will live forever.

"God loved the world so much," said Jesus, "he gave his only Son. People who believe in him will not die. They will live forever. God didn't send his Son to blame the world. He sent his Son to save the world. People who believe in him will not be blamed. But people who don't believe are blamed already, because they don't believe in God's Son.

"People have to choose between light and dark," said Jesus. "Light is in the world, but people love the dark because they do what's wrong. So they hate light. They are afraid their sin will show clearly. So they won't come into the light. But people who live in truth come into the light. They want to show that they live with God's help."

WEEK 5

 Monday

The Jordan River

The Jordan River is the only true river in Palestine. "Jordan" means "the one that goes down," which is exactly what the Jordan does. It starts in hills north of the land where Jesus grew up and winds in a twisting, turning path southward, down into Lake Galilee. South of the lake, it comes out again as a river and snakes its way on toward lower land. So the Jordan is always going south and down, down, down. It ends at the Dead Sea, called the Salt Sea in Jesus' time. No river comes out of the Salt Sea. The water just stagnates there.

The place by the Jordan where John was baptizing is called Aenon, which means "double spring" (as in a spring of water). So, as the story says, there was lots of water there.

Rabbis and other teachers like John had their own followers, who were very loyal to them. Their followers sometimes got into arguments over which teacher was right or best. It would have been hard for John's followers to see lots of people leaving John and follow Jesus instead, listening to His teaching and being baptized where He taught.

The Groom
John 3:22–4:3

Jesus and his friends went into the country. There Jesus spent time with his friends. They baptized people.

John was still dipping people in water too. He was at a place where there was lots of water, and people kept coming to be baptized.

John's followers went to him. "Remember the man you told us about? He baptizes too. Everybody goes to him now."

"A person has only what God gives him," said John. "I told you I'm not the Promised One. I was sent to make things ready for him. It's like a bride and groom. The groom's best friend waits for him. He's happy to hear the groom coming. That's the kind of joy I feel.

"Jesus has to become more and more important," said John. "I have to be less and less important. Jesus is from above. He is above everything. I'm from the earth. So I talk like a person from the earth. Jesus talks about things he has seen and heard. But nobody believes him. People who believe Jesus show that they know God tells the truth. The one God sent speaks God's words. There is no end to God's Spirit in him.

"The Father loves the Son," said John. "He gave everything to him. People who believe in him will live forever. But people who don't obey God's Son won't have life that lasts forever. They live in God's anger."

Some people said Jesus was getting more followers than John. The Jewish teachers heard about it. They heard that Jesus baptized too. But it was really Jesus' followers who were baptizing people. When Jesus heard all this, he went back to Galilee.

 Tuesday

Wells and Water

When cities were first built, one of the most important things people looked for was a source of water. In Jesus' time, they dug wells or got water from natural springs, rivers, or lakes. Women had go to the well every day to get the water their families needed. In the bigger cities, there were men who worked as water carriers. They would carry water from the public wells to water-storage tanks or pools in different parts of the city. This tank water was not always safe to drink, which is one reason they drank a lot of wine. Water from a tank was used mostly for cleaning and washing. The safest water to drink came straight from a well dug into the ground or from a spring or brook where water bubbled up from underground.

Water from a Well
John 4:3-26

On his way to Galilee, Jesus went through the land of Samaria. He was tired, so he stopped at a well to rest. It was about noon. Jesus' friends went into town nearby to get lunch.

It wasn't long before a woman came to the well to get water.

"Would you give me a drink?" Jesus asked.

Jews don't like people from Samaria. So the woman said, "Why do you ask me for a drink? You are a Jew. I'm from Samaria."

"God has a gift for you," said Jesus. "If you knew who I am, you'd ask me for a drink. I would give you water that brings life."

"You don't have anything to get water with," she said. "So where are you going to get this water? You're not greater than Jacob, are you? He dug this well. He drank water from it. So did his sons and his sheep and cows."

"People who drink this water get thirsty again," said Jesus. "But they can drink the water I give and never get thirsty again. In fact, my water will turn into a fountain inside them. It will become life that lasts forever."

"Then give me this water," said the woman. "That way, I won't get thirsty again. I won't
have to keep coming back to this well."

"Go and get your husband," said Jesus. "Then come back."

"I don't have a husband," said the woman.

"That's true," said Jesus. "You've had five husbands. But the man you live with now isn't one of them."

"You're a prophet!" said the woman. "So what do you think? Here on this mountain is where my people worship. You Jews say we have to worship in Jerusalem."

"Someday you won't worry about where to worship," said Jesus. "But you people don't really know the one you worship. We Jews do know the one we worship. It's through the Jews that the world will be saved.

"Someday true worship will come from the spirit," said Jesus. "In fact, the time is already here. God is spirit. So worship must come from the spirit. It must be true. That's the way the Father wants it."

The woman said, "Someday the Promised One will come and tell us all about it."

"I am the Promised One," said Jesus.

Wednesday

Samaritans

In Old Testament times, Samaria was part of the Northern Kingdom, called Israel. The Assyrian army captured them and carried away most of the people. Assyrian captives from other lands were brought in and settled in their place. (This happened a lot in ancient times.) So the few Jews who were left in Samaria married non-Jewish settlers. When the Jews of Judah came back from their own captivity in Babylon, they said the Samaritans were no longer true Jews and would not let them help rebuild Jerusalem or the Temple. As a result, the Samaritans chose their own mountain to worship on.

Jews hated Samaritans and often insulted them. They said a Samaritan was worse than a foreigner, and a Samaritan's bread was worse than pig-meat (which Jews would never eat). But Samaria was right in the middle of Palestine. So if you traveled between Galilee (where Nazareth was) to Jerusalem or Bethlehem, the fastest way would be to go through Samaria. Even so, many Jews went out of their way, even crossing the Jordan River, to stay out of Samaria.

Bringing in Crops
John 4:27-42

About that time, Jesus' friends came back. They were surprised to see Jesus talking with this woman. But they didn't ask him why he was talking to her.

Then the woman left her water jar there. She went back to town and told people, "Come with me! Come and see a man who knows everything I've ever done. Do you think he might be the Promised One?"

The people went with the woman to see Jesus.

Now Jesus' friends were trying to get him to eat something. But Jesus said, "I already have food. It's food you don't know about."

"Do you think somebody gave him food?" his friends asked.

"Doing what God wants is like food to me," said Jesus. "Finishing God's work fills me. You say that in four more months you can bring in the crops. But look! Look at the fields! They are ready. It's time to bring crops in now. People are like crops. They can be gathered and helped to find life that lasts forever.

"The planter and the one who gathers are happy together," said Jesus. "One person plants and another brings in the crops. I'm sending you to bring in what you didn't plant. Other people have done the hard work. Now you can gather what they planted."

Lots of people from that town believed in Jesus because of what the woman told them. They asked Jesus to stay with them for awhile. He stayed two days. Many more people heard what Jesus had to say. They believed too. They talked about it with the woman. "At first we believed just because of you," they said. "But now we have heard Jesus ourselves. We know he really did come to save us."

Measuring Time

If you were Jewish in Jesus time, you would say that a day went from one evening to the next evening. Saturday would start at sundown on Friday night and end at sundown on Saturday night. You would divide a day into "watches," each measured by the position of the sun in the sky. There were two "watches": darkness and light. (Jesus often talks about darkness and light, which gives a spiritual meaning to the people's common concept of these "watches.") The watch of light began at sunrise, making the seventh hour about 1 p.m. In the old original writings of scripture, we can read about things happening "at the sixth hour" or "at the third hour." If you start counting at 6 a.m., the sixth hour is noon, and the third hour is nine in the morning.

The Jews learned to count hours from the Romans. Both Greeks and Romans used sundials and water-clocks. With a sundial, the sun would shine on a metal "hand" that stood in the center of a flat disk. This would make a shadow on the dial, which pointed to a numeral written on the edge of the disk to show what time it was. With a water-clock, a container was filled with water, which dripped out a little at a time. The water level showed what time it was. But most people measured the passage of time by the sun's position in the sky. They were not as concerned as we are today about staying "on time."

A Sick Son
John 4:43-54

Jesus went back to Galilee. People were glad to see him there. They had been at the Passover holiday and had seen the things Jesus did there.

Jesus went to the town of Cana again. That's where he had turned water into wine.

A man who worked for the king lived in Capernaum. He heard that Jesus was nearby, so he went to see Jesus. This man's son was sick. It looked like he wouldn't live much longer. So the man asked Jesus to come to Capernaum. He asked Jesus to make his son well.

"You people have to see wonders, don't you?" said Jesus. "Then you will believe."

"Please come before my son dies," said the man.

"You can go back to him," said Jesus. "He will live."

The man believed Jesus. He left to go home. On the way, his servants came and met him. They told him his son was alive.

"What time did he get better?" asked the boy's father.

"At one o'clock yesterday afternoon," they said. "That's when his fever was gone."

The father knew that's when Jesus said, "He will live." So the man believed in Jesus. Everyone who lived at his house believed too.

That was the second wonder Jesus did in Galilee.

Synagogues

Every Jewish village had a synagogue. Larger towns had more than one. But a synagogue was not really considered a place to worship. To worship, you would go to the temple in Jerusalem. The synagogue was a place to learn God's laws and pray.

Synagogues were open three times a day for anyone who wanted to come in and recite the "Shema" and other prayers. In fact, Jewish men were required to recite the Shema three times a day, so Jesus would have done this too. Shema means "Listen" or "Hear." It's the first word of this verse in Hebrew. Here is the first part of the Shema:

> Deuteronomy 6:4-7
> "Listen, people of Israel! The Lord is our God. He is the only Lord. Love the Lord your God with all your heart, soul and strength. Always remember these commands I give you today. Teach them to your children. Talk about them when you sit at home and walk along the road. Talk about them when you lie down and when you get up."

The entire Shema is longer than this. But when Jesus visited a synagogue, He would recite the Shema with everyone else. At some point after that, a man in the group would be chosen to read from a scroll. In the following story, the man chosen was Jesus.

Jesus' Home Town
Matthew 4:12-17; Mark 1:14-15; Luke 3:19-20; 4:14-21

John had been teaching in the desert. Something he said made King Herod angry. John had told Herod he shouldn't marry the wife of Herod's brother. John named other things Herod shouldn't have done. So Herod put John in jail.

Jesus heard about this. That's one reason he went back to Galilee. He went to live in the town of Capernaum by Lake Galilee. So Isaiah's words came true: "The way to Lake Galilee is by the Jordan River. People who lived in the dark now see a bright light. It's beginning to shine on people living in death's shadow."

Then Jesus started teaching: "Turn away from your sins. Heaven's kingdom is near."

People everywhere heard about Jesus. He went to teach at their worship places. Everyone said good things about him.

Then Jesus went to Nazareth, the town where he grew up. On the worship day, he went to the town's worship house, where he always went. Jesus stood up and got ready to read. Someone gave him the book of Isaiah. The words were on a long roll of paper.

Jesus unrolled it and read, "God's Spirit is on me. He chose me and sent me to teach good news to poor people. He sent me to tell people in jail they can be free. He sent me to help people who can't see so they can see again. He sent me to help people who have had a hard time. He sent me to tell about a new time, a time when God will save his people."

Jesus rolled up the paper and handed it to the man who was helping. He sat back down. Everybody was watching him. "These words have come true today," he said.

WEEK 6

 Monday

Nazareth

Nazareth was a Jewish village in a Gentile part of Palestine. It sat in a quiet, out-of-the-way place on the lower slope of the foothills of a line of mountains. Nazareth's streets were laid out like terraces. It may have been an outpost for the larger towns nearby. That means if an enemy attack was coming, people in Nazareth would see it first and warn the larger towns.

From the top of Nazareth's hill, you could look north and see the tall, snow-capped Mount Hermon in the far distance. A rich, farmed plain stretched out in front of it. The fields around Nazareth grew flax, so if the flax was in bloom, you would see fields of blue flowers. If you looked west toward the horizon, you could see the Great Sea (the Mediterranean). You would also see seaports and the roads that led to them. Turn east and you would see the long caravan-road traveled by strings of pack-carrying camels and donkeys as well as strangely dressed travelers from different countries.

In the following story, the crowd in Nazareth pushes Jesus out of town. They are probably swarming around him like angry bees, following, pushing, right out to the edge of town. They probably mean to "accidentally" crowd him right off the cliff that falls 40 feet into the valley below.

Pushed by the Crowd
Luke 4:22-30

The people had only good things to say about Jesus. But they were surprised at the way he talked. "This is Joseph's son, isn't it?" they asked.

Jesus said, "I'm sure you'll tell me the old saying, 'If you're a doctor, make yourself well.' You heard about what I did in Capernaum and want me to do the same things here. But here's the truth. People in a prophet's home town don't say good things about him.

"Remember what happened when Elijah lived?" asked Jesus. "For three and a half years there was no rain. No food grew. There were many women whose husbands had died. God sent Elijah to one of these women. But she was not Jewish. Later, when Elisha lived, many people had a skin sickness. But Naaman was the only one God made well. He was not Jewish."

Everyone was angry when Jesus said this. They all stood up and pushed Jesus out of town. The town was on a hill. They pushed Jesus right to the edge of the hill. They were going to throw him over the edge. But Jesus passed right through the crowd and walked away.

 Tuesday

Fishing

Fish was one of the most important foods in Jesus' time. Jews did not like the sea, so they did not fish in the Mediterranean or "Great Sea." But non-Jews did. They took the fish they caught to market in Jerusalem.

Jewish fishing was big business in Lake Galilee. Fishermen often worked at night as part of a team. Boats and nets and crews could be expensive, so it helped if you had other fishermen to help share the cost. Besides, it took a team to set out and pull in the big nets.

Fishermen had to know the best places in the lake to make a catch, and they had to be patient. They also had to understand the winds and the boats, know which nets to use to catch different kinds of fish, and be able to mend their nets, which were made of linen thread.

One kind of net they used was a dragnet. It was long and heavy and took two teams to use it. In the water, it formed a wall about 12 feet high and 100 feet long. To set it out, one team sailed out and circled around to spread one side of the net. The did the same with the other side. Together, they dragged it back to the shore to see what they caught.

Another kind of net was the cast net. It was round and about twenty feet across. Weights held the bottom edge down. It was thrown or "cast" from a boat or from shore. It would sink and trap fish under it. The fisherman would then dive into the water and gather the bottom of the net so the fish wouldn't be lost when he pulled it back up.

The third kind of net was a trammel net made of three sections. A section with narrow holes was sandwiched between two sections with wider holes. The boat sailed in a circle and let out the net. Fish tried to get away from the nets with wide holes, only to swim into a trap, the net with the smaller holes.

Nets Full of Fish
Matthew 4:18-22; Mark 1:16-20; Luke 5:1-11

Jesus stood by Lake Galilee. Many people stood around, listening to him teach. Peter and others who had been fishing washed their nets nearby. Their two boats were at the edge of the water. Jesus got into Peter's boat and asked him to row out on the lake. They went a little way from shore. Then Jesus sat down in the boat and began to teach the people.

When Jesus finished, he told Peter, "Take the boat into deep water. Then put out your nets. We can catch some fish."

"We fished all night," said Peter. "It was hard work, and we didn't catch anything. But if you say so, I'll put the nets out."

The men threw out their nets. Right away, hundreds of fish swam into the nets. The fish were so heavy, the nets began to break. Peter called for James and John to come and help.

James and John brought the other boat. Together, they filled both boats with fish. The boats were so full, it looked as if they might sink. The men were surprised to see so many fish.

Peter bowed down in front of Jesus. "You should leave me, Lord," he said. "I am sinful!"

"Don't be afraid," said Jesus. "You'll catch men after this. Follow me, and I'll show you how to fish for men."

So they pulled their boats up onto the land. Then they followed Jesus.

Wednesday

How News Spread

Sometimes ancient people needed to signal each other. For example, in a battle, the captain might send a signal by certain blasts on a trumpet. Soldiers would know what to do by listening to the number of blasts, some long, some short. Or they might signal by holding up a particular flag or by holding up a sword a certain way. They might light a torch on a tower or city wall or even send smoke signals or light fires on hilltops.

But what about everyday news? It spread by people telling each other face to face. Women often shared news when they got together at the well to get water. Sometimes people shouted news to neighbors from rooftop to rooftop. If a message traveled by word of mouth, it was said to be sent by "the bird's wing."

Some people wrote letters to each other. But in Jesus' time, Palestine did not have a postal service, so letters had to be sent by messenger. This might be a person hired for the job, or it might be a friend going on a journey. But because travel was so slow, news also traveled slowly. Even the most exciting news, like earthquakes or shipwrecks, would never be heard by most people. Most news traveled only about 20 miles.

Many Sick People
Matthew 8:14-17; Mark 1:21-34; Luke 4:31-41

Jesus and his friends went back to Capernaum. The worship day came. Jesus went to the worship house and began teaching. People were surprised. Jesus didn't sound like other teachers of the Law. He sounded like he knew what he was talking about.

Suddenly, a man yelled, "Jesus of Nazareth! I know who you are! You are God's Holy One! What do you want here? Did you come to get rid of us?" A bad spirit controlled the man.

So Jesus said firmly, "Hush! Come out of that man!"

The bad spirit made the man shake. Then the spirit came out with a loud yell.

The people were surprised. "This is a new teaching," they said. "Jesus talks like a man in charge. Bad spirits obey him!" The news about Jesus soon went all over the place. People all around Galilee heard about him.

Jesus and his friends left the worship house and went to Peter and Andrew's house. James and John were with them. Peter's wife's mother was at the house. Peter told Jesus that she was in bed with a fever.

Jesus went into her room and held her hand. Then he helped her get up.

Right away, she was well. She started taking care of her visitors.

After the sun set, the whole town seemed to be coming to Peter's door. They brought all kinds of sick people and people who were controlled by bad spirits. Jesus made them well. He sent many bad spirits away from people. But he did not let the spirits talk, because they knew who he was.

 Thursday

Leper Laws

Leprosy was a common disease in ancient times. But several types of skin problems were called leprosy: white patches on the skin, or open sores, or the disease that caused the loss of fingers and toes. Anyone who had leprosy was considered "unclean." That meant they were thought to be unfit to worship God. If you came near a leper or touched one, you were considered unclean too.

According to law, lepers could not cover their heads. They had to wear special clothes and live far away from towns and villages. When they went anywhere, they had to call, "Unclean! Unclean!" so other people would know to stay away from them.

The amazing thing is that Jesus actually touched a leper. The man was healed, but Jesus told him not to tell anyone what had happened. If people knew Jesus had touched a leper, they would consider Jesus unclean for a period of time. And that's probably what happened. Because the man told. Then Jesus couldn't go into the towns for awhile.

People from Everywhere
Matthew 4:23-25; 8:1-4; Mark 1:35-45; Luke 4:42-44; 5:12-15

Jesus got up very early the next morning. He went to find a place to pray alone.

Later, Peter and his friends looked for Jesus. When at last they found him, they said, "Everybody is looking for you!"

Jesus said, "Let's go to other towns where I can teach. That's why I came."

So Jesus traveled through Galilee. He spoke in worship houses and told the good news about God's kingdom. He made people well. Even people to the north, in Syria, heard about Jesus. People brought sick friends and family to him. Some were hurting very badly. Some had bad spirits in control of them. Some couldn't move. Jesus made them well. Big crowds came from Galilee and the Ten Cities. They came from Jerusalem and from around the Jordan River. Many people followed Jesus.

One day a man with a skin sickness came to Jesus. "You can make me well if you want to," he said.

"I do want to," said Jesus, and he touched the sick man. "Be well," he said.

Right away the the man was well.

Jesus said, "Go to the priest. Let him check your skin. Give him the offering you're supposed to give for getting well. And don't tell anyone how you got well."

But the man went and told, and the news went all over the place. So Jesus couldn't go into the towns for awhile. Still, people came to see Jesus from everywhere. They came to be made well.

Roofs

In Jesus' time, roofs were flat. You would climb a stairway or wooden ladder outside the house to get to the roof. You might work on your roof, because the breeze would cool you there. On hot nights, you and your family might sleep on your roof.

To make a roof, you would first lay out beams, long boards that crossed from the top of one wall to the other. You covered these beams with mud mixed with straw, which hardened when it dried. After a hard rain, you had to roll a heavy stone cylinder across the roof to repack it so it wouldn't leak. Jesus probably had to do that at his own house when he was growing up. Being a carpenter, he probably laid out many roof beams. In the following story, people dig through the straw and dried mud and let a sick friend down through the roof to get to Jesus.

What Jesus says to the sick man makes more sense when we understand that people in Jesus' time thought they were sick because of something bad they had done. One rabbi said, "Offend your maker by doing wrong, and you will have many visits to doctors." Another said, "The sick don't get well until their sins are forgiven." So when Jesus told a sick man, "Your sins are forgiven," it was the same as saying, "You're well now." The man's healing proved to the people that the man's sins really had been forgiven.

A Hole in the Roof
Matthew 9:1-8; Mark 2:1-12; Luke 5:18-26

Jesus went back to Capernaum. News went around that he was home. Crowds gathered at the house where he was staying. Soon the house was full of people and there was no more room. There wasn't even room around the door outside. But Jesus taught the people right there.

Then four men walked up carrying a mat. On the mat lay a friend who couldn't move. But it was so crowded, they could not get to Jesus. So they dug through the roof. They made a hole right above Jesus. Then they let the sick man down through the hole on his mat.

Jesus saw how much they believed. He told the sick man, "Your sins are forgiven."

Some teachers of God's laws were watching. They thought, "How can Jesus say that? Only God can forgive sins."

Jesus knew what they were thinking. He said, "Is it easier to say, 'Your sins are forgiven'? Or to say, 'Get up, take your mat with you, and walk'? I have the right to forgive sins here on earth. You'll see."

Then Jesus looked again at the man who couldn't move. He said, "Get up. Take your mat with you. You can go home now."

The man stood up, picked up his mat, and walked out. Everyone was very surprised. They praised God. They said, "We never saw anything like this before!"

WEEK 7

 Monday

Matthew and the Tax Collectors

In ancient Palestine, people respected some jobs and thought other jobs were lowly. The high priest was the most respected. Traders, men who bought and sold spices, cloth, and other goods from different lands, were rich and respected. Weaving was not considered respectable, because it was women's work. The baker was not respected either. But the tax collector was hated, because he worked for the Roman government and was allowed to take more money than the tax really was. Tax collectors could grow richer while taxed people grew poorer.

Matthew was considered one of the worst kinds of tax collectors. He sat at a tax booth in a busy part of town, taking the taxes for people who traveled. He could ask people to pay a tax on what they were bringing into town or on what they were taking out of town. He made them pay for using bridges and roads and boat landings. He could even invent a tax if he wanted to. It was said that this kind of tax collector had almost no hope of repenting and becoming a good Jew.

Because of his tax collecting, Matthew was probably rich. So at Matthew's party, Jesus would have eaten on a plate, maybe one made of gold or silver. If you had gone with Jesus to Matthew's, you probably would not eat with your fingers like you would at home. Instead, you would use knives and spoons of ivory or wood. But no forks. They didn't have forks at all in ancient times.

A Party at Matthew's
Matthew 9:9-15; Mark 2:13-20; Luke 5:27-35

Jesus walked out by the lake. Lots of people came to see him there, so he started teaching them. Then Jesus saw Matthew sitting at his tax table. Matthew was a tax worker. He took the tax money that people had to pay. "Follow me," Jesus said to Matthew.

So Matthew followed Jesus. He even gave a big dinner party for Jesus at his own house. Tax workers and many other people came to his party. Some of the Jewish leaders came too. But they didn't like tax men, because they took more money than they should.

The leaders talked to Jesus' friends about it. "Why do you eat and drink with tax workers? They're sinners."

Jesus heard what the leaders said. "People who are well don't need a doctor," said Jesus. "Sick people do. Why don't you go and learn what this means? 'I want your kindness, not your gifts.' I didn't come to find people who are doing right. I came to find people who are doing wrong."

Then the leaders said, "John's followers go without food to help them pray and worship God. Our followers do too. But your followers eat and drink."

"The groom is with his friends," said Jesus. "Why should his friends stop eating now? One day the groom will be gone. Then there will be days when they don't eat."

 Tuesday

Pools in Jerusalem

Jerusalem was in a dry area of Palestine. At times, like during the "dry season," very little water came in from the spring they depended on. So the people of Jerusalem had built water storage tanks, called cisterns, and pools to collect rain water. In Jesus' time, there may have been more water storage tanks than houses. Most of the pools were carved from stone, and at least some of them were deep enough to swim in. A stone trough, channel, or gutter sloped into the pool, carrying rainwater to it.

Pools were a common meeting place. It was easy to say, "I'll meet you at the Pool of Siloam after lunch." There was also the Pool of Towers, near Herod's palace. And there was a pool near the Sheep Gate. That pool held water that bubbled once in awhile. People believed that whoever could get into the water first when it bubbled would be healed. Some people claimed that an angel stirred the water to make it bubble.

At the Pool
John 5:1-15

Jesus went to Jerusalem for a Jewish holiday. Now in Jerusalem there was a gate called the Sheep Gate. Near the Sheep Gate there was a pool. Five covered sidewalks led to the pool. Lots of sick people gathered there, thinking the water could make them well when it bubbled.

One man lying by the pool had not been able to walk for 38 years. Jesus saw him and asked, "Do you want to get well?"

"Yes," said the man. "But no one will help me into the pool. The water bubbles, and I try to get in. But somebody else always gets in first."

"Get up," said Jesus. "Pick up your mat. Walk."

Right away, the man's legs got strong. He picked up his mat, and he walked.

Now this happened on a worship day. So when people saw the man carrying his mat, they said, "This is a worship day. God's law says not to carry mats on a worship day."

"A man made me well," he said. "He told me to pick up my mat and walk."

"Who was this man?" asked the leaders. "Who told you to pick up your mat and walk?"

The man with the mat didn't know who had made him well. Jesus had quietly moved away into the crowd.

Later, Jesus saw the man at the worship house. Jesus said, "You're well now. Don't sin anymore. Not being able to walk is bad. But it's not as bad as what could happen if you keep sinning."

The man went and found the Jewish leaders. He told them that Jesus had made him well.

☐ Wednesday

Fathers and Sons

In Jesus' time, a boy grew up to do whatever his father did. If your dad was a baker, you grew up to be a baker. If your dad was a merchant-trader, you grew up to be a merchant-trader. You would keep your same job all your life.

Since Joseph was a carpenter, Jesus was trained to be a carpenter. Until He was about thirty years old, that's what He did for a living. But when Jesus was twelve, He let Mary and Joseph know that He knew God was His Father. Jesus said His Father was always working. Like a good son, Jesus grew up to do exactly what His Father did.

Father and Son
John 5:16-47

The Jewish leaders got angry at Jesus, because he made someone well on a worship day.

"My Father is always at work," said Jesus. "He is working even today. So I work too."

The leaders were angry that Jesus was calling God his own Father. He was making himself the same as God. So they tried to find a way to kill Jesus.

Jesus said, "The Son can't do anything by himself. He does only what he sees his Father do. Whatever the Father does, the

Son does too. The Father loves the Son. He shows the Son everything he does. He will show the Son even greater things than you've seen. The Father gives life to the dead. In the same way, the Son gives life too.

"The Father doesn't judge anyone," said Jesus. "He lets his Son judge. If the Son is not important to you, then the Father is not important to you. The Father sent the Son. So believe him. Then you'll have life now and forever. You won't be blamed. You'll move out of death into life. It's time for the dead to hear the Son's voice. Everyone who hears will live. Someday, people in their graves will hear the Son's voice and will come out. People who did good things will get up and live. People who sinned will get up and be blamed.

"You went to see John," said Jesus. "He told you the truth. He was like a lamp that gave light for awhile. You chose to enjoy his light. But I can tell about my Father better than John. My work shows that the Father sent me. You didn't hear his voice or see how he looks. His word doesn't live in you, because you don't believe me.

"You work hard at studying God's words," said Jesus. "You think that's the way to have life forever. Those words tell about me. But you won't come to me to have life. God's love is not in your hearts. Other people come in their own names, and you believe them. I come in my Father's name, but you don't believe me. You want other people to cheer for you. But you don't even try to get God to cheer for you."

The Sabbath

When the first evening stars appeared on Friday, the hazzan, the synagogue leader, blew three sharp blasts on the ram's horn. Everyone stopped working and the Sabbath began. On Saturday morning, you would go to the synagogue. There the prayer leader prayed aloud:

> We bless and praise God,
> the eternal and mighty,
> who gave his promises
> to Abraham, Isaac, and Jacob,
> and who will bring a redeemer
> and give peace to his people, Israel.

When he finished, everyone said, "Amen," then, "Hear, O Israel: The Lord our God is one Lord."

The hazzan then brought out a box containing a Torah scroll, one of the first five books of the Old Testament. He held the scroll up for everyone to see. The prayer leader chose three men to read each of three parts. After the reading, the hazzan placed the scroll back in the box. A speaker would now talk about what was just read. After that, someone would be called on for the "haftarah," a reading from the prophets. The reader would then sit down and comment on what he had read.

The last blessing of the day had to be said without stopping to take a breath: "May God bless you and keep you and make his face shine upon you and give you peace" (Numbers 6:24, 25). Another blast on the ram's horn called an end to the Sabbath.

On the Worship Day
Matthew 12:1-8; Mark 2:23–28; Luke 6:1-5

One worship day, Jesus and his friends walked through some wheat fields. His friends were hungry, so they picked some of the wheat and ate it.

Some Jewish leaders saw them. "You can't pick wheat on a worship day," they said. "It's against God's law."

"Remember when David and his men were hungry?" said Jesus. "They ate some of the priests' bread in the worship house. Or maybe you remember that priests work on the worship day, and God doesn't blame them. There's someone here who is greater than the worship house. God's word says he wants your kindness, not your gifts. If you knew what that meant, you wouldn't be mad. We didn't do anything wrong. People were not made for the worship day. Instead, the worship day was made for people. Besides, I am Lord of the worship day."

Pharisees

As a reminder: Pharisees were men who had studied God's laws and tried to make sure all Jews knew and followed these rules. The rabbis said there were seven kinds of Pharisees:

1. "What do I get out of it?" Pharisees

2. "I look the part" Pharisees

3. "Oh, my poor head" Pharisees
   (because they walked along the street with their head down in order not to see women, so they banged into walls)

4. "Pestle" Pharisees (who walked so bent over they looked like a pestle in a
   mortar)

5. "What is my duty so I may do it?" Pharisees

6. "I do one good deed every day" Pharisees

7. "Respect and love God" Pharisees (which they said were the only true Pharisees)

Watching Jesus
Matthew 12:9-14; Mark 3:1-6; Luke 6:6-11

Another worship day came. Jesus went to the worship house and began to teach. A man was there whose right hand was small and twisted. The leaders watched Jesus to see what he would do. They wanted a reason to blame Jesus for doing something wrong.

At last they asked Jesus, "Is it right to make people well on the worship day?"

Jesus said, "Let's say you have a sheep, and it falls into a pit on the worship day. Wouldn't you pull it out? A person is a lot more important than a sheep. So it's right to do good on the worship day."

Jesus looked at the man whose hand was small and twisted. "Stand up," said Jesus. He turned to the people. "Should we do good or bad on the worship day? Should we save lives or kill on the worship day?"

Nobody answered. The people were all quiet.

Jesus looked around. He was very upset because their hearts were hard. He could see that they didn't care about God. He looked at the sick man. "Hold your hand out," he said.

The man held his hand out. It reached out all the way. It was well.

But the people got very angry. They began planning to get even with Jesus. The leaders talked about killing him.

WEEK 8

 Monday

Galilee

Jesus is sometimes called "the Galilean" because the part of ancient Palestine where he grew up was nicknamed Galil ha-Goyim. That meant the "circle of unbelievers." Over time, Galil ha-Goyim was shortened to Galil and then became Galilee. It earned its nickname by its mixed population. Lots of non-Jews lived there, and caravan travel from all over the known world passed through, bring their different ideas, customs, and languages. Several Greek cities had been founded there, and the Romans had moved in too. The Jews of Judea, where Jerusalem was, considered Galileans to be lower class on the scale of true Jewishness. Galileans were thought to be either country folk or rebels, undisciplined and tainted because of living among non-Jews.

Actually, the soil was better in Galilee than down south near Jerusalem. There were more springs and they got more rain. The land was hilly, but there were stretches of plains, too. Wheat, barley, fruit trees, and flax grew well there. And of course, the lake was rich with fish.

The following story takes place on the shores of Lake Galilee, often called the Sea of Galilee. It's also called the Sea of Chinnereth, Lake Gennesaret, or Kineret, names that come from the Hebrew word that means "harp." Lake Galilee is shaped like a harp.

Crowds
Matthew 12:15-21; Mark 3:7-12

Jesus and his friends went to the lake. Many people from Galilee followed him. Some came from across the Jordan River. Some came from Tyre. Some came from Jerusalem and other places. The crowd was huge. Jesus had made many people well, so sick people kept pushing toward him, wanting to touch him. People controlled by bad spirits fell down before Jesus. They called out, "You are God's Son!" But Jesus was very firm with them and told them not to tell anyone who he was.

So the words of Isaiah came true: "Here is my servant, the one I chose, the one I love. I'm happy with him. I'll put my Spirit on him, and he will tell all nations what is right and fair. He won't fuss or fight or cry out. People in the streets won't hear his voice. My servant won't hurt bent plants, people who are sad. He won't blow out glowing candles, people who are glad. He will stand up for what's right, and he will win. The nations will hope in his name."

Jesus' Twelve Friends

Jesus had many followers, but He chose twelve of them to be his closest helpers. Just as we do, Jesus had many different, interesting friends.

Peter: a fisherman whose name means "the rock;" sometimes spoke without thinking

Andrew: a fisherman, Peter's brother, brought people to Jesus

James: a fisherman, John's brother (the brothers were called "sons of thunder")

John: a fisherman, one of Jesus' best friends

Philip: spoke Greek well

Nathanael: an honest man

Matthew: a tax collector

Thomas: eager to follow Jesus, even to die

James the Younger: may be related to Jesus

Simon: ready to fight against Rome

Thaddaeus: asked about Jesus' plans

Judas: kept the money bags

These are not the only people who followed Jesus, traveled with Him, and helped Him. But these are the ones Jesus chose to train and teach especially for carrying on the Father's work when Jesus was gone.

*F*riends and Helpers
Mark 3:13-19; Luke 6:12-19

Jesus went up on a mountain to pray and spent all night there, praying to God.

In the morning Jesus called his friends. He picked twelve of them to be in his closest circle of friends and helpers. He chose Peter and his brother Andrew, James and his brother John. He chose Philip and Nathanael, Matthew, Thomas, and Simon. He chose another James, who was the son of Alphaeus and Judas, whose father's name was James. Then Jesus chose another Judas, called Judas Iscariot. He turned out to be an enemy.

Jesus led these men to a big, flat place. A large crowd of his followers stood there. People had come from all over the place to listen to Jesus. Some had come to be made well. People bothered by bad spirits were set free. Everyone tried to touch Jesus, because power was coming from him, and he was making everyone well.

How Rabbis Taught

Rabbis taught about God's rules and ways to please God. They often became quite famous. Disciples followed them in order to learn from them. ("Disciple" means "learner.") Rabbis often taught their disciples as they walked along a road. Or the rabbi would sit and his disciples would gather around to hear him teach. That's just what Jesus did. He taught as he walked, and He also sat to teach. Lots of people called Him "Rabbi."

Some of Jesus teachings sound like what other rabbis taught. On the other hand, people said there was something different about Jesus. They said He spoke with authority, that He sounded like He knew what He was talking about. How was Jesus different?

1. Other rabbis usually quoted each other or the old scriptures to prove their points. They would say things like, "So-and-so says . . ." But Jesus said, "Truly, truly I say to you –." He was speaking with His own authority and God's.

2. Other rabbis would go by what the doctors of the law had said and written. Jesus often said, "You've heard that you should . . . But I tell you to . . ." He would often change what had been written in order to encourage people to do better than what was written.

3. Jesus raised the standard. He said people should do better than scribes and Pharisees.

4. No rabbi would have dared to say that 'one greater than the temple' is here. To all good Jews, rabbis especially, there was nothing greater than the temple except God. In the same way, no rabbi would dare say that there would be a time coming when the true worshiper would worship not in Jerusalem, but "in spirit and truth."

5. Jesus said one thing that even the greatest rabbis never taught: Love your enemies.

Up the Mountain
Matthew 5:1-12; Luke 6:20-23

Jesus saw how many people were coming to hear him. So he went up on the side of a mountain and sat down. His followers gathered around him. Then he began to teach.

"God will bring good to people who know they need him. The kingdom of heaven belongs to them," said Jesus. "God will bring good to people who cry. They will feel better. Good will come to people who think others are important. The earth will belong to them. Good will come to people who are hungry and thirsty for what's right. They'll be filled. Good will come to people who are kind. God will be kind to them. Good will come to people whose hearts are clean and not dirty from sin. They'll get to see God. Good will come to people who make peace. They'll be called God's children. Good will come to people who get hurt for doing what's right. The kingdom of heaven belongs to them. Good will come when people laugh at you. They might hurt you for doing good or lie about you because of me. But God has great gifts for you in heaven. So be happy. People also hurt the prophets who spoke God's words."

Salt and the Table "Barrel"

Many spices were grown in Palestine: mustard, capers, cumin, mint, dill, garlic, onions, and salt. In Palestine, salt came from the salt pits near the Salt Sea (Dead Sea). Romans said that because salt came from pure sun and pure sea, salt was the purest element in the world. Greeks said it was divine. The Jews valued it and used it to season food, preserve food, and season their grain offerings.

It seems strange that Jesus talked about salt losing its savor, because that usually doesn't happen with salt. But it may be that the salt from near the Salt Sea was not pure. Some people have said that the sodium chloride (salt) could seep out of the crystals, leaving a tasteless stuff behind. Other people think maybe Jesus was talking about the salt used in outdoor ovens. To help keep the heat in, people would add a layer of salt under the tile floor. After the oven had been used a lot, the salt would not work as well to keep heat in, so they would put new salt in and throw the old salt out on the road. Either way, Jesus' teaching still means the same thing.

In Jesus' time, every family had a container large enough to measure out a bushel of barley or wheat that they needed for bread. Poor people often turned this container upside down and used it as a low table. That's what Jesus was talking about when He said, "No one lights a lamp and puts it under a bushel (some people say bowl or barrel)."

Salt and Light
Matthew 5:13-16; Luke 6:24-26

"Watch out if you are rich," said Jesus. "That means you have your gifts already. Watch out if you have plenty of food now. You may go hungry. Watch out if you laugh now. You may end up crying. Watch out when people say good things about you. That's what people said about prophets who lied."

"You're like salt here on earth," said Jesus. "But what if the salt stops being salty? Can it get salty again? No. It's good for nothing. It has to be thrown out. Then it's good only for walking on.

"You're like a light to this world," said Jesus. "You're like a city high on a hill. It's up where everyone can see it. People don't put a lamp under a basket. Instead, they put it where it will shine and light up the house. So let your light shine where people can see it. They'll see the good you do and cheer for God your Father."

Friday

Law and Prophets

In Hebrew, the Jewish language, the word "prophet" means "one who is called to speak." In Greek, the word means "to speak for." In the Old Testament, prophets could tell what was going to happen. They gave advice to kings and rulers, and they reminded God's people to follow His ways. You might say they were a "moral compass" for the Jews. People often made fun of them or disrespected them (especially people the prophets were criticizing). Still, prophets had great influence.

So while the law told people how to live ("Do this and this and this"), the prophets told people they were not living by the law ("You're in trouble because you're not doing this and this and this"). But nobody could live a perfect life. No one ever followed all the laws all the time. So everyone was in trouble. That's why Jesus came: to live a perfect life for us. Jesus' perfect love fulfilled the law and the prophets.

You Have Heard
Matthew 5:17-28

"Don't think I came to get rid of the Law or what the prophets wrote," said Jesus. "I didn't come to get rid of these words. I came to make them come true. Even the smallest law is important until everything happens the way God planned. If people break the smallest law, they'll be the smallest in the kingdom of heaven. If people teach others to break God's laws, they'll be the smallest in the kingdom of heaven too.

"But people who obey God's laws will be great in heaven. So will people who teach others to obey," said Jesus. "You must be even better than your Jewish leaders. If not, you'll never get into heaven's kingdom. You've heard that the Law says not to kill. But I say this. Anyone who is angry with another person gets in trouble. Anyone who isn't kind answers to the judge. If someone says, 'You fool,' he will be in danger of hell fire. You've heard, 'Don't have sex with someone you're not married to.' But I tell you not to let your mind even think about it. If you think it, you've done it in your heart.

"Let's say you bring a gift for God to the altar," said Jesus. "Then you remember someone is angry at you. Leave your gift, and go make peace with that person. Then come back and give your gift. Make peace quickly with a person who blames you for something. Do it before you get to the judge. If you don't, the judge will give you to the officer, and you might be put in jail. There you'll stay until you've paid the last penny.

WEEK 9

 Monday

Rabbis' Sayings

Jesus had heard rabbis' teachings, so He probably knew some or all of the following sayings of rabbis, which were common in His time:

Repenting is like the sea. You can bathe in it at any hour.

If you break a promise, you're as bad as a person who worships idols.

If you pray in your house, you build a wall around it stronger than iron.

If you welcome the wise, it's like greeting God.

If two study the Law together, the glory of God is among them.

If you beg someone to forgive you, don't do it more than three times.

God lets the poor be here always, so we'll have lots of chances to do good.

A child should get fat on the Law, as an ox gets fat in the stall.

It's better to burn in fire than to insult your neighbor in public.

If you repent, you reach the throne of God.

Fools bring a sacrifice for sin, but they do not repent.

If you judge your neighbor well, God will judge you well.

Do not judge a man until you have been in his place.

God is as near to his creatures as the ear to the mouth.

There is no death without sin and there is no pain without sin.

An Eye for an Eye
Matthew 5:29-42; Luke 6:27-31

"Is your eye making you sin?" asked Jesus. "Then it would be better not to have an eye. Is your hand making you sin? Then it would be better not to have a hand. You don't want to sin and be sent to hell someday. You've heard that a man who leaves his wife is supposed to give her a divorce paper. I say anyone who leaves his wife and marries another woman is sinning. He is sinning unless she left him first. Anyone who marries a divorced woman is sinning.

"You've heard that you're to keep promises you made to God," said Jesus. "When you say yes, mean 'yes.' When you say no, mean 'no.' Anything more than that comes from Satan. Don't make promises in heaven's name. That's where God sits to rule. Don't promise by the earth's name. It's the stool for God's feet. Don't promise by Jerusalem. It's a great king's city. Don't promise by your own head. You can't even make your hair white or black.

"You've heard that if somebody hurts you, then you can hurt that person," said Jesus. "But I tell you not to fight a sinful person. What if someone hits you on your right cheek? Then turn your left cheek to him. What if someone takes your coat? Give him your shirt, too. What if someone makes you walk a mile with him? Go two miles. Give to people who ask you for something. Don't say no to people who want to borrow something. Treat other people the way you want to be treated."

Roman Numerals

In Jewish schools, the goal was for boys to be able to read the Torah. So learning to read was the most important task. But boys were also taught enough math to calculate dates and read the Jewish calendar. After that, they just needed to know enough to add and subtract the values of coins in order to buy and sell in the marketplace and pay their taxes.

Ancient people had different ways of keeping track of numbers when they were adding or subtracting. Some used their fingers. Some used pebbles. Others tied knots in a rope. Sometimes they made marks on a tablet. A common way to do large sums was to use an abacus, a frame with beads strung on wires or rods. With practice, you could get very fast sliding beads and calculating on an abacus.

To write numerals, ancient Jews used a combination of letters like Roman numerals. The numerals we use every day were invented in the land of Arabia, so our numerals are called Arabic numerals. But in Jesus' time, the Romans were in charge, so they used Roman numerals. In Roman numerals, when two or more numerals come together, you have to figure out what they mean. If the lesser numeral comes first, you subtract it from the next numeral. V is five. So IV would be four. If the greater numeral comes first, you add the next numeral to it. VI would be six. Ten is X. Fifty is L, so forty is XL. Sixty is LX. One hundred is C.

If your father was a merchant or banker or money-changer,

he would train you to do the math necessary to learn that business. People who loaned money had to keep track of what they were owed by writing down the numerals in ledgers, keeping their "accounts."

Loving and Lending
Matthew 5:43-48; Luke 6:32-36

"You've heard that you're to love your neighbor and hate your enemy," said Jesus. "I say, love your enemies. Pray for people who hurt you. Then you will be children of your Father in heaven. Your Father makes the sun shine on all people, bad and good. He sends rain for people who do right and for people who do wrong. What if you love only the people who love you? What good does that do? Even sinners love people who love them. What if you're friendly only to people you like? How is that different? Even people who don't believe in God do that.

"Let's say you lend money to someone, knowing he'll pay you back," said Jesus. "What good does that do? Even people who don't believe in God do that. They lend money when they know they'll be paid back. Love your enemies. Do good to them. Lend to them. Don't look for anything back. Then God will plan good things for you. You will be his children. God is kind to people who are not even thankful. He is kind to sinful people. So be kind like your Father."

Rabbis' Prayers

Jewish men (thirteen years old and older) prayed in the morning, at noon, and in the evening. (Women, children, and slaves did not have to pray at these times.) Before praying, the good Jew would cover his head with a prayer-shawl, a kind of scarf so large that it draped to the waist. Then he would turn toward Jerusalem, or if he was already in Jerusalem, he would turn toward the Temple. If he was in the Temple, he would turn toward the inner room, the Holy of Holies. Usually he would stay standing and raise his hands toward heaven, but sometimes he would lay on the ground. He usually prayed aloud.

Farmers would not plow before praying something like, "Lord, my task is the red, the green is yours. We plow, but it is you who give the crop." (Red is for the reddish dirt.)

Rabbis usually taught their disciples to pray long prayers. One rabbi said, "The person who prays a long prayer is heard." Another said, "Whenever good people make their prayer long, their prayer is heard." Jesus did not agree.

Your Secret
Matthew 6:1-8

"Don't do good things just so people will see you. If you do, God your Father won't do good things for you," said Jesus. "Don't show off when you give. Some people give so other people will say good things about them. The truth is, that's all the good that will come to them. Give to the poor. Don't tell your left hand what your right hand does. That way, it will be a secret. Your Father sees things that are done in secret. So he will do good things for you.

"What about praying?" said Jesus. "Some people pray just so others will see you. The truth is, being seen is all the good that will come to them. Go to your room when you pray. Close the door. Then pray to the Father you can't see. Your Father sees everything you do in secret. He will do good things for you. Don't just chatter away when you pray. People who don't believe in the true God do that. They think their god hears them if they use lots of words. But your Father knows what you need even before you ask."

Thursday

Common Prayers

Good Jews were supposed to say a prayer of thanks after every meal. Rabbis said that "a meal without a prayer is a meal accursed." People also commonly prayed asking-prayers. They felt that asking-prayers were very important, because they believed they needed God's help in everything. They knew God's gifts were necessary for their daily lives. Jesus was saying exactly that when He prayed, "Give us this day our daily bread."

Jesus also called God "Father." Jews only spoke of God as their Father in the sense of God being the Father of their nation. They never called God "Father" when they they talked to God in prayer. But Jesus told His followers to call God "Father" when they prayed.

This is How
Matthew 6:9-21

"This is how you should pray," said Jesus.

> Our Father in heaven,
> your name is wonderful.
> Bring your kingdom here to earth.
> We pray that what you want
> will be done on earth like it is in heaven.
> Give us the food we need each day.
> Forgive us for our sin
> as we forgive people who sin against us.
> Don't let anyone dare us to do wrong.
> Save us from Satan, the enemy.

"Forgive other people when they treat you badly," said Jesus. "Then God your Father will forgive you, too. What if you don't forgive? Then your Father won't forgive you."

"You can choose to go without food to worship God," said Jesus. "But don't frown about it. Some people make faces. They show everyone that they're going without food. The truth is, that's all the good that will come to them. When you go without food, put sweet-smelling oil in your hair. Wash your face. Then other people won't notice that you're going without food. But God will. He sees what you do in secret. He will do good things for you."

"Don't store up riches for yourself here on earth," said Jesus. "Moths and rust tear down things on earth. Robbers break in and steal riches. Store up your riches in heaven. Moths and rust can't tear things apart in heaven. Robbers can't break in and steal. Your heart will care about the place where you keep your riches."

 Friday

Birds and Flowers

White doves, ibis, pigeon, crows, chickens, eagles, vultures, quail, ravens, and sparrows – all these birds made Palestine their home. As for flowers, there were several kinds of lilies, including the white ones we call "Easter lilies." Then there were yellow jasmin and crocus with purple specks or stripes, different-colored tulips, bright blue nutmeg, and purple-red cockle flowers from a weed that grew in grain fields. Tall, feathery reeds and even papyrus grew in some areas. Calamus was a sweet-smelling cane, often called ginger-grass for its ginger smell.

Pink blossoms on the almond trees were a sure sign that spring had arrived. Large, orange-red pomegranate blossoms were a showy sign of a good crop of fruit to come. Fragrant, cream-colored camphire flowers hung in clusters like grapes on a small plant and were used for orange dye. The white myrtle flower was used to make perfume. Mint had dense white or pink flowers. People sprinkled its leaves on the floors of their houses or synagogues to make the room smell fresh. The saffron flower was often used to perfume halls during banquets.

Birds' Food and Flowers' Clothes
Matthew 6:22-34; Luke 6:37-38

"Your eye is like a lamp for your body," said Jesus. "If your eye is good instead of sinful, your body is full of light. If your eye is sinful, your body is full of darkness. Light is supposed to be inside you. If there is darkness instead, then it's really, really dark!

"You can't follow two leaders at one time," said Jesus. "You'll hate one and love the other one. Or you'll obey one and not the other. You can't serve God and money, too.

"So I tell you not to worry," said Jesus. "Don't worry about what you'll eat or drink. Don't worry about what you'll wear. Life is much more important than food. Your body is much more important than clothes. See the birds in the air? They don't plant food. They don't bring in crops. They don't save food in barns. God your Father feeds them. You're more important than birds. Can anyone make his life last an hour longer by worrying?

"Why worry about clothes?" said Jesus. "Look at the flowers in the field. They don't work or make their own clothes. King Solomon had beautiful clothes, but not as wonderful as one of these flowers. That's the way God dresses the grass in the fields. Grass is here today and gone tomorrow. So God will give you clothes too, won't he?"

"Your faith is so small!" said Jesus. "Don't worry. Don't say, 'What will we eat? What will we drink? What will we wear?' People who don't believe in God worry about those things. But your Father in heaven knows what you need. Put God first in your life. Then he will make sure you have everything you need. Don't worry about tomorrow. Tomorrow can worry about itself. Each day has enough trouble of its own. Why add tomorrow's worries to today?"

"Don't blame people for what they do," said Jesus. "Then you won't be blamed for what you do. Forgive people. Then you will be forgiven. Give, and good things will come to you in return. You will get plenty. God will shake it up and push it down to make room for more. God will give you so much! It will run over and flow out onto your lap. God will be fair to you. He will give to you the same way you give to others."

WEEK 10

 Monday

Humor and Word Pictures

If you lived in Jesus' time, you might wear something that showed the kind of work you did. People who sewed clothes wore a needle slipped through their tunic. A carpenter wore a chip or shaving of wood behind one ear. Jesus probably did that. He probably also carried logs and beams of wood through the street over his shoulder. If the log was long and the person carrying it wasn't careful, he could knock things down with the back end of the log.

Some of our first comedy movies had that kind of scene. Of course, there were no movies in Jesus' time. But He used the same idea of the big log to make a word picture: telling someone you'll get the dust out of his eye, when a whole log blocks your own eye. The funny picture had a serious meaning: Don't criticize someone when you're not dealing with your own problems.

Although people did not have tv, radio, or cartoons in Jesus' time, they did tell funny stories. They probably thought it was funny to think of birds planting and harvesting their own food. Or flowers making their own clothes. When Jesus said, "What good is it for one blind person to lead another?" they probably laughed at the thought. When he said, "Don't give pearls to pigs," He created a funny picture. Jesus laughed and enjoyed good humor with people.

The Dust and the Log
Matthew 7:1-14; Luke 6:39-42

"Can a blind man lead another blind man?" asked Jesus. "Wouldn't they both fall into a hole? The learner is not greater than his teacher. But when he has learned everything, he will be like his teacher.

"Why point at a bit of dust in someone's eye? You don't see the big log in your own eye. How can you say, 'Let's get that dust out' when you have a log in your own eye? First get rid of the log in your eye. Then you'll see clearly. You'll be able to get rid of the other person's dust.

"Don't give dogs something special that is for God," said Jesus. "Don't give beautiful pearls to pigs. If you do, they'll step on them. They'll mash them under their feet. Then they'll run over you, too.

"Ask, and God will give you what you ask for," said Jesus. "Look for him. Then you'll find him. Tap on his door. He will open it for you. Everyone who asks, gets. The person who looks for God finds him. The door opens for the person who taps on it.

"Let's say your son asks you for bread," said Jesus. "Will you give him a rock? What if he asks you for a fish? Will you give him a snake? You know how to give good gifts to your children. So, of course, your Father in heaven gives good gifts when you ask.

"Treat people the way you want them to treat you," said Jesus. "This is the whole message of the Law and the prophets. Go in through the small gate. There is a wide gate and a wide road. But people who take the wide road will be in trouble. Many people follow that road. There is also a small gate and a narrow road. This road leads to life. Only a few people find it."

 Tuesday

Fruits of Ancient Palestine

Figs and grapes may have been the most popular fruits in Jesus' time. He referred to both quite often, and used them to make a funny word picture: figs growing on thorn bushes, grapes growing on bramble bushes.

Besides grapes, people probably ate a kind of banana that was a little different than ours. They also had a kind of citrus fruit, something probably related to the lemons and oranges we eat. Melons were a common food, and once in awhile, people could find apples at the marketplace. Apples were brought into Palestine from the island of Crete.

Dates were common. They grow on a kind of palm tree. The people of Jesus' time made mats and baskets from leaves of the date palm. Since they didn't use sugar, they sweetened food with dates, as well as honey and grape syrup (which was much like our grape jelly but probably not as sweet).

The carob tree also grows in Palestine. It's an evergreen tree with small red flowers and pods that contain a pulp that tastes like chocolate. One legend says that John the Baptist ate carob in the desert. Sometimes it's called "St. John's bread." Jesus probably ate carob. It can be eaten raw, but most people eat it after it's roasted and ground into a powder or made into chips.

Good Fruit and Bad Fruit
Matthew 7:15-20; Luke 6:43-45

"Watch out for prophets who lie," said Jesus. "They may pretend to be sheep. But inside, they are mean wolves. You will know them by the way they act. What they do is like bad fruit.

"People don't pick grapes or figs from weeds," said Jesus. "Good trees make good fruit. Bad trees make bad fruit. A good tree can't make bad fruit. A bad tree can't make good fruit. Trees get cut down if they don't make good fruit. They get burned up. So you will know trees and people by their fruit. You can tell what they are like by what they do.

"Good things happen when good people are around," said Jesus. "That's because they have good stored up in their hearts. But bad things happen when bad people are around. That's because they have sin stored up in their hearts. People's words come from their hearts first. Then the words come out of their mouths."

Rains

If you lived in Palestine in Jesus' time, you would experience two main seasons: summer and winter. Spring and fall came but did not last long. Summer was the longest season. Winter was often rainy.

If you lived in Jerusalem, on the last day of the Festival of Booths, around the middle of the month we call October, you would go up onto your flat rooftop and look toward the temple. You would watch to see which way the smoke from the temple offerings was blowing. People said that the direction of the smoke would show whether the coming year would be rainy or not.

In Galilee, heavy rains would often fall in October and again in March. These rains could turn dirt roads into rivers of mud. This was not so important to people who lived in big cities, because many streets were paved with stone and many houses were built of stone. But smaller towns and villages had mud roads. Houses were made of mud brick with a dirt floor. Seasonal rains were sometimes so heavy that gullies gushed with water, and if a house had not been built on a solid foundation, it could be washed away.

Jesus, being a carpenter, probably laid the roof beams and set the door frames of many houses. He knew how important it was to build a house on a strong foundation. In fact, the following story He tells may be based on something that really happened.

Standing in the Rain
Matthew 7:21-29; Luke 6:46-49

"Just calling me 'Lord' won't get people into God's kingdom," said Jesus. "People must do what my Father wants. Many people will say, 'Lord, we spoke in your name. We sent away bad spirits in your name. We did wonders in your name.' But I'll tell them, 'I never really knew you. Get away from me. You do wrong things. Why do you call me "Lord"? You don't do what I tell you.'

"Some people hear me and obey," said Jesus. "They are like the wise man. He built his house on a rock. Rain came down, and rivers got high. Wind roared and beat on his house. But his house didn't fall down. It stood safe on the rock. Other people hear me, but they don't obey. They are like the foolish man. He built his house on sand. Rain came down, and rivers got high. Wind roared and beat on his house, and it crashed down."

People were surprised to hear what Jesus was teaching. He sounded like he knew what he was talking about. He didn't sound like any teachers they knew.

 Thursday

Centurions

Roman captains were called *centurions*, because *century* means 100, and centurions were captains over 100 men. Jews did not like being ruled by Romans, but Roman soldiers did do some good things for Palestine. First of all, as we learned earlier, they helped keep the peace. They were the policemen of Jesus' day. They also brought interesting things with them to Palestine. Carrots were probably brought into Palestine from Germany by Roman centurions. They also brought in a game that became quite popular and is even played today: hopscotch. Roman soldiers invented hopscotch. They would often play it with loads on their backs. They numbered their hopscotch spaces with Roman numerals. Children in Palestine probably played hopscotch, having learned it from watching the soldiers.

The following story tells about something good that a Roman centurion did: He built a synagogue.

The Captain's Servant
Matthew 8:5-13; Luke 7:1-10

There was once a Roman army captain who lived in Capernaum. He had a servant who was very special to him. But his servant got very sick. He was so sick, he was almost dead.

The captain heard that Jesus was in town. So he sent some Jewish leaders to ask Jesus to come to his house. He wanted Jesus to make his servant well.

When these leaders came to Jesus, they begged him to help. "The captain is a good man," they said. "He loves our nation. He even built our town's worship house. So you should help him. You should make his servant well."

Jesus went with the leaders. But the captain had sent some friends to Jesus too. They met him on his way to see the captain. They gave Jesus another message: "Lord, don't bother to come. I'm not good enough for you to come to my house. That's why I didn't come to you myself. I'm not good enough to see you. Just say the word. Then I know my servant will be well again. You see, I know about being in charge. I have a boss to obey. And I'm the boss of many other men. I tell one to come, and he comes. I tell another to go, and he goes. I tell my servants, 'Do this' or 'Do that.' And they do what I tell them."

Jesus was surprised to hear this. He looked at the crowd following him. "I haven't seen such great faith in the land of Israel before," said Jesus. "People will come from east and west. They'll eat a big dinner with Abraham in God's kingdom. Isaac and Jacob will be there. But other people will be thrown out into the dark. They will cry out there."

Then Jesus sent word to the captain. "You believed I would make your servant well. I will do just what you believed."

At that moment, the captain's servant got well.

Funeral Processions

In Jesus' time, if someone in your family died, you might hire professional mourners to walk with you as you carried the body through the streets to the grave. You might also hire a flute player to go with you. Even the poorest funeral had at least one mourner and two flute players. Mourners tore their outer clothes. Some put dust and ashes on their hair. Some shaved their heads or beards. They all cried out loud.

The dead person was carried to the grave on a kind of stretcher or litter so everyone could see him. If a small child had died, the child might be carried in someone's arms instead. Women usually walked in front of the litter, because it was said that since death came into the world through a woman (Eve), women should lead the victims of death to the grave.

Sometimes an important item was placed on the litter with the body to show something about the person who had died. For example, a girl who was engaged but not yet married might have a wedding-type canopy on her litter.

Getting a Son Back
Luke 7:11-17

Jesus and his friends headed toward a town called Nain. A big crowd was with them. As they came to the town gate, they saw people coming out. They were carrying a dead man.

The dead man was the only son his mother had. The man's father had died some time before. Many people were there with his mother.

Jesus saw the dead man's mother. "Don't cry," he said. His heart was very sad for her.
Jesus touched the long box that held the body.

The people who were carrying it stood still.

Jesus said, "Young man, get up."

The man who had been dead sat up. He began to talk. So Jesus gave him back to his mother. He was alive.

Everyone was surprised. They praised God. They said, "This man Jesus is a great prophet. God is here helping his people."

The news about Jesus went quickly all over the land.

WEEK 11

 Monday

Prophets

Many prophets wrote, or had scribes write what they said and did. They became the most famous prophets, the ones we hear about most often. Their sayings or the events of their lives are written in Old Testament books called by their names. But we can read of other prophets in the Old Testament who either did not write, or else their writings were lost.

It was not unusual for prophets to spend time in the desert. Moses did. So did Elijah, one of the most famous prophets, "a man of the desert who counseled kings." Prophets were willing to be different. Some of them actually acted out their teachings through what we might call object lessons. Ezekiel shaved his head. Jeremiah stayed away from "party-people" and never married. John the Baptist never married either. He dressed like a desert-dweller and was not afraid to speak the truth. Many people said John the Baptist reminded them of Elijah.

What Did You Come to See?
Matthew 11:1-19; Luke 7:18-35

John, the one who baptized people, had some followers. They told John what Jesus was doing. So John asked two of them to go to Jesus and ask a question. "Are you the one we've been waiting for? Or should I look for someone else?"

At that time, Jesus was making many sick people well. He was sending many bad spirits away. He was making many people see again. So Jesus said, "Go back to John. Tell him everything you've seen. Tell him everything you've heard. People who couldn't see before can see now. People who couldn't walk before can walk now. People with skin sickness are well. People who couldn't hear before can hear now. Dead people come to life again. Poor people hear the good news. Good things will come to people who keep following me."

So John's followers went back and told John.

Then Jesus talked to the people about John. "What did you go out to the desert to see? Did you go to see plants blown by the wind? If not, what did you think you would see? Did you think you'd see someone dressed in fine clothes? People who wear fine clothes are in palaces. So what did you go to see in the desert? Did you go to see a prophet? Yes. But John is more than a prophet. He is the one Malachi wrote about. Malachi said God would send someone with a message. That person would help people get ready for me. Here on earth there is nobody greater than John. But in God's kingdom, even the smallest is greater than John. The Law and the prophets told about all that was to happen until John came. John is the prophet like Elijah who was supposed to come. Hear this if you have ears."

People listened to Jesus. They said God's way was the right way. Even men who took tax money said this. They had been baptized by John.

Some Jewish leaders had not been baptized by John. So they wouldn't take what God had planned for them. They said they already knew all about the Law.

"What are these people like?" asked Jesus. "They are like children who sit in the market place. They call to each other. They say, 'We played the flute for you, but you didn't dance. We sang a sad song, but you didn't cry.'

"John came and didn't eat bread or drink wine," said Jesus. "So you say a bad spirit controls him. I come, and I do eat bread and drink wine. So you say, 'This man eats too much. He is a drunk. He is a friend of tax men. He is a friend of sinners.' But I say being wise is what's right. You can see that by watching a wise person."

Tuesday

Poor Meals, Rich Meals

In Jesus' time, the common family's floor was hard-packed dirt covered with rushes or straw or leather mats. The family sat on the floor around a common pot and ate from that pot. It was considered a sin not to wash your hands before you ate, so they poured water over their hands and dried with a cloth towel. As the family ate, the father might recite scripture or tell stories or teach about the rules that Jewish boys and girls were expected to know.

Poor people did not often eat meat, but rich people could afford it and had it regularly. People often ate stew (with meat if you were rich, without meat if you were poor). They would sop it up with bread or drink it out of a bowl. Some people used wooden spoons. Rich people might use metal spoons. They had no paper napkins. Instead, they used cloth towels. But they insisted on being clean when they ate. Sometimes, they washed their hands in between eating the different kinds of food. They might eat fruit, then wash their hands, eat meat, then wash their hands, eat a sweet cake, then wash their hands.

Perfume
Luke 7:36-50

There was a Jewish leader named Simon. He asked Jesus to come to dinner at his house. So Jesus went. He sat down at Simon's table.

Now there was a sinful woman in town. She heard that Jesus was having dinner at Simon's house. So she went too. She took a beautiful stone jar with her. The jar was filled with sweet-smelling perfume. The woman went into the house. She stood close to Jesus, at his feet, and she began to cry. Her tears dripped on Jesus' feet. They made his feet wet. So she wiped his feet with her long hair. Then she kissed Jesus' feet and poured perfume from the jar onto them.

Simon saw this. He said to himself, "Jesus can't really be a prophet. If he was, he would know this is a sinful woman."

Jesus said, "Simon, I want to tell you something."

"Tell me, Teacher," said Simon.

"Two men borrowed money from another man," said Jesus. "One man borrowed 500 coins. The other man borrowed 50 coins. But they couldn't pay it back when the time came. The man who loaned them the money said that was okay. 'I won't make you pay me back,' he said. Now, which man will love him more?"

"The man who borrowed the most money," said Simon. "He would be the most thankful. He would love him more."

"You're right, " said Jesus. "See this woman? She wet my feet with her tears. She wiped my feet with her hair. She kissed my feet and put perfume on them. You didn't even give me water to wash my feet. You didn't welcome me with a kiss when I came. You didn't put oil on my head. This woman has lots of love. She had many sins. But they have been forgiven. Some people haven't been forgiven for much. So they don't love very much."

Then Jesus said to the woman, "Your sins are forgiven."

Other people at Simon's house began to talk among themselves. "Who is this man?" they asked. "He even forgives people's sins."

Jesus said to the woman, "Go in peace. Your faith has saved you."

☐ Wednesday

Women Followers

Travelers in Jesus' time either took their food with them or bought food in towns along the way. If you were poor or were going a short way, you would carry your own food if you could. But if you passed through a big city, like Jerusalem, you would find snack shops with counters facing the streets so you could buy food and eat it there or take it out.

Women helped buy and bring food for Jesus' travels. That's one way Jesus was different from all other rabbis. He had women followers. They even supported Him with their own money. This does not sound strange to us. But in ancient Palestine, it was totally new. No teacher had women among His followers.

We don't know much about the women who followed Jesus. But we do know an interesting fact about Joanna. Her husband, Chuza, was in charge of King Herod's household. It's interesting to think about what this might have meant for Jesus. Herod put John the Baptist into prison and later killed him. Then Jesus was sent to Herod on the night He was condemned to die. We might wonder if Chuza and Joanna tried to keep her friendship with Jesus a secret so Herod would not find out. Joanna may have told Jesus and His other friends inside stories about what went on in Herod's court. It is very possible that Chuza was there the night Jesus came before Herod and that Jesus saw him and thought about Joanna and the things she had told Him.

Town to Town
Matthew 12:22-30; Mark 3:20-27; Luke 8:1-3

Jesus went from town to town. He taught the Good News about God's kingdom. His twelve closest friends went with him. Some women went with him too. Jesus had made many of them well. One was Mary Magdalene. Seven bad spirits had come out of her. Another was Joanna. Her husband was in charge of King Herod's whole house. Another was a woman named Susanna, and there were many others. These women spent their own money to help Jesus. They helped him and his friends get things they needed.

Jesus and his friends went to eat. But people began to gather around. The crowd got so big, Jesus and his friends couldn't eat.

Then some people brought in a man controlled by bad spirits. He couldn't see, and he couldn't speak. Jesus made the man well. The people were surprised. They said, "Could Jesus really be the one God promised to send?"

The Jewish leaders heard about this. They said, "Jesus gets power from the prince of the bad spirits. That's how he sends spirits away."

Jesus knew what they were thinking. He said, "If a kingdom fights itself, it can't last long. If a city or a family fights itself, it will be torn down. If Satan sends Satan away, he fights against himself. How could his kingdom last?

"You say my power comes from bad spirits," said Jesus. "You say that's how I send bad spirits away. Then how do your people send bad spirits away? I send bad spirits away by God's Spirit. That means God's kingdom has come. If you're not with me, you're against me. You can choose to work with me. If you don't, you choose to work against me."

A Sin that Can't be Forgiven

People sometimes find it strange that Jesus, who always talked about loving and forgiving, would say there is a sin that can't be forgiven. What might He be talking about?

Pretend you have a package of the sweetest, most delicious candy in the world. You offer it to your friend. Your friend takes one look at the package and says, "Those are bad. Awful. Bitter. Disgusting. I'll never touch the stuff."

"No, they're good," you say. "I've tried them. They're sweet. Delicious. The best candy I've ever eaten." You know your friend has a sweet tooth and would love these candies.

But if your friend keeps calling the candy *bad* and refuses to even touch it, will he ever eat it? Is that your fault or your friend's fault? Your friend is calling something that's good *bad*.

Now maybe we can understand what Jesus meant when He said people who speak against the Holy Spirit won't be forgiven. They are calling what's Holy *bad*. As long as they call the Holy Spirit of love and forgiveness *bad*, they will never accept forgiveness. They will never have forgiveness. That's the only reason they *can't* be forgiven. Because they keep pushing God and His forgiving love away, saying it's bad. Is that God's fault or theirs?

A Pack of Snakes
Matthew 12:31-37; Mark 3:28-30

"People will be forgiven for every sin. But if they say the Holy Spirit is a bad spirit, they won't be forgiven. Anybody who speaks against me will be forgiven. But anybody who speaks against the Holy Spirit won't be. Not now. Not ever." Jesus said this because they said he was controlled by a bad spirit.

"Make a tree good," said Jesus. "Then its fruit will be good. Or make a tree bad. Then its fruit will be bad. The fruit shows what kind of tree it is.

"You're just a pack of snakes!" said Jesus. "You're full of sin. So how can you say anything good? The mouth says what comes from the heart. Good things come from good hearts. Sin comes from sinful hearts. Someday God will judge the world. People will have to tell why they said words without thinking. You'll be made clean from sin because of your words. Or you'll be dirty with sin because of your words."

Jesus' family heard about what he said. So they went to take charge of him. They said, "He must be out of his mind."

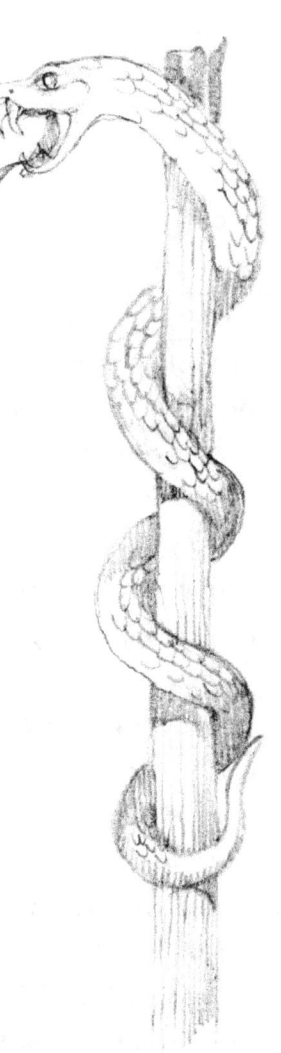

 Friday

Signs and Wonders

Many leaders in the ancient world asked their gods for a "sign." A sign is like a signal. It points to something else or means something important. Signs were sometimes called "omens" in ancient times. Anything out of the ordinary or anything that could not be explained might be seen as an omen. People actually looked for these kinds of signs to help them make decisions.

To the Jews, a sign was an event that showed God's greatness. It was something only God could do. A "sign" pointed to God. In the Old Testament, we read about many different signs that God sent His people: Moses' walking stick turned into a snake as a sign that God was with Moses. The sun's shadow went backward to show Hezekiah that he would get well. Gideon's fleece was wet one morning and dry the next as a sign that God was truly choosing Him to lead His people. Maybe that's the kind of sign the Jewish leaders wanted Jesus to show them.

The word for "sign" can also mean an event by which God shows something new about Himself. In that sense, Jesus Himself was the sign. He was showing who God is in all His life-giving love.

Wanting a Sign
Matthew 12:38-45; Luke 11:24-26

Some Jewish leaders and teachers came to Jesus. They said, "We want to see you do a wonder. It will be like a sign to us."

"Only sinful people ask for a wonder," said Jesus. "The only sign they'll see is the sign of Jonah. Jonah spent three days and nights inside a big fish. In the same way, I'll spend three days and nights in the earth.

"Someday, people from Jonah's time will be with the people of today," said Jesus. "It will happen when God judges everyone. Then they'll blame the people of today for what they have done. People from Nineveh heard what Jonah said. They were sorry for what they'd done. They stopped doing bad things. But someone more important than Jonah is here now.

"The Queen of Sheba will be with the people of today when God judges everyone," said Jesus. "Then she will blame the people of today for what they have done. She came from far away. She listened to Solomon. She heard the wise things he said. But someone more important than Solomon is here now.

"A bad spirit comes out of a person," said Jesus. "Then it goes through dry places. It tries to find a place to stay. But it might not find a place to stay. So it says, 'I'll go back to the place I left.' What if the place it left is empty? Then this spirit will go and get seven other spirits. They're even more sinful. They go and live in the person. Then the person is in even bigger trouble. That's how it's going to be with these sinful people."

WEEK 12

 Monday

Families

In Jewish tradition, the basic building block of all society was family. The laws and teachings of the rabbis were meant to keep the family pure and stable. Each family formed a mini-religious community, and many of the religious feasts were expected to be celebrated with the whole family. When good things happened to one member of the family, the whole family celebrated. When something bad happened, the whole family was unhappy.

In the following story, Jesus says something strange: "People who do what my Father wants are my brothers. They are my sisters and my mother." That may sound rude to us. But Jesus was not saying that His mother and brothers were not important. Instead, He was saying that His followers were just as important to Him as family. Jesus was not denying His earthly family. He was expanding it to include His spiritual family.

Family

Matthew 12:46-50; Mark 3:31-35; Luke 11:27-28

A woman in the crowd called out to Jesus. "God will be good to the mother who has you for a son."

Jesus turned to her. "God will be good to people who hear and obey God," he said.

As Jesus was talking to the people, his own mother and brothers came and stood outside. They wanted to talk to Jesus. So someone went in and told Jesus, "Your brothers are outside." They want to talk to you."

Jesus pointed to his followers. "Here's my family. My Father is in heaven. People who do what my Father wants are my brothers. They are my sisters and my mother."

Unmarked Graves

According to the law, a person who touched a grave was considered unclean for a week. That meant the person could not go into the synagogue or take part in any religious worship. That was the rule, whether or not the person knew he was touching a grave. So an unmarked grave was especially dangerous, because you might touch it and not know it until it was too late.

What Jesus is saying in the following story is that people who came into contact with the Pharisees and their teaching were touching evil, even though they didn't know it. Without suspecting it, they were learning wrong ideas through the teaching of the Pharisees. They were getting wrong ideas about the worship of God and wrong ideas about who God is and what He wants.

The Cup and the Dish
Luke 11:37-46, 52

One of the Jewish leaders asked Jesus to eat with him. So Jesus went. Jesus didn't wash the same way the leader did before he ate his meal. That surprised the leader.

Jesus said, "You leaders are like a cup and dish that you clean only on the outside. Inside yourselves, you're sinful. That's foolish. God made you on the outside. But he also made you on the inside. Give what you can to the poor. Then you will really be clean.

"How sad it will be for you leaders," said Jesus. "You give God a small part of what you earn. You even give him one out of every 10 garden plants. But you don't think about God's love. Think about what's fair and about loving God. After that, you can think about giving one out of every 10 coins.

"How sad it will be for you leaders," said Jesus. "You want to sit at the most important places. You want people to think you're the most important people. How sad. You're like graves that are not marked with stones. People walk over them without even knowing it."

One of these men knew a lot about the Law. He talked to Jesus. "Teacher, we feel put down when you say these things."

"You know a lot about the Law," said Jesus. "But how sad it will be for you. You give people all kinds of laws. It's very hard for people to do them all. You won't even lift a finger to help them. It's as if you took away the key to knowing. You don't try to learn and know. And you don't let other people learn and know."

Rooftop Teaching

Rooftops were flat in ancient Palestine. Stairs went up to the roof from the outside or from the inside courtyard. In poorer houses a ladder might go up to the roof. Because the weather was fairly mild, lots of daily activities took place on the rooftop. Besides, the indoors was dim, because the few windows were often high on the wall and narrow. So outdoors it was easier to see while doing the tasks of the day: weaving, grinding grain, drying fruits, washing and drying clothing, and even eating meals. People could also visit and share news with their neighbors, who were probably on their rooftops as well. If the night was nice, a family might even sleep on their rooftop.

A rooftop was also a good place to speak to a crowd of people who might stand below. Some rabbis taught in the streets and out in open areas. But there were, of course, no microphones or speaker systems, so the teacher's voice had to carry across the crowd. Being on a rooftop would help. Even then, if a rabbi was not a good speaker, or if he could not talk loudly, he might get a helper with a good, loud voice. The rabbi could quietly tell this helper what to say, and the helper could speak it loudly to the people who were listening. That's what Jesus may be referring to in the following story.

From the Roof Tops
Luke 11:53–12:12

The Jewish leaders began to talk sharply against Jesus. They asked him many questions, waiting for him to say something wrong. They wanted to trap him with his own words. But thousands of people were gathering. The crowd was pushing. People stepped on each other.

Then Jesus began to talk, first to his followers. "Watch out! What the leaders say and do is not right. One day people will know every-thing that has been hidden. Things you said in the dark will be told in daylight. You may have whispered in someone's ear. You may have said it in a room inside a house. But what you said will be shouted from the roof.

"Don't be afraid of people who can kill your body," said Jesus. "After that, they can't do anything else. Instead, be afraid of the one who can do more. He can kill the body. He can also throw you into hell. Yes, he is the one to be afraid of.

"You can buy five sparrows for two pennies," said Jesus. "They don't cost much, but God doesn't forget any of them. God knows all about you, too. He even knows how many hairs are on your head. So don't be afraid. You're more important than many sparrows.

"Tell people you know me," said Jesus. "Then I'll tell God's angels I know you. Are you afraid to tell people you know me? Then I'll tell God's angels I don't know you. Don't worry about what to say in worship houses or before the leaders. The Holy Spirit will tell you what to say."

 Thursday

Storing Treasure

If you lived in Jesus' times, you would bury money or valuables to keep them safe. Or you might hide money and valuables in a jar or under a mat or in a barrel inside your house. (But that was not as safe as burying it.) If you had to carry money, you would usually slip it into the folds of your belt or waistband.

Of course, kings had special rooms in their palaces where they stored their treasure. Another place where money was stored was in the temple. There was a special storage room there that served as a sort of bank. The temple loaned money to businesses and paid for construction and other public programs.

Towns often had a "storehouse," a rectangular building with thick walls. In a storehouse, small storerooms lined a main hall that went down the middle. In large cities, there might be one or more sections of the city set aside for storehouses. They lined the streets in that area of town. Then, of course, there were storehouses or barns on a farmer's property, built to hold the treasure of whatever the farmer harvested.

The Rich Man's Barns
Luke 12:13-21

Someone in the crowd said, "Teacher! Tell my brother to share with me."

"Who made me your judge?" asked Jesus. Then he told the people, "Be careful. Guard yourself against wanting more and more things. Life is not made of how many things you have." Then he told this story:

A rich man grew lots of crops on his farm. "What should I do?" he said. "I don't have a place to keep all my crops." Then he said, "I know! I'll take down my old barns. I will build bigger barns. Then I can store all my crops. I'll have plenty of good things stored away. They'll last for many years to come. I can take life easy. I can eat. I can drink. I can be happy."

But God said, "You are foolish. You will die tonight. Then who will get the things you kept for yourself?"

"That's the way it is for people who store things for themselves and are not rich in giving to God," said Jesus.

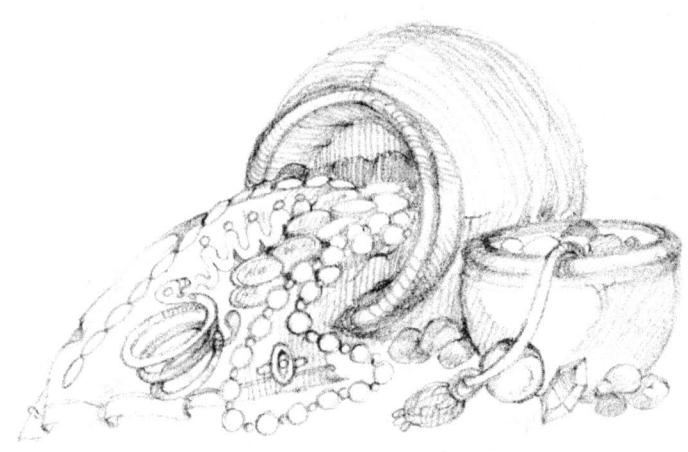

Friday

Servants and Slaves

In rich families, servants or slaves did most chores and served the food. If you were not rich, you did not own slaves, because it cost a lot of money to feed, clothe, and take care of them. Jews who owned slaves and had servants were usually kinder to them than Greeks and Romans were to their slaves. Jews were not supposed to treat their slaves badly. They were supposed to let slaves have a day of rest once a week, just like the Jews themselves had. Still, slaves and servants were bought to be workers. They were expected to work hard at doing whatever their master told them to do.

Every seventh year, Jews were supposed to set free any slaves who were Jews. Some of these slaves had been forced to sell themselves to pay off their debts. Setting them free was a way of saying that their debt had been paid. At other times, a slave might earn enough money to buy his freedom. Or a slave's family might help pay for his freedom.

The Wise Servant
Luke 12:35-48

"Be ready to help and serve," said Jesus. "Being ready is like keeping your lamp turned on. Be like servants waiting for their master. He comes back from a wedding party and taps on the door. His servants open it right away. They were waiting for him. That makes the servants look good. Then the master will serve and help them. He will tell them to sit at the table, and he will wait on them. It's good if the servants are ready for him. They should be ready even if he comes at midnight. A robber comes when no one is watching. You need to be ready. I'll come when you're not thinking about it."

Peter said, "Lord, is this story just for us? Or is it for everybody?"

"It's for people who do what they say they will do," said Jesus. "That's what a wise servant does. His master puts him in charge of all the servants. He even gives them their food. A good servant does what his master tells him. He will be following orders when his master comes back. Then his master will put him in charge of everything.

"Think about it," said Jesus. "What if he says, 'My master is taking too long'? Then he begins to eat and drink. He gets drunk. He beats the other servants. Then the master comes back. The servant wasn't thinking about him. The master will throw him out. He will be sent away forever. He will go to the place where people don't believe in God.

"The servant knows what his master wants," said Jesus. "If he doesn't do it, he will get in trouble. What if the servant doesn't know what his master wants? He will still get in trouble, but not as badly. If the master gives his servant a lot, he will want his servant to give a lot too."

WEEK 13

 Monday

A Time of Peace and Trouble

Jesus came during a time in history called the *Pax Romana,* Roman peace. Rome was firmly in control of its empire, and there were no major threats to Rome's rule. That was because Rome kept tight control of its provinces, using its army to quickly put down any rebellions. Palestine was one of the most rebellious parts of Rome's empire. The Jews were always restless when another nation was in charge. They always looked for the day when they could rule themselves.

At this time, many Jews were longing for someone to come and rescue them from the Romans. That's what many of them hoped Jesus would do. But Jesus told them truthfully that He didn't come to bring that kind of peace. He said there would still be family quarrels and arguments about whose side a person was on. But He came to bring a new choice to the discussion: the way of love. Of course, some families were sure to quarrel over whether the path of love was the right one or not!

Clouds from the West
Luke 12:51-56; 13:6-9

"Do you think I came to bring peace?" asked Jesus. "No. I came to shake things up. From now on, families will fight each other. Three will be against two. Two will be against three. Fathers will turn against sons. Sons will turn against fathers. Mothers will turn against daughters. Daughters will turn against mothers. Mothers-in-law will be against daughters-in-law. Daughters-in-law will be against mothers-in-law.

"You watch clouds coming up from the west," said Jesus. "Then you say it's going to rain, and it does. A south wind blows. Then you say it will be hot, and it is. You can tell what's happening with the earth and sky. Why can't you tell what's happening now?" Then Jesus told a story:

A man planted a fig tree in his garden. He watched for fruit to grow on it. But there was no fruit. At last he talked to his gardener about it. He said, "I've been coming here for three years. I've been looking for fruit on this fig tree. But I haven't found any. So cut it down. It's just using up the soil."

But the gardener spoke up. "Sir, leave the fig tree alone one more year. I'll see what I can do. I'll dig around it. I'll make the soil richer. Maybe it will give you fruit next year. If it doesn't, then you can cut it down."

 Tuesday

Oxen and Donkeys

In Jesus' time, you would keep your sheep and goats in pens at the edge of your village. But oxen, donkeys, and cows were kept near or in your house. If your house was fairly large, it would have an open courtyard in the middle with the rooms of the house around it. One of the rooms would be a stable for the animals, although chickens were likely to run around in the courtyard. If your house was small, donkeys, cows, and chickens might be kept in one end at night, while you and your family slept on a raised platform at the other end.

It is said that every poor Jew dreamed of having a pair of oxen and a plow, because that would allow him to make a better living. Oxen were usually the animals that pulled a plow, although sometimes people would use donkeys for this work. To be kind to animals, a law said you could not harness both an ox and a donkey to the same plow at the same time. You took good care of your animals, because they did so much of the work for you.

The Woman Who Couldn't Stand Up Tall
Luke 13:10-17

One worship day, Jesus was teaching in a town's worship house. A bent woman was there. She could not stand tall. A bad spirit had kept her bent for 18 years.

Jesus saw her. He called her to come over to him. He said, "You're now set free from your sickness." Then he put his hands on her.

Right away, she stood tall. She praised God.

The man in charge was mad because Jesus made this woman well on the worship day. The man in charge talked to the people. "There are six days for work," he said. "You can come and be made well any other day. But don't come to be made well on the worship day."

Jesus said, "All of you work on the worship day. Don't you take your ox or donkey outside on the worship day? Don't you lead it to water so it can drink? Satan kept this woman bent over for 18 years. Shouldn't she be set free on this worship day?"

Jesus' enemies felt put down when they heard this. But the other people were glad. They loved the wonderful things Jesus did.

 Wednesday

Farming

If you were a farmer in Jesus' time, you would loosen the dirt in your field by plowing it. Then you would put seeds in a bag, or hold the end of your mantle so the middle sagged, forming a big pocket where you would put the seed. Then you walked back and forth through your field, grabbing fistfuls of seeds and tossing them in all directions.

If your fields were not close to your house, you might set up a little tent or lean-to in your field. The boys and men of your family would live there during the months when the fields needed to be worked. After harvest, you would move back to town to live with the rest of your family. Farmers always had work to do. The reason Jesus tells so many parables about farmers is that people saw farms and farmers around them all the time.

Seeds and Dirt
Matthew 13:1-15; Mark 4:1-12; Luke 8:4-10

Jesus sat by the lake. Many people came to listen to him. So he got into a boat. The people stood on the shore. Then Jesus told them many stories. One was about a farmer:

Once farmer went out to plant his seeds. He threw them here and there. Some seeds fell on a path. Birds ate them. Some fell on rocky dirt. They grew fast. But there was not much dirt. The sun was hot on the little plants, and their roots were too short. They dried up.

Some seeds fell around weeds. The seeds grew, but weeds grew too. The weeds grew over the new plants. Other seeds fell on good, rich dirt. A crop of good plants came up. The farmer got much more than he planted.

"Why do you tell people stories?" asked Jesus' friends.

Jesus said, "You can understand the secrets of God's kingdom. Other people can't. Some people want to know and understand. They will be able to understand even more. Some people don't want to know or understand. They will understand less and less. That's why I tell stories. People seem to see. But they are not really looking. They seem to hear. But they are not really listening. They don't understand. What the prophet Isaiah said has come true:

> You will hear but never understand.
> You will see but not know what it means.
> These people's hearts are hard.
> They can't hear well with their ears.
> Their eyes are closed.
> If their ears and eyes were open, they might see.
> They might hear.
> Their hearts might understand.
> Then they would turn to me,
> and I would make them well."

Farming by the Months

Although the Jewish months are not exactly equal to ours, if we divide the farm year into months as we know them today, here's what it looks like in general.

September (Tishri) – first rains
>store grape juice in large pots or goatskin bags for making wine; plow the ground

October (Marchesvan)
>plow the ground; spread cloths under olive trees to catch ripe olives; repair field walls

November (Kislev)
>harvest olives in baskets; plant grain; plow vegetable gardens

December (Tevet) – the main rains come
>plant grain; repair farm tools

January (Shevat) – main rains continue plant peas, melons, and cucumbers

February (Adar)
>almond trees bloom light pink; plant cucumbers, peas, and melons

March (Nisan) – spring rains come
>harvest flax; wheat and barley grow tall

April (Iyyar) – spring rains continue
>harvest barley (barley is like tall grass); store barley grain in jars and cloth bags

- May (Sivan) – dry season begins (sunny)
  harvest wheat; feast and enjoy the harvest

- June (Tammuz) tend grape vines; pick first figs; build stone fences around grape fields to keep robbers out

- July (Av) – dry season still here (sunny)
  protect the grape vines from foxes; trim grape vines

- August (Elul) – summer heat is here
  pick dates from date palm trees; pick the grapes

The One Who Hears
Matthew 13:16-23; Mark 4:13-20; Luke 8:11-15

Jesus said, "Good things have come to your eyes. Your eyes see. Good things have come to your ears. They hear. Long ago, prophets and other good people wanted to see what you see. But they didn't get to see it. They wanted to hear what you hear. But they didn't get to hear it.

"So listen to the meaning of the story. Some people hear about God's kingdom. But they don't understand. Then Satan comes and takes away what was planted in their hearts. This is the seed that fell on the path.

"The rocky dirt is like the person who hears. He gladly takes God's word into his heart. But he doesn't grow. He has no roots. So he leaves God when trouble comes.

"Then there was the seed that fell around weeds. That's the person who hears God's words. But he has many worries about his life and his money. His worries become more important to him than God.

"But some seed fell on good dirt. That's like the person who hears God's words. He understands. In his heart, a great crop of God's love grows. It may be 30, 60, or even 100 times more than what was planted."

Friday

A Farmer's Year

A rhyme from about the time of Solomon has been discovered written on a stone plaque. Since the rhyme is so ancient, school boys in Jesus' time may have said it. Maybe even Jesus learned it when He was a boy.

> The two months are olive harvest.
> The two months are planting grain.
> The two months are late planting.
> The month is hoeing up flax.
> The month is harvest of barley.
> The month is harvest and feasting.
> The two months are vine tending.
> The month is summer fruit.

Weeds
Matthew 13:24-30, 36-43; Mark 4:26-29
Jesus told his friends another story. "God's kingdom is like this," he said.

A farmer planted wheat seeds. One night while he was sleeping, his enemy planted weeds in the wheat field. As the wheat grew tall, weeds grew tall too.

The farmer's servants said, "Sir, didn't you plant good wheat seeds? Where did all these weeds come from?"

"The enemy planted weeds," said the farmer.

"Do you want us to pull the weeds?" asked the servants.

"No," said the farmer. "You might pull up wheat with the weeds. Let the wheat and weeds grow together. Soon it will be time to bring in the crops. Bring in the weeds first. Pile them up, tie them together, and burn them. After that, bring the wheat into the barn."

Jesus left the group of people and went into a house. His friends followed. They asked, "What does the story of the weeds mean?"

Jesus said, "I'm the one who plants good seed. The field is the world. The good seeds are the people in God's kingdom. The weeds are the people who follow Satan. Satan is the enemy who plants those weeds. Bringing in the crop happens at the end of time. The angels bring in the crops. The weeds are pulled up and burned in the fire.

"That's how it will be at the end of time," said Jesus. "I'll send my angels. They will take everything evil and sinful out of God's kingdom. They will throw what's sinful into the fire. But good people will shine like the sun in God's kingdom. Hear this if you have ears."

"Here's what God's kingdom is like," said Jesus. "A farmer plants seeds. Night and day the seeds grow. They grow when the farmer sleeps. They grow when he is awake. They grow even if he doesn't understand how. All by itself, the ground grows wheat. First the stem comes up. Then it makes a head of grain. When it's ripe farmer cuts it. That's when the farmer brings in his crops."

WEEK 14

 Monday

Parables

In ancient Palestine, even though boys were taught to read, they had no books. They had only scrolls. Even then, there were not many scrolls to read, so you did not read stories for fun. With no tv, dvd's, radio, internet or cd's, the only way to have a story was to hear someone tell it or to make it up and tell it yourself. Rabbis often told the type of story called a parable. Long before Jesus was born, one rabbi told tales with a fox as the main character.

Jesus' parables were different. He told his stories about people's everyday lives. His stories were simple, but they had great meanings. If you lived in Jesus' time, you would never have read His parables. You would have only heard them. You would have to think about them and decide what Jesus meant. That's why Jesus said, "Listen to what the parable means." Jesus' stories were meant to help people remember and understand. Someone once called Jesus' stories and sayings "siren language," because they are meant to make people "stop, look, and listen."

Seeds, Yeast, Pearls, and Nets
Matthew 13:31-35, 44-52; Mark 4:30-34; Luke 13:18-21

"God's kingdom is like a mustard seed," said Jesus. "It's the smallest seed of all. But it grows into the biggest plant in the garden. It becomes a tree. The birds fly to it and sit in its branches.

"God's kingdom is like yeast that a woman mixed with flour. It mixed into all the batter.

"God's kingdom is like riches hidden in a field, under the ground. A man was digging, and he found them. He covered them up again. Then he sold everything he owned to buy that field.

"God's kingdom is like a man shopping for fine pearls. One day, he found a special pearl. There was no other pearl like it in the world. It cost a lot of money. So the man sold everything he owned. He bought the pearl.

"God's kingdom is like a fishing net. Different kinds of fish swam in and filled the net. The men who were fishing pulled the net to the shore. They took the fish out. They put the good fish in baskets. They threw the bad fish away. That's how it will be when time ends. Angels will come. They'll keep people who did what's right. They'll throw out sinful people. The sinful people will cry. Do you understand what I'm saying?" Jesus asked.

"Yes," said his friends.

"Teachers who know about God's kingdom are like people who own houses," said Jesus. "They have rooms where they keep things. Sometimes they bring out new things. Sometimes they bring out old things."

Jesus told many other stories. He almost never talked without telling a story. But he told his friends what the stories meant. So the psalm came true. "I'll talk in stories. I'll tell secrets hidden since the world was made."

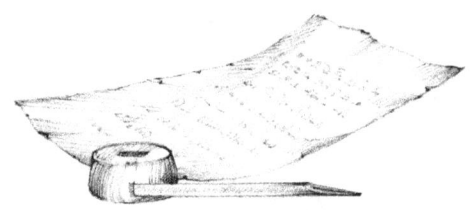

Tuesday

Beds and Sleeping

In Jesus' time, only very rich people had bedrooms and beds that stood up off the ground like ours. Their bed frames could be iron or wood or even ivory. But most people slept on cushions or mats. If you were poor, you rolled mats out on your flat roof or on the floor of the one room you and your family lived in. Your mat would probably be filled with straw. Or if you could afford it, your mat might be filled with wool.

When it was cold, you used your tunic or cloak as a blanket. Some people had camel-hair or goat-hair blankets. Rich people could afford fine wool blankets. As a pillow, you might use a piece of wood, or a stone under your neck. Even rich people used fancy stone neck-rests.

Foxes Have Dens
Matthew 8:19-22; Luke 9:57-62

A teacher who knew God's law told Jesus, "I will follow you anywhere you go."

"Foxes sleep in dens," said Jesus. "Birds sleep in nests. But I don't have a place to sleep."

Jesus told another man, "Follow me."

"Wait," said the man. "I can't come until my father grows old and dies."

Jesus said, "The person who waits is the one whose love for me is dead. You need to follow me. Tell other people about God's kingdom."

Another man said, "I will follow you, Lord. But first I want to have some time with my family."

Jesus said, "You're like a farmer. He was getting his field ready for planting. He looked back and wished he had stayed home. If you are going to wish you had stayed home, you are not ready to serve in God's kingdom."

Storms on Lake Galilee

The Sea of Galilee is a fairly small lake, thirteen miles north to south and eight miles east to west at the widest. As part of the Jordan valley, it's surrounded by hills. Normally in Palestine, wind blowing from the mountains and seas north and west brought rain and storms. Wind blowing from the deserts south and east could be warm or else so dry they dried out the land and plants. In winter, an east wind would be cold and dry.

But Lake Galilee, ringed with hills and deep valleys, could have very sudden weather changes. The valleys to the west of the lake have been compared to giant funnels. Blowing through these valleys, the wind presses together and then shoots out full force onto the lake. It's common for this to happen very suddenly. One minute the lake is glassy calm, and the next minute, waves are high enough to hide any boats on the lake.

In the following story, the Greek word in the Bible that describes the storm is *seismos*, which means *earthquake*. In this case, it's not the land but the sea that is shaking. The disciples' boat is said to be *kaluptesthai*, which means *enveloped* or completely hidden among the waves.

The Storm
Matthew 8:23-27; Mark 4:35-41; Luke 8:22-25

The sun began to go down. "Let's go across the lake," Jesus told his friends.

So they got into a boat. They left the crowd of people. Some other boats went with them.

But a storm roared in. Waves crashed over the boat. Water almost filled it. All this time, Jesus was in the back of the boat, sleeping on a pillow.

Jesus' friends woke him up. "We're about to die in this water!" they cried. Don't you care?"

Jesus got up. He spoke firmly to the wind. He spoke firmly to the waves. "Be quiet. Be still."

The wind died down. Everything became still.

Jesus looked at his friends. "Why are you so scared?" he asked. "Could it be that your faith is still very small?"

Jesus' friends were afraid. They said to each other, "The wind obeys him! The water obeys him! Who is this Jesus?"

Demons

People in ancient times, including Jews, did not know how the brain or the mind worked. So mental illness was usually blamed on the work of demons or evil spirits. People believed there were all kinds of demons everywhere. Jews said these demons were fallen angels. Some even said they were children that Adam had before he had Cain and Abel.

People said evil spirits lived mostly in ruined houses, in marshes, in the shade of certain trees, and in places people would use as toilets. (One rabbi always took a lamb with him for protection in the toilet.) The Jews' rules said people could not carry anything on the Sabbath, unless you thought a demon might give you trouble. Then the rabbis would allow you to carry a locust's egg, a fox's tooth, or a nail from a gallows as protection. You could also light a lamp on the Sabbath (which was normally not allowed) if you needed to get a demon to leave you alone. Or you could run farther than the allowed distance for Sabbath travel if you were running to get away from a demon.

Most Jews depended on guardian angels to protect them. They made sure to say their prayers before going to bed. They also thought it helped to wear a small leather case with scriptures written in it. There were men who were known for being able to command demons to leave people. Jesus did that too. But when Jesus was around, the demons recognized who He was. They knew right away that He was in charge and that they had no power against His word.

The Man Who Lived by Graves
Matthew 8:28-34; Mark 5:1-20; Luke 8:26-39

Jesus and his friends landed their boat. When Jesus got out, he saw a man controlled by a bad spirit. This man lived by the graves. Every day and night, he shouted around the graves and hills. He cut himself with stones. Many times people put chains on his hands and feet. But he just tore the chains off. No one was strong enough to hold him down. This man ran to Jesus.

Jesus said, "Bad spirit, come out of this man!"

The man fell down and shouted, "Jesus, Son of God Most High! What do you want with me? Please promise you won't hurt me!"

Jesus asked the spirit, "What's your name?"

"Many," answered the spirit. "There are many of us." The spirits begged Jesus not to send them out of that land. Pigs were eating on a hill nearby. "Let us go into the pigs," they said.

So Jesus let them go.

There were about 2,000 pigs. The spirits went into them. All the pigs ran down the hill, jumped into the lake, and drowned.

The pig keepers ran to town and told everyone what had happened. People went to see for themselves. When they reached Jesus, the man was sitting with him. The man's mind seemed to be working just fine. The people were scared. They begged Jesus to leave their land.

So Jesus got back into the boat. The man asked if he could go with Jesus. But Jesus said, "Go home to your family. Tell them what God did for you. Tell them about God's kindness."

So the man went home. He told people what Jesus had done. People were very surprised.

 Friday

Doctors

In ancient times, people did not know about bacteria or viruses. They knew very little about how the human body worked. Romans did have doctors and hospitals, but the best were in the city of Rome and in other large cities. Doctors could set broken bones, remove arrowheads, and perform amputations if necessary.

Sometimes doctors' remedies sounded more like superstition – like putting a coin under the sole of your foot to cure a foot pain. Or for the chills and fever of malaria, get seven splinters from seven palm trees, seven shavings from seven beams of wood, seven nails from seven bridges, seven ashes from seven ovens, and seven hairs from old dogs. Hang these around your neck from a white thread so they lay on your chest.

As for the woman in the following story, some doctors would have told her to sit at a fork in the road. Then they would come up behind her and yell to scare her sickness out of her. Others would have told her to eat a grain of barley found in the poop of a white mule. So she may have paid money for such advice. And she may have done these exact things to try to get well. Hearing what people went through when they tried to get well, we can see why so many of them crowded around Jesus, wanting Him to heal them.

Touching Jesus' Coat
Matthew 9:1, 18-22; Mark 5:21-34; Luke 8:40-48

Jesus took the boat to the other side of the lake. A big crowd of people came to see him.

A leader from the town's worship house was in the crowd. His name was Jairus. He bowed to Jesus. "My little girl is sick," he said. "She is going to die. Please come with me. Touch my little girl so she will live."

Jesus went with Jairus. Many people followed, pushing around Jesus.

A woman was in the crowd. She had been sick for 12 years. Many doctors had tried to make her well. In fact, she had given all her money to doctors. But instead of getting well, she got sicker. She pushed her way through the crowd. She crept up right behind Jesus. "I only need to touch his clothes!" she thought. "Then I'll be well." So she reached out and touched Jesus' coat. Right away she was well. She could feel it.

Jesus could tell that power had gone out of him. So he looked around. He asked, "Who touched me?"

"Many people are pushing you," said his friends. "Why do you ask who touched you?"

Jesus kept looking around. The woman came up to him. She bowed at his feet. She was so scared, she was shaking. But she told Jesus everything.

"You are well because you believe," said Jesus. "Go home now. You will have peace."

WEEK 15

 Monday

Medicines

If you lived in Jesus' time, you would probably live your whole life without ever being treated by a real doctor. Instead, you would use home remedies, medicines you would make yourself. Many medicines were made by crushing dried roots into powder or by soaking leaves and berries in water to make potions. Radishes were considered a medicine, and lettuce was used in more than 40 healing potions. Wine was often given to ease stomach problems and other ailments. Sometimes wine was mixed with myrrh to make a medicine. For many sicknesses, people took olive oil. They also rubbed olive oil or cumin onto wounds. A dark substance called asphalt was taken from the Salt Sea (Dead Sea) and used on boils. (It was also used to get rid of house pests.)

For a toothache, you would rub garlic, salt, or yeast on your gums. If your toothache was really bad, you could always find someone who knew how to pull teeth. And if you needed them, false teeth could be made from real human teeth or animal teeth.

The Sick Little Girl
Matthew 9:23-26; Mark 5:35-43; Luke 8:49-56

While Jesus was still talking to the woman who touched His coat, some men came to Jairus. "Your little girl has died," they said. "Don't bother Jesus anymore."

Jesus didn't listen to them. He told Jairus, "Don't be afraid. Just believe."

At Jairus's house, people were crying loudly. Jesus went in with Peter, James, and John. "Why is everyone crying?" asked Jesus. "Why are you making so much noise? The little girl isn't dead. She is just asleep."

The people laughed at Jesus. So he sent them all out. He took Peter, James, and John with him. He took the little girl's mother and father, too. Then he went into the little girl's room.

He held her hand. "Little girl, get up," he said.

Right away, the girl got up and walked! She was about 12 years old.

The people were very surprised. Jesus told them to bring the girl something to eat. He said, "Don't tell anyone else about this.

Sickness and Blindness

Blindness was common in Jesus' time. For one thing, people worked outdoors a lot, and they had only eye salves to protect their eyes from the sun's glare. They had no other eye protection. For another thing, they didn't know how important it was to keep clean and not rub their eyes with dirty hands. The dust was bad in Palestine, and flies swarmed everywhere, carrying infections. So it was easy to get dust in your eyes and touch germs carried by flies.

Some doctors really did help people get well. One doctor claimed to have cured eye cataracts by putting liver on the eyes. But no ancient doctor ever healed a blind person.

Because people thought sickness came from doing something wrong, they thought that if they could make up for what they had done, they could be well. But Jesus said, "Your faith has made you well." He was telling the person that they were well, not because of something they had done to deserve it, but simply because of God's love and forgiveness.

Two Men Who Could Not See
Matthew 9:27-33

Two men who could not see began to follow Jesus. They called out, "Jesus, be kind to us! Make us well!"

Jesus kept walking. He went inside a house. But the men followed him.

Jesus asked them, "Do you believe I can do this?"

"Yes, Lord," they said.

Then Jesus touched their eyes. He said, "You believe. So you will see."

And they could see again.

"Don't let anyone know about this," Jesus said.

But they left and told everyone about it.

Another man came in. He was controlled by a bad spirit. He couldn't talk. A friend brought him to Jesus. So Jesus sent the bad spirit out of the man.

Then the man talked.

People were surprised. "We've never seen anything like this," they said.

☐ Wednesday

Carpenters

Carpenters made and repaired benches and stools, cabinets, and tables. They made doors, window frames and shutters, and even put locks in doors. They also built plows and yokes for farmers and made wooden bowls for women to knead bread in. Carpenters built whole houses. In fact, they were often hired when cities were being built. They not only worked with wood, but with stone, too.

At the time Jesus grew up in Nazareth, a nearby city called Sepphoris was being rebuilt by Herod, the ruler of Galilee. Sepphoris was the capital of Galilee. Herod built a beautiful palace there. It stood on a high ridge and was a kind of fort. Although most of the people who lived in Sepphoris were Greeks, if there had been any danger of attack, Jesus and his family and all the people of Nazareth would have gone to Sepphoris for safety.

As carpenters, Jesus, Joseph, and even some of Jesus' brothers may have helped build parts of the city of Sepphoris. In addition to all the other buildings that had to be constructed by carpenters, there was a theatre with a wooden stage. Jewish carpenters may have worked on this building, too, although Jews did not approve of Roman and Greek theatres.

Sheep with No Shepherd
Matthew 9:35-38; 13:53-58; Mark 6:1-6

Jesus went back to the town where he grew up. He took his friends with him. The worship day came. So he taught in the town's worship house.

Many people heard him teach. They were surprised. "How can he say all these things?" they asked. "How can he be so wise? He even does wonders. Didn't he work in the wood shop when he was growing up? Isn't he Mary's son? James, Joseph, Judas, and Simon are his brothers. All his sisters live here!" Thinking about Jesus bothered them.

"Nobody says good things about a prophet in his own town," said Jesus. He made a few sick people well. But that's all he could do. He couldn't do any other wonders. He could hardly believe that their faith was so small.

Jesus traveled through many towns. He taught in worship houses. He told the good news of God's kingdom. He made people well.

Jesus looked at the crowds of people. He was sad for them. It seemed that they had no one to help them. They were like sheep with no shepherd.

"These people are like crops in a farmer's field," said Jesus. "It's time to bring in the crops. But there aren't many workers. Ask God to send workers into the field. The workers can bring in the people."

 Thursday

Transportation

Even though a donkey was the common transportation for most people, not everyone owned a donkey. If you had a donkey, you might need it to carry your packs as you walked. If you decided to ride the donkey, only one person could ride at a time (maybe two, if they were children). So you would probably walk wherever you wanted to go, even if you were traveling from one city or town to another. People could usually walk 15 to 20 miles a day.

Of course, there were other kinds of transportation, like farm carts and wagons drawn by oxen or donkeys. You could ride in these, but you would have to sit among the goods the carts carried. Only Roman soldiers, messengers, and wealthy travelers rode horses. Camels were used mostly by caravans. Then there were chariots, used by wealthy people. In large cities, a type of chariot was used like a taxi. If you had enough money, you could rent one and drive it yourself.

Like Sheep Going Where Wolves Are
Matthew 10:1-16, 40-42; Mark 6:7-11; Luke 9:1-5

Jesus called his twelve closest friends. He told them to go out two by two. He gave them power to send bad spirits away and make people well.

"Go to the Jews," said Jesus. "Teach God's message. Tell people that the kingdom of heaven is near. Heal people who are sick. Make dead people live again. Send bad spirits away.

"What you have, you got for free," said Jesus. "Now give it away for free. Don't take gold or silver. Don't take a bag. Take only one shirt and one pair of shoes. Don't take a walking stick. You are a worker. People should help you.

"Go into towns," said Jesus. "Look for people who will help you. Stay with them until you leave that town. Go into their homes. Be friendly and pray for peace to come to them. If they welcome you, keep praying for their peace. But what if they don't welcome you? What if people in town won't listen to you? Then shake the dust off your feet when you leave. The truth is, someday God will judge the world. The bad city of Sodom will be better off than that town.

"You are like sheep going where the wolves are," said Jesus. "So be as smart as snakes. But be as peaceful as doves. People who are friendly to you are being friendly to me. People who welcome me are welcoming God.

"Welcome a prophet just because he is a prophet. Then God will give you the same good things he gives the prophets," said Jesus. "Welcome people who do what's right because of the right things they do. Then God will give you the same good things he gives them. It might be only a cup of cold water that you give. But you'll still get good things from God."

Friday

The Fortress of Machaerus

The Herod family built several forts and palaces in different places around the land of Palestine. It seems they wanted several places to which they could escape if they were in danger. With so many forts, no matter where attack might come from, the Herods would have a place nearby where they could hide and be safe. One fort-palace was known as Machaerus. It was on a high "wild hill" overlooking the Salt Sea (Dead Sea). This hill was surrounded by ravines and was not too far from where John the Baptist spent most of his time in the desert. So it's not surprising that Machaerus is where Herod put John into prison. The dungeons of Machaerus had iron hooks in the walls to which prisoners were bound. John spent ten months there. Then came Herod's birthday. He had his birthday party at the palace at Machaerus, and John did not live through it.

John in Trouble
Matthew 14:1-12; Mark 6:14-29; Luke 9:7-9

John, who baptized people, was still around. He had talked to many people about God's way. He had even talked to King Herod, who had married his own brother's wife. Her name was Herodias. John had told Herod, "It's not right to marry your brother's wife."

So King Herod had put John into jail. Herodias was angry at John too. In fact, she wanted to have him killed, but she couldn't. That's because Herod was afraid of John. He was also afraid that people would be upset if he killed John. So he kept John safe.

King Herod knew that John was a good man. He knew that John did what was right. Herod liked to listen to John. The things John said were like a mystery to him.

On King Herod's birthday, he had a party. All the leaders of the land came. Herodias had a daughter who came too. She danced for the people. They all liked the way she danced. So Herod promised to give her anything she wanted. "Just ask me," he said. "I'll give you anything, even half of my kingdom."

The girl went out and asked her mother, "What should I ask for?"

"Ask Herod to kill John," said Herodias. "Tell him you want John's head."

So the girl went to King Herod. "I want John's head on a plate," she said. "Right now!"

Herod was very upset. But he had promised. He didn't want to say no in front of everyone. So he sent a man to the jail to kill John.

The man put John's head on a plate. He brought it to King Herod. The king gave it to the girl. She gave it to her mother.

John's friends came and got his body. They put it in a grave.

At this time, Jesus and his friends were traveling from town to town. They told people the good news. They made many people well, too. People talked about Jesus everywhere.

Some people said, "Jesus is really John. He came back to life! That's why great powers work in him."

Other people said, "Jesus is really Elijah!"

Other people said, "Jesus is a prophet. He is like one of the prophets from long ago."

Even King Herod heard about Jesus. He said, "It's John. I cut off his head, but he is alive again!" Herod tried to see Jesus for himself.

WEEK 16

 Monday

Marketplaces

In most towns and villages, shops were at the front of the houses where people lived. For example, the potter would live in the back of the building. He would make and sell his pottery in a room at the front, which opened to the street.

Sometimes the people of a town would get together just inside or outside the town gate to form a marketplace. This would be especially important if the town was on a well-traveled road where they might expect travelers to stop and buy or sell.

Larger cities were usually built in the Greek form, with an open area where people could gather. Sellers from in and out of town would set up booths there. They would sell grain and fruits, wine and sheep. They would buy tools and clothes, jewelry and perfumes.

Jewish market inspectors walked around in these markets, ready to settle arguments about what the price of something should be. The tax station would be there, too, where the different kinds of products would be weighed and taxed. That meant that the money-changer had a booth there as well, because there were so many different kinds of coins used at that time.

From All the Towns
Matthew 14:13-15; Mark 6:30-36; Luke 9:10-12; John 6:1-3

Jesus' twelve closest friends had been going from town to town. After some time, they came back. They told Jesus what they had done. But many other people crowded around. They didn't even have time to eat.

"Come to a quiet place with me," said Jesus. "Let's get some rest."

So they got into a boat and sailed across Lake Galilee. They headed to a place away from the crowds.

People saw Jesus and his friends leave. They came from all the towns. They ran to the place where Jesus' boat would land. They got there before Jesus did.

When Jesus and his friends landed, there were the people in a big crowd. Jesus felt sorry for them. They looked like sheep who had no shepherd. So he started teaching them. He told them about God's kingdom. He made sick people well.

At last, Jesus' friends came to him. "It's getting late," they said. "We're not in town. We need to send the people back to town. Then they can buy their supper."

 Tuesday

Barley Bread

In the following part of the story, Jesus' friends wanted to send the people back to town to buy their supper. But Jesus had something else in mind. A boy who had brought his own supper was part of the answer to the problem.

The rolls the boy had were probably barley bread, which was the cheapest bread, poor people's bread. The fish were probably pickled and small like sardines. So it wasn't much that the boy shared. But it was plenty for Jesus to use to feed the crowd of more than 5,000 people.

Bread was so important to ancient people that, in Jesus' time, you were not allowed to throw away crumbs the size of an olive or larger. You were not supposed to cut bread, either. You "broke" bread: you tore off the amount you expected to eat.

Bread for Everyone
Matthew 14:16-21; Mark 6:37-44; Luke 9:13-17; John 6:4-14

Jesus looked at the crowd of people. Then he looked at Philip. "Where can we get bread for these people?" he asked. Jesus already knew what he was going to do. But he asked to see what Philip would say.

"We would need lots of food," said Philip. "We could work for eight months. Even then, we would not have the money to buy enough for each person to have one bite!"

"Look at this little boy," said Andrew. "He brought his own supper. He has five rolls and two small fish. But that won't feed many people."

Then Jesus told his friends to put the people into groups. Some people got in groups of 100. Some got in groups of 50. They sat down on the grass.

Jesus took the five rolls and two fish. He looked up to heaven and thanked God. Then he began to hand the rolls to his helpers. There were a lot more than just five rolls.

Jesus' friends began to give the rolls to the people. Then Jesus handed the fish to his friends. They gave fish to the people. There was more than enough. All the people got to eat as much as they wanted.

After supper, Jesus' friends cleaned up the leftovers. They filled 12 baskets. About 5,000 men had eaten there. Women and children had eaten there too. They said, "This is the prophet we've been looking for!"

Wednesday

Boats

The west side of Palestine is coastline along what people called the Great Sea (the Mediterranean). But ancient Palestine did not have many good harbors or seaports. The Jewish people did not like the sea anyway, so they did not do much business there. But if they visited the coast or traveled any of the trade roads along the coastline, they probably saw Roman warships, which were long and narrow. Although these boats had square sails to catch the winds, below deck dozens of rowers sat, pulling on their oars. These Roman ships protected the Great Sea from pirates and kept the shipping lanes open for trading ships. Trading boats were shorter than warships, and rounder. They depended on their sails, although they also had oars so they could row if necessary.

The boats that Jesus' friends used on Lake Galilee were, of course, smaller than the seafaring ships. One boat from Jesus' time has been discovered. It is wide and has three or four bench seats across it, with wider platforms at the front and back. It was made of seven kinds of wood, including cypress and cedar, and looks as if it was repaired a lot. Many boats in Jesus' time had sails, but they also held oars for rowing. These kinds of boats were probably solid, though not very fast. Still, they could usually cross Lake Galilee in 30 minutes. But sometimes, as we've learned, winds blast through the hills west of the lake without any warning, creating whirlwinds and huge waves.

On Top of the Water
Matthew 14:22-36; Mark 6:45-56; John 6:15-21

Jesus sent his friends out in the boat. Then he sent the crowd of people home. He knew they wanted to make him their king. He went up on a hill to be alone and pray.

It was already dark. Out on the lake, a strong wind was blowing. Waves were growing bigger. From the hill, Jesus saw his friends in their boat. They were rowing hard, trying to go one way. But the wind was blowing them the other way. About three o'clock in the morning, Jesus went to them. He walked on top of the water.

Jesus' friends had rowed about three and a half miles. Now they looked up and saw Jesus coming. They thought he was a ghost going past. They cried out, scared.

"It's just me," said Jesus. "Don't be afraid."

"If it's really you, tell me to come to you," said Peter. "Let me walk on the water too."

"Come on," said Jesus.

So Peter got out of the boat. He stepped onto the water and began to walk to Jesus. When he saw the waves, he got scared and started to sink. "Lord! Save me!" he cried.

Right away, Jesus reached out to Peter. He lifted Peter up. "Your faith is so small!" said Jesus. "Why didn't you believe?"

They both climbed into the boat. Then the wind stopped blowing so hard.

Jesus' friends were surprised. They really had not understood the wonder Jesus did with the rolls and fish. But now they worshiped Jesus. They said, "You really are God's Son!"

At last they reached the other side of the lake. When they left their boat, people saw them. They ran to tell everyone that Jesus was there. People brought their sick friends.

In the country, people brought sick friends to Jesus. In town, they brought sick friends to him. They wanted just to touch the edge of his coat. Everyone who touched him got well.

 Thursday

Bread

Bread was one of the most important foods in the ancient world. You were never to set raw meat on top of a loaf of bread or to set a pitcher of water on it or a hot plate against it.

Before bread could be baked, grain had to be ground between two round, flat stones called "millstones." Women and girls did the grinding, usually every day, or at least every two or three days. It took about an hour to grind enough to make the coarse flour used for making the day's bread. After you had ground the flour, you would sift it to get bits of dirt out.

Then you would mix the flour with water or olive oil plus some leftover dough from the day before. The old dough was the yeast that would make the new dough rise (puff up). If you wanted the bread to be sweet, you would add a bit of honey to the dough. Then you shaped the dough into rounds about 1/2 inch thick and 12 inches across. Each one was called "a round of bread" or just "a round." You left these dough rounds to rise in the warm sunlight. Sometimes you left them overnight to rise, then baked them the next day.

Bread from Heaven
John 6:22-40

The next day, people on the other side of the lake wondered where Jesus was. They knew only one boat had left. They knew Jesus wasn't in it. So they began to look for him. At last they took their own boats to the other side of the lake. There was Jesus. "When did you get here?" they asked.

"You're looking for me only because I gave you food," said Jesus. "Don't work for food that will rot. Work to get life that lasts forever. That's what doesn't rot. I can give this life to you, because God is pleased with me."

"What does God want us to do?" they asked.

"God wants you to believe in me, because he sent me," said Jesus.

"Show us a wonder," they said. "Then we can believe. Long ago, God's people got food in the desert. It was bread that came down from heaven."

"It wasn't Moses who gave them bread from heaven," said Jesus. "It was God, my Father. Now he gives you true bread from heaven. I'm like bread from heaven. I give life to the world."

"We'd like to have this bread," they said. "We'd like to have it from now on."

"I am the Bread of Life," said Jesus. "Come to me. Then your heart will never be hungry. Believe in me. Then your spirit will never be thirsty. But you saw what I did, and you still don't believe. I didn't come from heaven to do what I want. I came to do what God wants. He wants me to care for people who trust me. He wants me to give them life that lasts forever. I'll never send away people who come to me."

 Friday

Ways of Baking

There were several ways ancient people could bake bread. They could bake it over hot wood coals in a small oven. Or on heated rocks. Or on a clay or iron griddle or pan over heat. Poor people who didn't have their own ovens would take their bread rounds to the town's community oven. Sometimes women made a hole in the center of their rounds of bread so they could store them on a pole. The pole also made it easy to carry the stack of bread rounds.

Who Will Leave?
John 6:41-71

People began to give Jesus a hard time, because he said he was the Bread from heaven. They said, "This is Jesus, Joseph's son. We know his father and mother. How can he say he came from heaven?"

"Stop making a fuss," said Jesus. "People can't come to me unless my Father brings them. I will give them life that lasts forever. Isaiah the prophet wrote that God will teach everyone. So when people hear from God, they come to me . When they learn from my Father, they come to me. I'm the only one who is from God. I'm the only one who has seen the Father. The truth is, the person who believes has life forever.

"I am the Bread of Life," said Jesus. "Long ago, God's people ate manna in the desert. But they still died. I came from heaven too, like manna. But you'll never die if you eat this kind of bread.

This kind of 'bread' is my body. I will give my body so the world can live."

The Jews fussed among themselves. "How can he give us his body to eat?" they asked.

Jesus said, "I'll give my blood, too. My body and my blood give life. This gift can feed your spirit like food feeds your body. So let your spirit feed on my gift. Then you'll have life forever. Your last day on earth will come. Then I'll make you live again."

Jesus talked about this at the worship house in Capernaum. Many of Jesus' followers said, "This is too hard to understand. Who can go along with this?"

"Does this upset you?" Jesus asked. "What if you see me go where I was before? You see, it's the Spirit who gives life. The body doesn't count for anything. The words I speak are spirit. They are life. But some of you don't believe."

Many people turned away after this. They didn't follow Jesus anymore. But Jesus already knew which followers would not believe. He had known from the first who would become his enemy. Jesus asked his 12 closest friends, "Do you, too, want to leave me?"

"Lord, where would we go?" asked Peter. "You teach us about life that lasts forever. We believe you. We know you are God's Son."

"I chose 12 of you," said Jesus. "But one of you is a devil." He was talking about Judas. Jesus had chosen him as one of his 12 closest friends. But later, he would turn against Jesus. He would become an enemy.

WEEK 17

 Monday

The Pharisees' Way of Washing

Many Jews in Jesus' time would not approve of the way we wash our hands. Even though we wash our hands with soap and water, they would say we are unclean. That's because they had rules about exactly how to wash before you ate. (It was ritual washing – like a ceremony. A ritual is a way of doing something according to religious law.) The Pharisees thought that being ritually clean was the way to please God. That's why they were upset that Jesus didn't wash His hands the right way.

The water they used had to come from special large stone jars. Keeping the water in these special jars was a way of making sure it had not been used for anything else and nothing had been mixed with it. The amount of water you used each time you washed your hands had to be equal to one and a half eggshells full. Normally a slave, servant, or woman of the household poured the water over your hands. Here's the way you would do it:

1. Your hands have to be clear of any sand or grit.

2. Hold your hands over a basin with your fingers pointing up. Let the water drip off your wrists. (Pour 1 1/2 eggshells' worth of water over the hands.)

3. Make a fist with your right hand. Rub it into the palm and over your left hand.

4. Make a fist with your left hand. Rub it into the palm and over your right hand.

5. Now the water on your hands is unclean, because it touched your unclean hands. So hold your hands over the basin again, wrists bent, fingers pointed *down*. (Pour 1 1/2 eggshells of water over the wrists so that the water runs off at the finger tips.)

The Leaders' Rules
Matthew 15:1-9; Mark 7:1-13

There was a special way that Jewish leaders washed their hands. They wouldn't eat until they had washed in this way. They even made a washing rule. Everyone had to wash that same way. The leaders had many other rules like this. They had a rule for washing cups, jugs, and pots. The rule told the special way to wash these things.

Some of the leaders had seen Jesus' friends eating. Jesus' friends had not washed their hands that special way. So the leaders went to Jesus. They asked, "Why don't your friends follow the leaders' rules? They don't wash their hands like we do."

"Isaiah talked about you," said Jesus. "He was right. He said, 'These people say good things about me. But their hearts are far away from me. They worship me for nothing. Their teachings are just rules made by people.' You're not obeying God's rules," said Jesus. "Instead, you're following your own rules. Moses said, 'Treat your mother and father like important people.' But you say you don't have to help your mother and father. You say you'll give your help to God instead. You make God's rules seem like nothing, because you think your made up rules are more important."

 Tuesday

Roads

One great thing the Romans did was build good roads. The roads they built were meant to connect the different countries they ruled to the city of Rome. "All roads lead to Rome" became a famous saying. Building such long roads meant they had to build bridges and tunnels, too. Romans wanted these roads so they could send their armies quickly to other parts of the world and so their messengers could travel fast. (The fastest a messenger could travel was about 75 miles a day.)

Roman roads were paved with flat stones or blocks of rock cut to fit. Since these well-paved roads went only where Rome chose them to go, most other roads were still not paved. These were dirt roads that had been packed down by travelers over hundreds of years. When Jesus went from Judea to Galilee or the other way around, He probably traveled over both kinds of roads.

Angry Leaders
Matthew 15:10-20; Mark 7:14-23; John 7:1

Later, Jesus' followers told him, "The leaders were angry when you said that."

"Plants that God didn't plant will be pulled up by the roots," said Jesus. "Just leave them alone. They may be leaders, but they can't see. When one man who can't see leads another man who can't see, they both fall down."

Jesus went on. "Nothing a person eats can make him dirty from sin. That's because it's not going into his heart. It's going into his stomach, then out of his body."

"What do you mean?" asked Peter.

"Don't you understand yet?" Jesus asked. "It's the words that come out of a person that make him dirty. Bad thoughts come from inside him, from his heart. Sinning with sex, stealing, and killing come from the heart. Being greedy, hating, and lying come from the heart. Wanting what's not yours, bragging, foolish thinking – all these come from inside a person. That's what makes people dirty."

Then Jesus went to Galilee. He stayed away from Judea, because some of the leaders there were waiting to kill him.

Pets

In ancient Egypt, cats were common pets. They were even worshiped there. But cats were not pets in Palestine. There's not even a word for "cat" in the Bible's Old Testament Hebrew language. Sometimes rich people in the ancient world made pets of certain kinds of monkeys. Hyenas were also sometimes kept as pets. But most people considered hyenas to be unhealthy animals, because in the wild, they dug up graves.

In ancient Palestine, most people did not have pets. Still, animals were around all the time. A family might make a pet out of a favorite lamb or chicken or even doves. Doves were sometimes sent out with messages attached to them and always were able to make their way back home. Some people kept small dogs as pets, and others probably used dogs to herd sheep. But most dogs were seen as scavenger animals, so they were considered unclean. Dogs often ran wild in packs through the streets. Jewish people called non-Jews "dogs."

Making People Well
Matthew 15:21-31; Mark 7:24-37

Jesus went to a house in a town called Tyre. He didn't want anyone to know he was there. But he couldn't keep it a secret.

A woman who was not Jewish lived near Tyre. She came to Jesus. "Lord," she said, "be kind to me. Bad spirits control my daughter."

But Jesus didn't answer her.

Jesus' friends told him, "This lady keeps crying to us. Tell her to go away."

Jesus looked at the lady. "I was sent only to God's people," he said.

The woman bowed to Jesus. "Lord, help me," she said.

"I shouldn't take what belongs to God's people," said Jesus. "I shouldn't toss it to the dogs. It wouldn't be right."

"Yes, Lord," she said. "But even dogs get tiny bits of food. They eat what falls off their master's table."

Then Jesus said, "You have a lot of faith. I'll give you what you asked for."

At that very moment, her daughter got well.

Then Jesus traveled to the Ten Cities. Some people led a man to Jesus. This man couldn't hear. He could hardly talk. The people asked Jesus to touch this man.

So Jesus took the man away from the people. He put his fingers into the man's ears. Then Jesus spit. He touched the man's tongue, looked to heaven, and took a deep breath. "Open," he said.

Right away, the man's ears opened. His tongue was set free. He started talking clearly.

Jesus told the crowd not to tell anyone. But the more Jesus said, "Don't tell," the more they told.

People were very surprised. "Jesus does everything just right," they said. "He can even make people hear. He can make people talk."

Big crowds of people came to Jesus. They brought sick people, and Jesus made them well. People who couldn't walk ended up walking. People who couldn't see ended up seeing. People who couldn't hear or speak were listening and talking. Everyone was very surprised. The people cheered for God.

Thursday

Meat and Fish

As we have seen, poor people, including Jesus' family, did not often eat meat, not because they were vegetarian, but because meat was expensive. Sometimes they had chicken, especially on a special occasion. On feast days they would eat lamb. Yogurt was a common food. So were "curds," which we would call cottage cheese. But the milk and cheese that people had in Jesus' time came from goats. Crushed garlic on bread was a favorite food as well. At special times of festival or celebration, you would eat honey-coated pastries.

In Galilee, it would be more common to have fish. Fishermen would carry their big fish to the market hanging on a ring or string. They would carry smaller fish in baskets or small barrels. Rabbis gave advice on which kinds of fish were right to eat for which occasion.

People enjoyed fresh fish, of course, but they would often eat their fish dried or pickled. Sometimes they made a special sauce out of fish. They also ate fish eggs.

Seven Rolls
Matthew 15:32; Mark 8:1-7

The crowd around Jesus hadn't had anything to eat. So Jesus called his friends to him.

"I feel sorry for these people," said Jesus. "They've been with me for three days. They don't have anything left to eat. Many of them came a long way to get here. They'll get hungry if I send them home. They might be too weak to get home."

"We're not close to any town," said his friends. "Where can we get enough bread to feed all these people?"

"How much bread do you have?" Jesus asked.

"We have seven rolls," they said.

Jesus told the people to sit on the ground. He took the seven rolls. He thanked God. Then he pulled the rolls apart. He gave them to his friends. His friends gave them to the people.

Someone had a few small fish. Jesus gave thanks for them, too. Then he told his friends to pass the fish to everyone. All the people got plenty of food. There were about 4,000 men. There were many women and children, too.

Friday

Superstitions

Many Jews of Jesus' time were superstitious. Some believed they should hang a red rag or fox's tail between the eyes of their horse or donkey to make sure they didn't fall as they rode. They believed that even numbers were unlucky, but not odd numbers. They said that if you got into a food fight and threw little balls of bread at each other, you would get sick.

In the ancient world, it was said that if you sneezed going across the gangplank to get to a ship, bad things would happen. Clipping your nails or trimming your hair in good weather aboard a ship was bad luck. Birds coming to sit among the ship's ropes was a good sign. Unless the birds were crows or magpies. Then it was a bad sign.

People often asked Jesus for a "sign." But Jesus refused to act like a magician. He did not feed their superstitions. When He answered them, He used a saying about signs in everyday weather: Red sky in the morning, sailors take warning; red sky at night, sailor's delight. He was saying the sign is here; you're just not seeing it. God sent Jesus as a sign of His love. Jesus was saying that He Himself was the sign.

The Evening Sky
Matthew 15:39–16:4; Mark 8:8-12

After everyone had eaten, Jesus' friends picked up the leftovers. All in all, they got seven baskets full of leftovers.

Then Jesus sent the people away. He got into a boat with his friends. They sailed across the lake.

Now the leaders wanted to test Jesus. They wanted him to show them a wonder.

Jesus said, "You say, 'The evening sky is red. So we'll have good weather tomorrow.' You say, 'The morning sky is red. There are clouds. So we will have a storm today.' You know what will happen by looking at the sky. But you cannot see what's happening right now," said Jesus. "Sinful people look for wonders. But you will get just one sign: the sign of Jonah."

WEEK 18

 Monday

Baskets

Jesus fed thousands of people two different times. The first time, there were 5,000 men plus women and children. Afterward, Jesus' friends picked up twelve baskets full of leftovers. The word for "baskets" used in that story is *kophinoi*. Those were baskets shaped like bottles. They had narrow necks. When Jews traveled or went out for a long day, they often carried food with them in these kinds of baskets so they wouldn't have to buy food that might have been touched by the hands of non-Jews. (That would have made the food "unclean" to them.)

When Jesus fed 4,000 people, there were seven baskets full of leftovers. That word for "baskets" is *sphurides*. We might call that kind of basket a hamper. The apostle Paul later used a basket like that to escape over the wall of the city of Damascus. So we know it was big enough to hide a person in. It was the kind of basket a non-Jew might use. This makes sense, because when Jesus fed the 4,000 people, he was in a part of the country called the Decapolis. That means "ten cities." These ten cities were Greek cities, so the 4,000 people Jesus fed may have been mostly non-Jews.

Yeast
Matthew 16:5-12; Mark 8:13-21

Jesus and his friends got into a boat and sailed back to the other side of the lake. They took only one loaf of bread with them.

"Be careful about the leaders' yeast," said Jesus.

His friends looked at each other. "Did he say that because we're running out of bread?" they whispered.

Jesus knew what they were saying. "Why do you talk about having no bread? Don't your eyes see? Don't your ears hear? Don't you remember? I gave five rolls to 5,000 people. How many baskets of leftovers did we have?"

"Twelve," they said.

"I gave seven rolls to 4,000 people," said Jesus. "How many baskets of leftovers did we have?"

"Seven," they said.

"Don't you understand?" asked Jesus. "I wasn't talking about bread. Be careful about the leaders' yeast."

Then they understood. He wasn't talking about the bread's yeast. He meant, "Be careful about what the leaders teach."

Keys in Ancient Palestine

In Jesus' time, most houses had doors of wood hung by hinges of leather. The doors either didn't lock, or they had a sliding bolt. Only rich people had doors that locked with a key. Because carpenters often installed locks in doors, Jesus probably had experience working with locks and keys. He may have also made wooden chests that locked with a key. Jewish keys were quite large. People sometimes wore them on a necklace as a sign that they were wealthy.

In the following story, Jesus and his followers are visiting a non-Jewish city that had fourteen temples to ancient gods. There was also a cave there that was supposed to be the place where the Greek god Pan was born. As Jesus and His friends sat there, no doubt within view of at least some of these temples, Jesus asked His followers who they thought He was. Peter said, "You are the Son of the *Living* God." He probably said, "*Living* God" because there were so many not-alive "gods" honored in that city. Peter was contrasting the *living* God with those idols. He was basically saying, "You're the Son of the one true, real God who is alive, not like all these other pretend gods."

Keys
Matthew 16:13-20; Mark 8:22-30; Luke 9:18-21

There was a man who couldn't see. People led him to Jesus. They asked Jesus to touch the man and make him well.

So Jesus took the man's hand. He led the man to a place outside the town. Then Jesus spit on the man's eyes and touched them. "Can you see anything?" asked Jesus.

"I see people," the man said. "They look like walking trees."

Jesus touched the man's eyes again. Then the man could see clearly. Jesus sent the man home. "Don't go into town," he said.

Jesus traveled on with his friends. "Who do people say I am?" he asked.

"Some people say you're John who baptized," they said. "Some say you're Elijah. Others say you're Jeremiah or one of the other prophets."

"Who do you think I am?" asked Jesus.

"You're the one God promised to send," said Peter. "You're the Christ. You're the Son of the Living God."

Jesus said, "God will be good to you, Peter. My Father in heaven showed you who I am. You're Peter. You are like a rock. I'll build my church on this rock. The power of hell will never get rid of it. I'll give you the keys to God's kingdom. If you lock anything on earth, it will be locked in heaven. If you open anything on earth, it will be open in heaven. But for now, don't tell anyone I'm the one God promised to send."

Getting Behind Jesus

Even though Peter believed that Jesus was the Messiah, the Son of God, he did not expect Jesus to be any different from his own ideas of what the Messiah would be: a warrior king who would save the Jews from the Romans. What Jesus said to Peter when Peter pulled Him aside sounds rude, even shocking. Was He calling Peter *Satan*? The word *satan* means "the accuser" or "the one who comes against." Peter was trying to argue with Jesus, and Jesus' answer told Peter that Peter was coming against Jesus, accusing God's plans of being wrong. What Jesus says is, "Get behind me, Satan." He is saying, "Peter, you are in the way. You are supposed to be behind me, following me, not trying to lead."

Then Jesus talks about God's *kingdom*. A kingdom is a place where a king rules. When Jesus talks about God's kingdom or the kingdom of heaven, He is talking about God's life-giving love at work all around the world. Within a little over thirty years from the time Jesus died and rose again, the news about Jesus had spread throughout the known world.

What's Coming
Matthew 16:21-28; Mark 8:31–9:1; Luke 9:22-27

Jesus now began to get his friends ready for what was going to happen. He told them he had to go to Jerusalem. He said the leaders and teachers of God's laws would treat him badly. He said he would be killed. But he said he would come alive again on the third day.

Peter pulled Jesus to one side. "Never, Lord," he said. "This will never happen to you."

"Get out of my way, Satan!" said Jesus. "This does not help me. You're not thinking of what God wants. You're thinking of what you want."

Then Jesus called to everyone around him. "Do you want to be with me? Then you'll have to give up what you want. You'll have to do what God chose you to do. Do you want only to save your own life? You'll end up losing it. Give up your life for me and God's kingdom. That's the way to save your life. What if you got all the riches in the world but lost your soul? What good would your riches be? What could you give to buy your soul back?"

"Some people are upset about me," said Jesus. "They are upset about my words. I'll be upset about them when I come again with angels and my Father's power. Some people here will see God's kingdom. They will see it before they die."

Fullers, the Law, and the Prophets

In ancient Palestine, women washed clothes by dunking them into a river or a brook or a large tub of water. Then they would beat the clothes with a stick or rub them across rocks. Another way to get clothes cleaned was to take them to men called "fullers." Fullers cleaned clothes for rich people. Instead of rubbing or beating the wet clothes, they often stepped all over them (with clean feet, of course). They tried to whiten and brighten the white robes that some people wore. In fact, in Mark's book, he writes that when Jesus was on the mountain with Moses and Elijah, His clothes became whiter than any fuller could make them.

Two interesting people met Jesus on the mountain that day: Moses and Elijah. All good Jews in Jesus' time would have known the Ten Commandments. They greatly admired Moses, the man God gave the Ten Commandments to. Jews also greatly admired the prophets. Elijah was one of the most famous prophets. To Jews, Moses represented the Law and Elijah represented the prophets. Jesus represented the "fulfillment" of the law and the prophets. His life completed all that the law and the prophets set out to do. Jesus lived a perfect life for us, fulfilling the law by loving perfectly.

As White As Light
Matthew 17:1-13; Mark 9:2-13; Luke 9:28-36

Six days later, Jesus took Peter, James, and John with him. They went up on a high mountain. All of a sudden, Jesus changed. His face began shining as bright as the sun. His clothes turned as white as light. Then Moses and Elijah showed up and talked with Jesus.

"Lord!" said Peter. "This is wonderful. If you want, I can make three tents here. One for you, one for Moses, and one for Elijah!"

Then a bright cloud came down around them. A voice from the cloud said, "This is my Son. He is the Son I love. I'm happy with him. Listen to him."

Peter, James, and John fell to the ground, afraid. They didn't look up.

Jesus came over and touched them. "You can get up," he said. "Don't be afraid."

They looked up and saw no one but Jesus.

Then they all came down the mountain. Jesus said, "Don't tell anyone what you just saw. I will die. But I'll come back to life. Then you can tell about it."

"The Jewish leaders say Elijah has to come first," they said. "Why?"

"Elijah already came," said Jesus. "They didn't know him. They treated him any way they wanted to. They'll treat me badly too."

Then Jesus' friends understood what he was saying. He was talking about John, who baptized people. Jesus was calling him Elijah.

Peter, James, and John did what Jesus asked. They didn't tell anybody what they saw on the mountain.

Mustard Seeds and Mountain Movers

A mustard seed is part of a word picture Jesus uses in this next story. In Jesus' time, mustard seeds were considered to be the smallest in the world. People used these hot seeds to spice their food. When the tiny seeds were planted, they grew very quickly. They could grow large enough for birds to nest in.

The other word picture Jesus uses is "moving mountains." That's how people in Jesus' time described a great teacher who could help you solve problems. They called that kind of teacher an *uprooter* or *mover* of mountains. So "moving mountains" meant solving difficult problems.

Combining both word pictures, the mustard seed and mountain-mover, Jesus made His point: With even a little faith, we can solve difficult problems.

Everything Is Possible
Matthew 17:14-21; Mark 9:14-29; Luke 9:37-43

Jesus walked back with Peter, James, and John. They found a big crowd around their other friends. Teachers of God's law were fussing at them. When the people saw Jesus, they ran to meet him.

"What are you fussing about?" asked Jesus.

One man said, "I brought my son here to see you. A bad spirit controls him. It won't let him talk. It throws him to the ground. His teeth rub together. His arms and legs get tight. I asked your friends to send the spirit away. But they couldn't."

"You people don't believe in me," said Jesus. "How long will I have to put up with you? Bring me the boy." So they brought the boy to him.

When the spirit saw Jesus, it threw the boy down. He fell on the ground and rolled around.

"How long has he been like this?" asked Jesus.

"This started when he was very little," said his father. "Sometimes the bad spirit throws him into the fire. Sometimes it throws him into the water. It tries to kill him. Please be kind to us. Help us if you can."

"If I can?" said Jesus. "Everything is possible for the person who believes."

"I do believe!" said the father. "Help me get past the part of me that doesn't believe."

Jesus saw that a crowd was gathering. So he talked to the bad spirit. "You spirit, come out of that boy," he said. "Never go into him again!"

The spirit yelled and shook the boy. Then it came out.

The boy was so still, people said, "He is dead."

But Jesus took the boy's hand, and the boy stood up.

Jesus went into a house. His friends asked, "Why couldn't we send the spirit away?"

"It's because your faith is very small," said Jesus. "Even faith the size of a small mustard seed is strong. With it, you can move a mountain. You can say, 'Move from here to there!' It will move. Nothing will be impossible for you. But this kind of spirit comes out only by prayer."

WEEK 19

 Monday

Taxes

If you lived in Jesus' time, you would pay lots of taxes.

1. Each person paid a "poll" tax ("poll" means "head") to Rome. Richer people paid more.
2. You paid Rome taxes on the property you owned.
3. You paid taxes on what you carried to market to sell; taxes were collected at certain bridges, roads, entrances to towns, and in marketplaces.
4. You tithed to the temple. That means you paid a tenth of whatever you grew, whether it was sheep, barley, eggs, or herbs like mint and dill.
5. Each male over 13 paid a temple tax every year.

The last one, the temple tax, was what the tax collectors asked Peter about. Peter was trained to fish. That was his job. So Peter found the money to pay the tax by doing what he was trained to do. Your family pays taxes. They get the money to pay taxes by working at their jobs.

Fishing for Money
Matthew 17:22-27; Mark 9:30-32; Luke 9:44-45

Jesus and his friends traveled through Galilee. Jesus was teaching these friends. He didn't want anyone to know where they were. "One of my twelve closest friends will turn against me," said Jesus. "He will take money from some of the leaders and show them where I am. They will kill me. But on the third day, I'll come back to life."

Jesus' friends didn't understand what he was talking about. They were afraid to ask Jesus about it.

They came to the town of Capernaum. Some tax men saw them and came up to Peter. They said, "Doesn't Jesus pay the worship-house tax?"

"Yes, he does," said Peter. Then he went to Jesus.

But Jesus talked first. "What do you think, Peter? Who do kings get taxes from? Do they get taxes from their own family? Or do they get taxes from other people?"

"From other people," said Peter.

"Then their own family doesn't pay taxes," Jesus said. "But we don't want to make these men mad. So go fishing. Throw your line into the lake. Take the first fish you catch. Open its mouth and look inside. You'll find money in there. Then you can pay our taxes."

Rulers and Leaders

In ancient Rome, people considered the emperor to be the greatest person alive. He was even seen as a god or "god's son." There were all sorts of other rulers under him, including men called senators. Under the emperor and senators came the leaders of the lands Rome controlled. Some were called kings. In Palestine, Herod was a king. But he was not as great as the emperor. There were also procurators like Pilate, who ruled as governors. Pilate ruled Judea where Jerusalem was. Herod ruled Galilee, where Jesus grew up and spent much of His time. But Pilate and Herod were more like enemies than friends.

The next important official was the man in charge of the Jewish religious system, the High Priest. He had great power as long as he went along with the Romans. (Just to let the high priest know he'd better go along with them, the Romans kept his special holy-day clothes locked away until he needed them.)

Under the High Priest were the other priests and law-makers and the judges known as the Sanhedrin. Most of them were rich, and many lived, dressed, and acted in the popular Greek and Roman style. They were allowed by the Romans to keep their positions as long as they did nothing to offend Rome or the emperor.

Then there were the Pharisees, the Jewish leaders. Some of them were also in high positions. They loved to be seen around town and to be known for their good works and for following the rules exactly. They wanted to be treated as very important people.

Among all these people, there was plenty of jealousy. Men tried to move into higher positions or into greater authority and wealth. There were plenty of arguments, which at times got violent. So we can see why Jesus didn't want his own followers quarreling about who was greatest.

Who Is the Greatest?
Matthew 18:1; Mark 9:33-35; Luke 9:46; 17:7-10

Jesus and his friends were walking down the road. His friends began fussing with each other. So Jesus asked them, "What are you fussing about?"

Jesus' friends didn't answer. They had been fussing over who was the greatest.

Jesus sat down. "Do you want to be first?" he asked. "Then make yourself last. Serve others. Suppose you had a servant who took care of your garden. Or he watched your sheep in the field. At the end of the day, he comes in. Would you say, 'Come in. Sit down. Have something to eat'? No, you would say, 'Make my supper first. Serve me while I eat and drink. Then you may have your supper.'

"Let's say your servant does what you tell him to do. Is that anything special? I don't think so," said Jesus. "It's that way with you, too. You say you did only what you were told to do. To be a great servant, you must do more than you were told."

 Wednesday

Games

As we learned earlier, children in Jesus' time probably played hopscotch, a game invented and played by Roman soldiers. They also had races and played blind-man's bluff and probably tag and tug of war, too. One game, kind of like our game of checkers, was played with stones as checkers. The squares were drawn on stone, in dirt, or on wood. Another game, like our game of jacks, was played with a ball made of leather and the knucklebones of sheep instead of jacks.

Games of throwing were popular. For one game, children dug a hole in the dirt and tried to toss stones into the hole from a distance. They also had a game similar to our game of bowling: they rolled round stones at wooden or clay figures, trying to knock them down. Sometimes they would shoot arrows and throw stones from slingshots. But these games were also serious practice, since bows, arrows and slingshots were real weapons.

Tops to spin and hoops to roll were popular toys. Younger children pulled carved toys. Children also had simple musical instruments like drums, tambourines, rattles, and whistles. They often made these instruments themselves. Dancing was a fun pastime as well. Men danced in one group, and women danced in another.

All these were games that Jesus may have played growing up.

A Little Child and a Little Sheep
Matthew 18:2-14; Mark 9:36-37; Luke 9:47-48

Jesus called a child to come to him. Jesus' twelve closest friends were there too. He asked the child to stand with them. Then Jesus said, "You must change from what you're like now to go into God's kingdom. You must become like little children. A little child knows there are others who are greater. So treat others like they're greater than you are. Then you'll be the greatest in God's kingdom.

"If you welcome a little child, you are welcoming me," said Jesus. "If you welcome me, you are welcoming God. If you make a child sin, you're in trouble. It would be better to drown in the deepest sea. Don't treat these little ones as if they aren't important. Their angels always see the face of their heavenly Father.

"Suppose you had 100 sheep," said Jesus. "One walked off and got lost. Wouldn't you leave 99 sheep on the hill? Wouldn't you look for your lost sheep? What would you do if you found that sheep? You'd be happy about that one sheep. You'd be happier for it than for 99 that didn't walk off. That's the way your Father in heaven is. He doesn't want any little ones to be lost.

Thursday

The Value of a Name

In the ancient world, if you talked about a person's "name," you might not be talking about the label given them by their parents, like "Peter" or "Paul" or "Mary." Instead, when you talked about someone's "name," you might mean their character or reputation, the kind of person they were. In the Old Testament book of Proverbs, it says, "Let love and faithfulness never leave you . . . Then you will win favor and a good name in the sight of God and man" (Proverbs 3:3, 4). That doesn't mean you will win a name like "Bethany" instead of "Bitsy" or "Evan" instead of "Eugene." It means you will win a good reputation. People will think well of you and say good things about you. "A good name is more desirable than great riches; to be esteemed is better than silver or gold" (Proverbs 22:1). "A good name is better than fine perfume" (Ecclesiastes 7:1). That doesn't mean you hope your mom and dad chose a good name for you, a name you like. It's talking about your reputation, your character, how you act, what you say.

So when we read about doing something "in Jesus' name," it doesn't just mean saying the name of Jesus. It means that what we do or say shows Jesus' character, His life-giving love, to others. When we pray and ask "in Jesus' name," it means we ask according to His character of love. It means that we plan to use what we ask for to show His life-giving love.

In Jesus' Name
Matthew 18:15-20; Mark 9:38-41; Luke 9:49-50; 17:1-2

"How sad it is for the world that there are things that make people sin," said Jesus. "These things will always be around. But how sad it is for the people who make others sin. They should know they'll get in trouble with God.

John said, "We saw a man send bad spirits away by saying your name. We told him to stop, because he is not one of us."

"Don't stop him," said Jesus. "He does wonders in my name. So he won't say bad things about me. Anyone who isn't against us is for us. Someone may give you water in my name. They may do it because you're my friend. If they do, God will do good things for them.

"Someone may do something wrong to you," said Jesus. "Then you should go to see him. Show him what he did wrong. Keep it just between the two of you. If he listens, then you have won a friend. If he won't listen, go back later. Take one or two people with you. Maybe he will listen to them. If he doesn't listen to them, tell my followers. If he doesn't listen to my followers, stop trying. He is like someone who doesn't believe in God."

"Two of you might agree when you pray," said Jesus. "Agree about anything you ask for. Then my Father in heaven will do it for you. Two or three people might come together in my name. Then I'm right there with them."

 Friday

Lending and Debts

Jews were supposed to loan money to other Jews without making them pay interest (extra money when the loan is paid back). That rule did not apply if the borrower was not a Jew. Either way, if you could not repay what you owed, you might be seized and sold as a slave. Or your whole family might be sold as slaves. Or you might be put in jail, at least until the year of release, which came around every seven years. During that year, slaves were to be set free. Debts were to be cancelled as well. Even the land was given a rest from plowing and planting.

In the following story, Peter probably thought he was being generous when he asked about forgiving seven times. The rabbis said you must forgive only three times. But Jesus answered that people should forgive "70 x 7." The number 7 was considered to be holy. The seventh day of the week was the Sabbath, a holy day, and every seventh year was special. The expression "7 x 7" or "70 x 7" meant infinity, forever and ever.

The Servant Who Would Not Forgive
Matthew 18:21-35; Luke 17:3-4

Peter asked Jesus, "How many times should I forgive someone? Seven times?"

"Not just seven times," said Jesus. "Seventy-seven times. Tell the person what he did. If he is sorry, forgive him. He may sin against you seven times in one day. He may come back seven times saying, 'I'm sorry.' So forgive him. Then Jesus told this story:

God's kingdom is like a king. This king wanted his servants to pay what they owed him. One man owed him millions. But he couldn't pay the money back. The king said he would sell that man. He would sell the man's whole family. He would sell everything the man owned. Then the king would have the money the man owed him.

But the servant bowed down in front of the king. He begged, "Please wait a little while longer! I'll pay back all the money!"

The king felt sorry for the man. He told the man not to worry about what he owed. The king wouldn't make him pay it back. He let the man go.

"The servant left. He owed no money! But he met a man who owed him just a little money. He caught this man and started choking him. "Pay me what you owe me!" he said.

The man bowed and begged, "Please wait a little while longer. I'll pay you back!"

But the servant wouldn't listen. He sent the man to jail. Other servants saw what happened. They were angry. They told the king about it."

The king called the servant. "You are a sinful servant!" he said. "I did not make you pay what you owed me. That's because you begged me not to. I was kind to you. So shouldn't you have been kind to this other man?' The king was angry. He sent his servant to jail. He wouldn't let him out until he paid back everything."

"Forgive other people from your heart," said Jesus. "If you don't, my Father in heaven will treat you this same way."

WEEK 20

Monday

Holidays

The word "holiday" means "holy day." That's because in ancient times, the first holidays were special times to celebrate or worship gods (in lands that believed in more than one god) or God (for the Jews). The Jews had lots of holidays, also called "feasts" or "festivals." Jesus celebrated several feasts every year with His people:

◆ The Feast of Trumpets: Ram's horns (shofar) were blown; it was a time of rest and thinking about how awesome God is.

◆ Purim: The story of Esther was celebrated by reading the book of Esther and giving each other gifts.

◆ Hanukkah or the Feast of Lights: In the Bible, it's called the "Feast of Dedication." One candle is lit each day to celebrate a war that the Jews won.

◆ Pentecost or the Feast of Weeks: This thanksgiving feast marked the end of harvest time.

The following story happens at the time of the Holiday of Tents or Festival of Booths. This festival lasted eight days. On the first day, families gathered fresh branches. They used the branches to build huts or booths on their flat roof or in their yard. Families lived in their booths for the whole week of the festival to remind them of the time when the Jews lived in tents as they traveled to the Promised Land. The booths represented God's protection and shelter.
Whispering about Jesus

John 7:2-13

The Holiday of Tents was coming up soon. Jesus' brothers told him, "You should go to Judea for the holiday. Then your followers can see your wonders. You want people to know who you are, don't you? Don't keep these things a secret. You can do all these wonderful things. So why don't you show yourself to all the world?" Jesus' brothers said this, but they didn't really believe in him.

"The right time hasn't come yet," said Jesus. "Any time is all right for you. The world can't hate you. But the world hates me. It's because I tell them that they sin. You go on to Judea. I'm not going yet."

So Jesus stayed in Galilee. His brothers went to Judea. Later, Jesus went too. But he didn't let anybody know he was going. He went in secret.

But the leaders of God's people were watching for Jesus at this holiday. "Where is that man?" they asked.

There was a lot of whispering about Jesus. "He is a good man," said some people. "He is just fooling everybody," said others. But nobody talked out loud about him. They were afraid of the leaders.

Rebels

Over the years before Jesus came (and for several years after), many adventurous rebels claimed to be the Messiah and got Jews to follow them. When Jesus was eight or nine years old, Judas of Gamala claimed to be the Messiah and led a group of rebels against the Romans. The Romans caught him and killed him, just like they did to anyone leading people against Rome. They hated these troublemakers.

> "He must be the one God promised to send," they said. "Look at all the wonders he has done."

Is He the One?
John 7:14-31

Jesus stayed out of sight until halfway through the holiday. Then he went to the worship house and began to teach.

People were surprised. "How did this man learn so much?" they said. "He didn't learn these things in school."

"This isn't my teaching," said Jesus. "It comes from God who sent me. Choose to do what God wants. Then you'll find out if my teaching is from God. If I speak just for me, then I make myself important. But if I make God important, what I say is true. Moses gave you God's laws. But you don't obey them. Instead, you try to kill me. Why?"

"Who is trying to kill you?" the crowd asked. "We think a bad spirit must be in control of you!"

"I did a wonder on the worship day," said Jesus. "I made a man well. Everybody was surprised. But you also work on the worship day. You do it to keep some of God's rules. So don't judge things just by the way they look."

People asked each other, "Aren't our leaders trying to kill this man? Here he is, speaking out loud in the crowds. The leaders are not stopping him. Do they think he really is the one God promised to send?

"We know where this man comes from," others said. "When the Promised One comes, nobody will know where he is from."

"Yes, you know me," said Jesus. "You also know where I'm from. But it wasn't my idea to come here. God sent me. He is true. You don't know him, but I know him. I came from him."

Then the leaders of God's people tried to find a way to catch Jesus. But nobody could, because it wasn't time yet.

Lots of people believed in Jesus. "He must be the one God promised to send," they said. "Look at all the wonders he has done."

 Wednesday

"Living Water"

One of the activities done during the Holiday of Tents (the Festival of Booths) was fetching water from a pool and pouring it out as an offering to God. This was part of celebrating God's care. It represented the water God gave His people when they wandered in the desert. The festival water was probably being poured out when Jesus said, "Streams of living water will flow out of you."

"Living water" was another way of saying, "running water," which was fresher than water that just sat in a pool. Jesus used "living water" as a word picture to describe the Holy Spirit in people who believe in Him.

Streams of Living Water
John 7:32–8:1

The Jewish leaders heard people whisper about Jesus. So they sent the worship-house guards to catch him.

"I'm here for just a little while," said Jesus. "Then I'll go back to the one who sent me. You'll look for me. But you won't find me. You can't come where I'm going."

"Where does he think he can go? Where could we not find him?" asked the leaders. "Will he go to another land to teach? What does he mean?"

The last day of the holiday was the most important. Jesus stood up in front of the people that day. He called, "If you're thirsty, come to me. Believe in me. Then streams of living water will flow out of you."

Jesus was talking about God's Spirit. God was going to send his Spirit to people who believed in Jesus. But God hadn't given them the Spirit yet. That's because Jesus wasn't finished with his work yet.

Some people said, "We're sure Jesus is the Prophet."

Some said, "He is the one God promised to send!"

Others said, "How could the Promised One come from Galilee? The Promised One is supposed to come from King David's family. Bethlehem is the town where David lived."

The people didn't agree about Jesus. Some wanted to catch him, but nobody even touched him.

At last, the worship-house guards went back to the leaders without Jesus.

"Why didn't you bring Jesus with you?" asked the leaders.

"Because nobody ever talked the way he talks," they said.

"Did he fool you, too?" the leaders asked. "Have any leaders believed in him? No! It's this foolish crowd! They don't know anything about the Law! Bad things will happen to them."

Nicodemus was one of the leaders. He had gone to visit Jesus one time. He asked, "What does our Law say? Can people be blamed before we even hear them? First we should find out what he is saying and doing."

"Are you from Galilee too?" asked the other leaders. "Look it up! You'll find out that a prophet doesn't come from Galilee."

Then the leaders went home. Jesus went to Olive Mountain.

Writing

In Jesus' time, the nearest thing to paper was papyrus. The papyrus plant grew in some parts of Palestine. When the plant was soaked a long time in water, the fibers of the stem came apart. The fibers were pounded and flattened and dried in sheets that could be glued together to make long scrolls. We get our word "paper" from papyrus.

You might also write on pieces of broken pottery or wooden tablets covered by soft clay or wax. Or you might write on leather scrolls or parchment (goat or sheepskin) with sections sewn together. Some scrolls were 40 yards long. You rolled them up to carry or store them.

The writing surface that Jesus uses in the following story is dirt. He writes on it with his finger. We don't know what He wrote, but somehow He was answering the problem that the leaders had brought to Him. They were trying to trap Him when they asked if they should kill the sinful woman by stoning her. If Jesus said yes, He would no longer be seen as loving and forgiving. (He would also have to face the Roman rules that said only Roman courts could put someone to death.) But if Jesus said no, the leaders could say He was ignoring the Jewish laws and saying that what the woman had done was all right.

We don't know what Jesus wrote, but the Greek word used to describe His writing is not just *graphein*, "to write," but *katagraphein*, "to write against." So it seems that Jesus wrote something against the men standing there. Or He may have written, "Where is the man?" The sin they accused her of involved another man. The law said that not only the woman, but the man, too, had to be killed by stoning.

Writing on the Ground
John 8:2-11

Jesus was at the worship house by sunrise the next day. Lots of people gathered around him. So he sat down and began to teach them. But the worship-house leaders pushed a woman in front of him. They had found her sleeping with a man the way a wife would. This man wasn't her husband. Now here she was, in front of everyone.

"We found this woman sleeping with a man the way a wife would. He isn't her husband," they told Jesus. "The Law says to throw rocks to make her die for that. What do you say?" The leaders were trying to trap Jesus with their question. They wanted to have a reason to blame him for what he said.

Jesus bent down. He started writing in the dirt with his finger.

But they kept on asking him about it.

So Jesus stood up. "Is there anyone here who has never sinned?" he asked. "If so, you can be the first to throw a rock at her." Jesus bent down and wrote in the dirt again.

People started leaving, one at a time. The older people left first. Soon only Jesus was left with the woman.

"Where did everyone go?" asked Jesus. "Isn't there anyone left to blame you for what you did?"

"No one, sir," she said.

"Then I won't blame you," said Jesus. "Go on home. But don't sin anymore."

 Friday

Lights and Lamps

If you lived in Jesus' time, you would go to bed soon after dark. When you needed light, you used a hearthfire or campfire, an oil lamp or torch. If you were rich, you might hang oil lamps from your ceiling. Jesus used lamps and light as a word picture in the following story. He was probably still at the Holiday of Tents or Festival of Booths. One of the ways they celebrated was by lighting the huge seven-branched lampstand in the temple in the courtyard of the women. The flames represented the cloud of fire that traveled with God's people as they wandered through the desert with Moses.

Jesus used the light as a word picture that referred to Himself. He may have been standing with people in the court of women, watching the flames from the lampstand there. Or He may have been at the Festival of Lights, which we call Hanukkah. At that time, every Jewish house had lamps lit in their windows. Maybe that's when Jesus said, "I am the Light of the World."

The World's Light
John 8:12-37

Jesus talked to the people at the worship house again. "I'm the World's Light," he said. "Follow me. Then you won't live in the dark. You'll have the light of life."

"You're telling about yourself," said the leaders. "So what you say can't be true."

"I may be telling about myself," said Jesus. "Still, what I say is true. The Law says to have two people tell about something. Then you know it's true. So I tell you about myself. My Father also tells you about me. That makes two."

"Where is your father?" they asked.

"You don't know me," said Jesus. "You don't know my Father. If you knew me, you'd know my Father, too."

"Who are you?" they asked.

"I'm just who I said I am," said Jesus. "You'll lift me up. Then you'll know I'm who I said I was."

Many people believed in Jesus. "Keep believing what I'm teaching," Jesus told them. "Keep obeying me. Then you'll really be my followers. You'll know the truth. The truth will set you free."

"We've never been anybody's slaves," they said. "So how could we be set free?"

"Anybody who sins is a slave to sin," said Jesus. "A slave is not one of the family. Only a son belongs to the family forever. If the Son sets you free, you really are free. I know you're ready to kill me. You don't have any room in your hearts for my word.

WEEK 21

 Monday

The "Fathers"

One of the most common things a rabbi would say is, "the merits of the Fathers." When rabbis said this, they were talking about the good things Abraham, Isaac, and Jacob had done. They believed that because all Jewish people had come from Abraham, all Jewish people got credit with God for Abraham's faithfulness. It was even said that Abraham sat at the gates of hell to save any Jew who looked like he might be sent there. It was said that the ships on the sea were kept safe because of Abraham's faithfulness. Rain came because of Abraham's faithfulness. Moses got the Ten Commandments from God because of Abraham's faithfulness. Daniel's prayers were heard because of Abraham's faithfulness. Even non-Jews who became Jewish believers were not as great as someone who was born a Jew. Because non-Jews did not come from the lineage of Abraham.

Whose Children?
John 8:38-59

" I do what I've heard from my Father. You do what you've heard from your father."

"Our father from long ago was Abraham," they said.

"Then you should do what Abraham would have done," said Jesus. "You want to kill me. Abraham didn't do things like that."

"At least we have a father," they said. "Our only true father is God."

"Then you should love me," said Jesus. "I came from God. But you belong to your father, the devil. You do what he says. He was a killer from the very beginning. He never had a bit of truth in him. Lies are the language he speaks. He is a liar and the father of lies. I tell the truth. But you don't believe me. If you belong to God, then hear what God says. You don't hear because you don't belong to God."

"We are right," said the leaders. "A bad spirit controls you."

"No," said Jesus. "I'm following my Father and making him the important one. Now he wants to make me the important one. He is the judge. If you obey my word, you'll never die."

"Now we know a bad spirit controls you," they said. "Abraham died. All the prophets died. But you say that whoever obeys your word will never die. Who do you think you are? Are you greater than Abraham?"

"My Father is the one you call your God," said Jesus. "He makes me the important one. Your father Abraham was happy to think about seeing me here. He did see this, and he was glad."

"You're not even 50 years old," the leaders said. "When did you see Abraham?"

"The truth is," said Jesus, "I lived before Abraham was born."

When Jesus said that, they picked up rocks to throw at him. But Jesus hid. Then he quietly left the worship house.

Spit

Jesus healed people in many different ways. On two occasions, He did something we might consider very strange. He used His saliva (spit or spittle) to heal. Once, He used spit to heal a man who was deaf and could not talk. In the following story, He made mud with His spit and put it on the man's eyes. In ancient times, people believed that spit had the power to heal, especially if it came from someone important. This isn't so strange if we think about what we do if we nick or burn a finger. We usually put it straight into our mouth.

Pliny, a famous Roman writer who lived around the time of Jesus, has a whole chapter about spit in one of his books. He says spit was a protection from snake poison. Spots of leprosy were supposed to be cured by the spit of someone who was fasting. Eye disease was thought to be cured by putting spit on the eyes every morning. Spit was even supposed to cure a crick in the neck. So it was common to use spit as a cure in the ancient world. Jesus was doing what a doctor of His time might do and, of course, adding God's own healing power.

Notice that as this story opens, Jesus' friends ask Him a question that shows something we learned about earlier. They asked, "Whose sin caused this man's blindness?" Remember that the Jewish people thought if a person was sick, it was because he or his family had done something wrong and the sickness was the punishment.

Seeing for the First Time
John 9:1-7

As Jesus walked along, he came to a man who couldn't see. He'd been that way since he was born.

"Why can't he see?" asked Jesus' followers. "Did he sin? Did his mother and father sin?"

"It's not because of anyone's sin," said Jesus. "It happened so God can show his power. I have to do God's work while it's day. Night will be coming. Then nobody can work. While I'm here, I'm the Light of the World."

Then Jesus spit on the dirt and made some mud. He put it on the man's eyes. "Go," said Jesus. "Wash the mud off in the pool."

The man went to the pool and washed the mud off. When he came back, he could see.

Sabbath Rules

God had told His people to respect the Sabbath day. It was a day to rest, not work. But the Jewish leaders were always trying to figure out what counted as work. What could you do or not do on the Sabbath day? They said you couldn't walk any farther than 2,000 cubits, about half a mile. They said you couldn't tie or untie a knot, because that was work. You couldn't carry a mat or anything heavier than two dried figs. They wondered if it was okay to eat an egg that a hen laid on the Sabbath, because the hen worked to lay the egg. They said you couldn't kill an animal on the Sabbath, but they wondered: Did that include bugs?

A bigger problem was the question of what to do if someone got sick or hurt on the Sabbath. What if a wall of stones fell on someone? They said you could see if the person was dead or not. If the person was dead, you left them until after the Sabbath. If they were not dead, you could do something so they would not get worse. But you could not do anything to make them better, because that would be working. The same went for someone who got sick. You could do what you needed to make sure they didn't get worse. But you could not do anything to make them better. Until the Sabbath day was over. That's the kind of thinking Jesus was dealing with every time he healed on the Sabbath.

How Could This Happen?
John 9:8-17

People were used to looking at this man who couldn't see, the one Jesus healed. They used to watch him beg. But now he could see. People said to each other, "Isn't this the same man? He couldn't see before. He used to sit and beg."

Some said he was the same man. Others said, "No, he just looks like that man."

But he said, "I am that man."

"How can you see now?" they asked.

"The man named Jesus made some mud," he said. "He put the mud on my eyes. Then he told me to go to the pool and wash. So I did. Then I could see!"

"Where is Jesus?" they asked.

"I don't know," said the man.

The people took the man to the leaders at the worship house. That's because this was a worship day.

The leaders asked the man how he could see.

"A man put mud on my eyes," he said. "I washed it off. Now I can see!"

Some of the leaders were angry. "The man who did this can't be from God. He is not obeying the law of the worship day."

Other leaders said, "If he is not from God, how could he do such a wonder?"

The leaders didn't agree. At last they turned to the man. "What do you have to say about the healer? It was your eyes that he made well."

"I think he is a prophet," said the man.

Kicked Out

The synagogue was a daily part of every Jew's life. It was where the scriptures were taught. It was where the community of true Jews, the saved and approved people of God, gathered. Boys were taught there. Local judges and leaders were chosen there. Problems of the daily life of the community were discussed and solved there. So to be kicked out of the synagogue was a disgrace. It meant being shut away from God and the community.

Because the blind man had been healed on the Sabbath, these synagogue leaders had a problem to deal with. They were never able to win the argument. So they kicked the man out of the synagogue, out of the most important place in the community. They may have thought they were shutting him away from God. But Jesus heard about it and found the man. So the man ended up face to face with Jesus, closer to God than he had ever been in his life.

The Men Who Could Not Believe
John 9:18-38

The leaders still could not believe it. A man couldn't see before. Now he could see. The leaders called for the man's mother and father. "Is this your son?" they asked. "Could he see when he was born? How can he see now?"

The man's mother and father were afraid of the leaders. That's because the leaders had a rule. People couldn't call Jesus the Promised One. If they did, they would be kicked out of their town's worship house. "We know he is our son," they said. "We know he couldn't see when he was born. But we don't know why he can see now. We don't know who made him well. You'll have to ask him. He is old enough. He can speak for himself."

Again the leaders called for the man who had been made well. They said, "Tell us the truth. We know the man who made you well is a sinner."

"I don't know if he is a sinner or not," said the man. "I do know one thing. I couldn't see before, but now I can see."

"What did he do to you?" they asked. "How did he make you see?"

"I told you already, and you didn't listen," said the man. "Do you want to hear it again? Do you want to follow him too?"

Then the leaders made fun of the man. "You follow the man who made you well," they said. "We follow Moses. We know God spoke to Moses. But we don't even know where this man comes from."

"That's funny," said the man. "You don't know where this man comes from. But he made me well. We know God doesn't listen to sinners. God listens to people who do what he says. Who ever heard of someone making a person see? This man had to come from God. If he didn't, he couldn't have made my eyes well."

"You were a sinner when you were born," they said. "How dare you tell us what's wrong and what's right!" Then they kicked him out.

Jesus heard what happened. So he looked for the man and found him. "Do you believe in God's Son?" asked Jesus.

"Who is he?" the man asked. "Tell me so I can believe in him."

"You've already seen him," said Jesus. "He is the one talking to you right now."

"Lord!" said the man. "I do believe!" Then he worshiped Jesus.

 Friday

Shepherds

If you were a shepherd in Jesus' time, you would probably join other shepherds and their flocks at night to put the sheep all together into a sheep-fold with stone walls. Then you and the other shepherds could take turns sleeping. Someone always had to be awake to watch for robbers and wild animals. A sheep-fold often had no gate, so after the sheep were in the fold, a shepherd would lie down across the opening. The shepherd was the gate.

Because you spent so much time with your sheep, you knew them well. And they knew you. Some sheep were tame and would come when you called their names. Each shepherd would have a different call for his own sheep. Shepherds would cry out as they led their sheep to water and pasture. Your own sheep would follow your particular call.

The Shepherd's Voice
John 10:1-12

"A shepherd goes into the sheep pen by the gate," said Jesus. "The guard opens the gate for the shepherd. Another man climbs in over the wall. He is a robber. The sheep listen for the shepherd's voice. He calls his sheep by their names. He leads them all out. Then he walks in front of them. The sheep follow the shepherd. They know his voice. They'll never follow a stranger. In fact, they run from strangers. They don't know the stranger's voice."

People didn't understand what Jesus was talking about. So He said, "I am like a gate for the sheep. People are like the sheep. Anyone who goes in through me will be saved. He can come in and go out. He will find green fields. The robber comes only to steal and kill. He comes to tear things apart. I came so my sheep can have a full life.

"I am the Good Shepherd," said Jesus. "The Good Shepherd will die to save his sheep. Some people are paid to watch sheep. They're not like the shepherd who owns the sheep. If the paid person sees a wolf, he runs away. He leaves the sheep with the wolf. The wolf jumps at the sheep. The sheep run this way and that. The man runs too. He is only being paid to watch sheep. He doesn't really care about them."

WEEK 22

 Monday

More About Shepherds

If you were a shepherd, during the winter you would keep your flock near the town where you lived. But about March, you would lead them out into the hills. You would live with them out there all spring, all summer, and most of the fall. About November, you would bring your sheep back near town.

Shepherds had to protect their flocks. Hyenas, jackals, wolves, and bears lived in the hills near where the sheep grazed. There were also robbers around. So each shepherd usually carried an iron cudgel and a big knife for protection, and maybe a slingshot, too. Some shepherds truly did die fighting for their sheep.

Dying for the Sheep
John 10:13-21

"I am the Good Shepherd," said Jesus. "I know my people. They are my sheep. My sheep know me, just like the Father knows me. I know the Father. I will even die to save my sheep. I have other sheep too. They're not in this sheep pen. I'll also bring them, and they will listen to my voice. Then there will be one group of sheep and one shepherd.

"My Father loves me, because I give up my life," said Jesus. "Nobody is going to take my life away from me. I choose to give it up."

The leaders who heard Jesus couldn't agree. Some said, "A bad spirit controls him. He is mad. Why do we listen to him?"

Others said, "Listen. He wouldn't talk this way if a bad spirit controlled him. A man couldn't see before. But now he can see. Can a bad spirit make a man see?"

 Tuesday

Proving Someone was Healed

If you had a skin disease, you were not allowed to be near people. You were considered unclean. That meant, of course, that you could not attend a synagogue or go to the temple. So not only were people with skin disease shut away from people, they also thought they were shut away from God. Remember that many different kinds of skin diseases were called "leprosy." With the worst kinds of leprosy, the sick person got worse and worse and died of it. But it was possible for someone with one of the less serious kinds of skin disease to get well.

The law gave very exact instructions on what to do if you got well. There was a "leper room" in the temple in the corner of the court of women. If you had been healed, you would go there, bringing three sacrifices for the priest to offer. The last offering was to be burned on the altar. (For a rich person, it would be a lamb. For a poor person it would be a bird.) After the sacrifices, the priest came back to the door of the leper room. You would stick your head out of the room, and the priest would touch your ear, your thumb, and your foot with the blood of your sacrifice. (Or sometimes, the priest would touch you with spit.) Then you were officially proclaimed to be healed. You could go back to your friends and family. You could also attend the synagogue again.

Ten Men and One Thank-You
Luke 17:11-19

Jesus headed toward Jerusalem. As he came near a town, he saw ten men. They had a very bad skin sickness. So they stood a little way off. They called loudly, "Jesus! Master! Feel sorry for us!"

"Go to the priests," Jesus called. "Let them look at your skin."

So the men started out to see the priests. While they were walking, they looked at their skin. Their skin was well!

One of the men ran back to Jesus. He cheered loudly for God. He bowed down at Jesus' feet. He thanked Jesus. He wasn't even Jewish. He was from Samaria.

"Weren't there ten men who got well?" asked Jesus. "Where are the nine others? Are you the only one who came back to praise God?"

Then Jesus said, "You can get up and go. You're well because you believed in me."

 Wednesday

Yokes

Yokes were wooden frames that went across the necks of animals like oxen or donkeys. Attached to the center of the yoke was a bar that ran back to a plow, a sharp metal wedge that dug into the dirt and churned it up so the ground would be ready for planting.

Being a carpenter, Jesus probably made many yokes. If the yoke was not the right size or was not made well, it could irritate or hurt the animal wearing it. In the following story, after Jesus tells people to come to Him if they are tired, He uses a yoke as a word picture. He says, "My yoke is easy." The Greek word for "easy" is *chrestos*, which means a good one, gentle, excellent, and useful. Jesus is saying, "I know how to make yokes. My yokes fit perfectly." His word picture of the yoke meant, "My plans for you are good, gentle, excellent, and useful. My plans for you will fit you perfectly."

Seventy-Two Men
Matthew 11:25-30; Luke 10:1-11, 16-21

Jesus chose 72 helpers. He sent them ahead of him two by two. They went to every town where Jesus was going.

Before they went, Jesus told them, "People are ready to come into God's kingdom. It's like the time when farmers bring crops in. But there aren't many workers. Ask God to send workers into the fields.

"You are like lambs going into a world of wolves," said Jesus. "Don't take a bag or shoes Don't stop to talk with people on the road. Don't move from house to house. Stay in one place. Eat whatever the people feed you. Drink what they give you. They should give you food for the work you do. Your work is to make sick people well. Tell people that God's kingdom is near.

"You might go into a town where you're not welcome," said Jesus. "Then stand in the street. Say, 'We wipe the dust of this town off our feet! But you can be sure that God's kingdom is near.' Anyone who listens to you is listening to me. Anyone who won't listen to you is not listening to me. He is not listening to God, who sent me."

Sometime later, the 72 helpers came back to Jesus. They were full of joy. They said, "Lord! Even the bad spirits left in your name."

"I saw Satan fall from heaven like a flash of lightning," said Jesus. "I've given you power to walk over snakes and spiders that can kill you. I've given you power greater than the power of Satan, the enemy. Nothing will hurt you. But don't be glad just because the spirits follow your orders. Be glad because your names are written in heaven."

Then Jesus was full of joy. He said, "I praise you, Father. You're the Lord of heaven and earth. You hid your truth from people who thought they were wise. You showed it to people who look foolish to the world. Yes, Father, this is what you enjoy."

Then Jesus said, "Come to me if you're tired. Come to me when you have too much to do. I'll give you rest. Learn by watching and listening to me. I'm thoughtful and kind. My heart is not proud. You'll find your soul can rest with me. My yoke will be easy to carry."

Thieves and Bandits

There were different kinds of robbers in Jesus' time. Housebreakers would dig through the walls of a house, which was fairly easy since most houses were made of mud and straw or clay bricks. There were also cattle-thieves and sheep-thieves, who would watch for sheep or cattle to stray from the flock or herd. Then the thieves would run in and steal the animal.

Some thieves and robbers formed groups or bands that robbed for their living. They would hide in caves and ravines and attack travelers. That's why most people didn't travel by themselves. They went in groups or caravans for protection and often sewed their money or valuables into the hems of their clothes or into their sashes.

Caravans sometimes hired a guide. They called him "the eye of the caravan." His job was to stay on the lookout for thieves. In fact, caravan leaders might hire one band of robbers to protect them from another band of robbers.

When a thief was caught, he might be sold as a slave, or he might be killed. The two men crucified with Jesus were thieves.

The Neighbor
Luke 10:25-37

One day, a man who knew the Law stood up. He tried to test Jesus. "What do I have to do to live forever?"

"What does the Law say?" Jesus asked.

"Love the Lord your God with all your heart," said the man. "Love him with all your soul and strength. Love him with all your mind. Love your neighbor as much as you love yourself."

"You're right," Jesus said. "You'll live if you do that."

But the man wanted to show that what he did was right. So he asked, "Who is my neighbor?"

Then Jesus told him a story:

There once was a man who was on a trip. He was going from Jerusalem to Jericho. But robbers jumped out at him. They took his clothes. They beat him. Then they left. There the man was, lying by the road, half dead.

Soon a priest came down the road. He saw the hurt man. But he moved to the other side of the road. He just passed by. A man who knew the Law came down the road. He saw the hurt man too. But he moved to the other side of the road. He passed by.

Then a man from another land came down the road. He was a Samaritan. He saw the hurt man too and felt sorry for him. The Samaritan took care of his hurts. Then he put the man on his own donkey and took him to an inn. The man could rest there until his hurt places were well.

The next day, the Samaritan took out his money. He gave some to the person in charge of the inn. "Take care of this man," he said. "I'll come back. I'll pay back whatever it costs to take care of him."

"Which man was a neighbor?" asked Jesus.

The man who knew the Law said, "The man who was kind."

"Right," said Jesus. "Now you go and do the same thing."

Women Disciples

Jesus traveled a lot, so He knew about traveling in groups and watching out for robbers. He knew about staying in inns and about staying with friends. Something interesting happened when he stayed with His friends Mary and Martha. Mary sat at Jesus' feet to listen to Him. That's where a disciple, a follower, of a rabbi would sit. The unusual thing was that no rabbi or teacher had women disciples, as we learned earlier. By sitting at Jesus' feet, Mary was saying she wanted to be His follower, His disciple. Martha was upset. She said Mary should be with her, making the food and serving the guests. Martha may have been saying that she needed Mary's help. But she may also have been upset that Mary was ignoring "women's work" and was instead doing something Martha thought only a man should do.

All This Work
Luke 10:38-42

Jesus and his followers came to a town called Bethany. A woman named Martha lived there. She said Jesus was welcome to stay at her house. So He did.

Martha had a sister named Mary. She sat down at Jesus' feet. She listened to what he said.

But Martha was thinking. She thought about all the things she had to do. She wanted things to be just right for Jesus' visit. At last, Martha came to Jesus. "Lord," she said. "My sister left me to do all the work by myself. Don't you care? Tell Mary to help me."

"Martha, Martha," said Jesus. "You're upset. You're worried about so many things. There is only one thing that's important right now. That's what Mary chose to do. She is taking time to be with me. I won't take that away from her."

WEEK 23

 Monday

Winter at Solomon's Walk

Winter time could be quite cold in ancient Palestine. Most houses did not have fireplaces. If it got too cold, you might light a charcoal brazier (like a bowl of burning coals). Some courtyards also had braziers for people to warm themselves by.

In the following story, it was winter, and Jesus went to the temple. If you went to the temple in winter, you might get an icy rain blown into your face from a chill wind gusting through the courtyards. It may have been cold the day Jesus went, because He walked under a covered porch called Solomon's Walk. That porch was in the area of the temple called the court of the Gentiles (non-Jews). It was the first courtyard you came to after you entered the temple grounds. There were two roofed walkways there, each lined by pillars almost forty feet high. One walkway, the "Royal Porch," ran along one side of this court of Gentiles. The other walkway, "Solomon's Porch," ran along the other side with three rows of columns, 268 in all.

Solomon's Porch had a good view of the Kidron Valley and the Mount of Olives. People would go to these walkways to pace and pray and meditate. Rabbis would also walk along these covered porches as they talked to their students and followers.

Throwing Rocks
John 10:22-33, 39-42

It was winter. There was a special holiday time in Jerusalem. So Jesus went. A covered porch called Solomon's Walk was at the worship house. Jesus began walking there.

The leaders of God's people came up to Him. "How long will you make us guess?" they asked. "If you're the Promised One, then just say so."

"I told you," said Jesus. "You didn't believe me. I do wonders in my Father's name. Those wonders tell you who I am. But you don't believe me. That's because you're not my sheep. My sheep listen to me. I know them. They follow me. I give them life that lasts forever. They will never die. Nobody can take them out of my hand. That's because my Father gave them to me. He is greater than anyone or anything. My Father and I are one and the same."

The leaders began to pick up rocks. They were going to throw them at Jesus.

"I've done great wonders," said Jesus. "I've done them with my Father's power. Which wonder makes you want to throw rocks at me?"

"We're not throwing rocks at you for doing wonders," they said. "We're throwing rocks at you because you're just a man. But you're calling yourself God."

The leaders tried to catch Jesus again. But he got away. He went back across the Jordan River where John had baptized people. That's where Jesus stayed now. Many people came to see him there.

People said, "John never did a wonder. But everything he said about Jesus is true." Many people believed in Jesus.

Tuesday

Doors and Gates

In Jesus' time, doorways between rooms were often narrow and low. The main doorway that led outside was wider and taller. The Shema might be written on the doorpost. Or it might be written on a small scroll placed in a container attached to the doorpost. The actual doors were usually made of wood. They might be covered with metal. Some doors were made of stone. Doors turned on hinges made of a pin that ran through a hollow stone.

Gates led through city walls or through walls around the temple courtyards. Each gate was named. City gates would be closed at night and would not be opened again until dawn of the next day. But a large city gate would have a small door in it, so even after the large gate was closed for the night, a person could enter the city. Of course, the person would have to convince the guard that he had a right and a reason to be allowed in after dark. The door in the gate is probably the kind of narrow door Jesus is talking about in the following story.

Like a Hen Gathering Chicks
Luke 13:22-35

Jesus went through many towns. He was teaching people on his way to Jerusalem.

Someone came to Jesus with a question. "Will only a few people be saved?"

"Try to go in at the narrow door," said Jesus. "Lots of people will try to go in. But they'll find out they can't. It's like a man who owns a house. He closes the door. People may stand outside and tap on the door. They may call, 'Open the door for us.'

"But the owner will say, 'I don't know you. I don't know where you came from.'

"They'll answer, 'We ate with you. We drank with you. We heard you teach.'

"The owner will say, 'Maybe you ate where I ate. Maybe you heard me teach. But you didn't get to know me. You still sin. You do what's wrong.'

"People will come from east and west," said Jesus. "They will come from north and south. There will be places for them in God's kingdom. They will come and sit at the dinner party. The ones who are last now will be first then. The ones who are first will be last."

"You'd better leave town," said some leaders. "King Herod wants to kill you."

"Tell that fox I'm going to send bad spirits away," said Jesus. "I'm going to make people well today and tomorrow. On the third day, I'll finish my plan. Whatever happens, I have to keep going," said Jesus. "It's not right for a prophet to die outside Jerusalem!"

"Jerusalem, Jerusalem!" said Jesus. "You killed the prophets. You hurt the people God sent to you. A hen gathers chicks under her wings. I've often wanted to get your children together like that. But you wouldn't come. Look. You have nothing left. You won't see me again until you tell me, 'Let God bring good to you. You come in the Lord's name!'"

A Dinner Party

If you were going to have a dinner party, a banquet, in Jesus' time, your slaves or servants would carry the invitations to whoever you wanted to invite. Usually there were no more than nine guests invited, all men. They would come some time in the early afternoon. They might walk or have their servants carry them on a cart or litter.

As the host, you would meet your guests in the open court of your house. You might give each guest "the kiss of peace." A servant would wash their hands and feet and maybe even pour a little oil or perfume on each person's head. When everyone had arrived, you would go into the dining room.

There were usually three tables in the dining room, arranged so they formed a U. The host's place was in the center of the U. The place of honor was to the host's right. People at the side tables were the less important guests.

People usually invited "good" guests to their banquets, guests who could invite them back or do something good for them in return. But Jesus encouraged people to invite the poor, the lame, and the blind. Remember that most people thought if you were blind or lame, you had sinned in some way. These were not the people that most hosts wanted at their banquets.

The Best Places at the Table
Luke 14:1, 7-14

On a worship day, Jesus went to a dinner party. It was at a Jewish leader's house.

Jesus was sitting at the table. He watched some of the people there. They took the best places at the table.

Jesus told the people, "What if somebody asks you to come to a wedding party? Don't take the best seat at the table. Somebody more important than you might come in. The person in charge will tell you, 'Give this person your seat, please.' Then you'll feel put down. You'll have to move to a different seat. Instead, take a place that's not important. The person in charge will tell you, 'Hello, friend. Move to one of these better seats.' Then you'll feel important in front of everyone.

"You see, some people try to make themselves important," said Jesus. "But they will end up feeling like nothing. Some people make others more important than themselves. They will end up feeling great."

Then Jesus talked to the man in charge of the dinner. "Let's say you want to ask people to come to lunch or dinner. Don't ask friends or family or rich neighbors. Later, they'll ask you to come to lunch with them, too. They'll pay you back. Instead, ask poor people to come to your party," said Jesus. "Ask people who can't walk or see. Then God will bring good to you. Those people can't pay you back, but God can."

Feasting

At a rich person's dinner party, you would lie on couches, leaning on your left elbow with your head near the table. (It was said that eating or drinking upright upset a person's whole body.) Everyone would eat with their right hand.

A Jewish dinner party always began with saying a blessing. Then servants or women of the house would serve the fancy food, as much as they could afford. The food would be served on the best dishes the host owned. But there would not usually have been spoons or forks. Guests would eat with their fingers. If the food was juicy, you would sop up the juice with bread. A servant would come around now and then with towels and bowls of water to wash everyone's hands.

A dinner party might last for five or six hours. There would be music and maybe dancing. A poet might be asked to say a poem. Or someone might be asked to make a speech or tell a story.

A Dinner Party in Heaven
Luke 14:15-24

A man at the table said, "I know what will make people happy. They'll be happy if they eat at the party in God's kingdom!"

"Once a man planned a party," said Jesus. "He asked lots of people to come. But no one showed up when it was time. So the man sent his servant to say, 'Come on. The party's ready.' But people gave different reasons for why they couldn't come. The first man said, 'I just bought a field. I need to go and see about it.' Another person said, 'I just bought 10 oxen. I'm on my way to try them out.' Another person said, 'I just got married. So I can't come.'

"The servant came back and told his master what the people said. The master got angry. 'Quick!' he said. 'Go to all over town. Get poor people. Get people who can't walk or see. Bring them to my party.'

"The servant went to the streets. He asked people to come to the party. Then he came back. 'I did what you told me,' he said. 'But there is still room.'

"The master said, 'Go into the roads. Go into the country. Bring people in. Let's fill my house! None of the people I asked first can come. They won't even get to taste my food!'"

 Friday

Measuring

Remember that carpenters often built buildings. So Jesus knew about planning and measuring. The measurements He used were different from what we use now. A "cubit" was the length from the elbow to the tip of the middle finger on an adult's arm. A "handbreadth" was the width of the hand at the base of the four fingers (a bit less than 3 inches). The width of the pointer finger was the smallest measure, called the "finger" (about 3/4 inch). The distance from thumb to little finger on an outstretched hand was a "span" (about 9 inches). Other distances were measured by how far an arrow could be shot, called a "bowshot," and how far a stone could be thrown, called a "stone's throw."

Types of measurement used in Jesus' day:

Cubit

Handbreadth

Finger

Span

Bowshot

Stone's Throw

Building and Going to War
Luke 14:25-33

Big crowds of people traveled with Jesus. He turned to them. "There's only one way you can follow me," he said. "I have to be the most important person in your life. I have to be more important than your family. I have to be more important than your own life. You must choose what is most important to you."

"What if you wanted to build a tall building?" said Jesus. "First you'd find out how much it would cost. Then you'd know if you had enough money to finish. What if you started the building and couldn't finish it? Everyone would make fun of you. People would say, 'He couldn't finish what he started!'"

"What if a king was planning to fight another king? First he would see if he had enough men to win. If he didn't, he would send some of his men to the other king to make peace.

"So you must give up everything for me," said Jesus. "If you don't, you can't follow me."

WEEK 24

 Monday

Coins

There were many different kinds of coins in ancient Palestine. Their differences were not just in value, like quarter, dime, nickel, and penny. The difference was in the entire culture the coin came from. Because people from so many countries lived and traveled through Palestine, you would commonly see Greek drachmas, the zuzim from Tyre, the Roman denarius (called dinar in Hebrew), and shekels of the Jews.

Roman and Greek money usually had the image of the ruler on one side. If the ruler changed, the image on the coins would be changed too. Jewish money did not have pictures of animals or people on them, because Jews were not allowed to make images of animals or people. Instead, Jewish coins were decorated with wreaths, baskets of fruit, or lampstands.

With all these different kinds of coins being used, "money-changing" was big business. Money-changers were a bit like bankers, except you paid a money-changer to change your coins for you. You took them one type of coin, asked for a different kind, and they would give you the right amount. At least they were supposed to give you the right amount. Sometimes they cheated and gave you less. In those days, what really counted was not the size or name of the coin, but the amount of gold, silver, or copper it contained. So instead of counting coins, they weighed them to see if the gold, silver, or copper was the right amount. It was not unusual for the person weighing the coins to cheat by using weights or scales that were not correct.

Lost and Found
Luke 15:1-10

Tax men and sinners came to hear Jesus. So the Jewish leaders and teachers said, "This man welcomes sinners. He even eats with them."

Then Jesus told some stories. "Suppose you're a shepherd. You have 100 sheep. But one of them gets lost. Wouldn't you leave the other 99 sheep to look for the lost sheep? When you found it, you would be so happy. You'd carry the sheep home on your shoulders. You'd call all your friends and neighbors. You'd say, 'Be glad with me! I found my lost sheep!'

"It's the same in heaven," said Jesus. "The angels are very happy about one sinner who is sorry. They're happy when one sinner turns to God. It's better than knowing 99 people who do what's right. Those people don't even need to say they're sorry."

"Suppose a woman has ten silver coins. But she loses one," said Jesus. "Won't she light a lamp? She will clean house. She will look carefully until she finds her money. When she finds it, she will call her friends and neighbors. She will say, 'Be glad with me! I found the money I lost!'

"It's the same in heaven," said Jesus. "The angels are very glad when one sinner is sorry. They're glad when one sinner turns to God."

Costs

One of the most common coins in Jesus' time was the silver dinar, which Romans called a *denarius*. We might compare it to our nickel. One hundred denarii was equal to a few dollars. A Roman soldier earned one denarius a week. A vineyard worker earned 6. A scribe (who copied scriptures or wrote letters or legal documents for people) earned 12. That may not sound like much, but things didn't cost as much back then. For fun, figure out how long it would take to earn enough money to do these things at the prices charged for them in Jesus' time:

Buy a cloak. 100 dinars
Rent a house for a month. 4 dinars
Buy a loaf of bread. 1/12 dinar
Buy a jug of olive oil. 1 dinar
Buy a ram. 8 dinars
Buy a lamb. 4 dinars
Buy a calf. 20 dinars
Buy an ox. 100 dinars
Pay the Temple tax. 1 dinar
Have friends over for a large meal. 1 dinar
Buy one pomegranate. 1 prutah (About 13 prutahs make a dinar.)
Buy a cluster of grapes. 1 prutah
Get a weaver to make you a tallit, a long, scarf-like outer cloak. 8 dinars

Pig Food
Luke 15:11-32

"A man had two sons," said Jesus. "His money would belong to his sons someday."

But one day his younger son said, "Father, give me my share of the money now."

So the man gave the younger son his share of the money. He gave the rest to his older son.

Soon after that, the younger son left home with his share of the money. He moved to a land far away. He lived a wild life there and used up all his money.

Now there wasn't enough food in that land. So he couldn't get enough to eat. . . . The only job he could get was feeding pigs. By that time, he was very hungry. He even wanted to eat the pigs' food. But no one would let him.

At last he started getting smart. He said, "People who work for my father have plenty to eat. Here I sit, dying of hunger! I'm going home. . . . I'll say that I'm not good enough to be called his son."

So the young man got up. He went back home. He wasn't even close to his house when his father saw him.

The father ran to his son, full of love. He hugged and kissed him.

The son said, "Father, I've sinned against heaven. I've sinned against you. I'm not good enough to be called your son."

But the father called his servants. "Hurry!" he said. "Bring me the best robe we have! Put it on my son! Put a ring on his finger! Put shoes on his feet! Remember the meat we were saving for a special time? Cook it! Let's have a party! I thought I would never see my son again! It's like he was lost. But now he is found!"

So they had a big party. All this time, the older son was out in the field. . . . He called to one of the servants. "What's happening?" he asked.

"Your brother came home, said the servant. "Your father is having a welcome-home party for him."

The older brother got angry. He would not go to the party.

So his father went out. He begged his older son to come in.

"Look," said the older son. "I worked for you all these years. I always did what you told me to do. But you never gave me a party. Now my brother comes home. He used up all the money you gave him. But you have a party for him."

The father said, "You don't understand, son. You're always with me. Everything I have is yours. But I thought I'd never see your brother again. So we need to have a party! We need to show our joy. He was lost, but now he is found!"

Unclean Jobs

The Pharisees said some jobs were "dirty" or "unclean." Sheep shearers were considered unclean. Tanners, who made leather out of animal hides, were said to be unclean. Tanning was a smelly job, so tanners had to work away from other businesses. Copper smelters, who melted ore to get copper, were thought to be unclean. So were dung-collectors, who gathered manure for the tanners to use in their job. Anyone who had the job of moving a dead body or preparing it for burial would be unclean, because they had to touch a dead person. Tax collectors did not have dirty or smelly jobs, but they were suspected of taking more money than they should. So they, too, were considered unclean.

There were other jobs that no good Jew would ever do. One was acting. Greeks loved to go to the theatre. In fact, there were several theatres in different cities around Palestine. Troupes of actors would travel through. But good Jews did not go to the theatre. Jesus often used a word that came from acting: *hypocrite*. A hypocrite is someone who pretends to be something he is not. In other words, an actor. Jesus often called the Pharisees hypocrites.

Jews would not take part in certain sports either, because athletes did their sports naked. They also often dedicated their sports-playing to their gods to honor them. Other sports were too violent for Jews to support. Roman crowds gathered in large arenas to see men fight wild animals or other men to the death. That, of course, did not fit with the Jews' honor for life or Jesus' teaching about a God of love. However, because Palestine was a Roman country, several cities had large sports arenas. Jesus probably saw sports arenas and theatres from the outside.

A Little and a Lot
Luke 16:1-12

Jesus told a story:

There once was a rich man who heard bad news: The man in charge of his business was using up his money. So the rich man called his worker. "What's this I hear about you?" he asked. "Tell me what you're doing with my money. If you're using it up, you can't be in charge anymore."

The worker was worried. He thought, "What will I do now? My boss will take my job away. I'm not strong enough to dig. I'd feel bad about having to beg for food. I know! I'll make friends with people who owe my boss money. I'll lose my job. But these people will let me stay with them."

So the worker called one man. "How much do you owe my boss?" he asked.

The man said, "I owe him 800 jugs of olive oil."

"Take your bill and change it," said the worker. "Make it 400 jugs."

The worker asked another man, "How much do you owe?"

The man said, "I owe 1,000 baskets of wheat."

"Take your bill and change it," said the worker. "Make it 800."

The boss saw what his worker had done. He said it was a smart idea. He said the worker had been wise.

"Worldly people are wise when they deal with worldly people," said Jesus. "They're wiser than God's people in dealing with the world. Use worldly money to get friends. Someday the money will be gone. But you will have friends.

"What happens when you can be trusted with a little?" asked Jesus. "Then you can be trusted with a lot. What happens when you can't be trusted with a little? Then you can't be trusted with a lot. What if people can't trust you with worldly riches? Do you think you'll be trusted with heaven's riches? What if people can't trust you with things that belong to them? Do you think you'll get things of your own?"

 Thursday

Beliefs About the Afterlife

In Jesus' time, the Jews had three different ways of looking at life after death:

1) Some believed in <u>Sheol</u>. The Old Testament talks about the souls of all people, good and bad, going to Sheol when they die. It was not a place of punishment, but just a land of the dead, who did nothing and felt nothing. (Note: The Greek 'Hades' is the same as sheol, although we often translate it 'hell.' The Sadducees and Samaritans held this belief about sheol. Like most Jews today, they didn't worry too much about the afterlife. It was life now that was important.)

2) Some believed in <u>Sheol and Paradise</u>: They believe the angel of death leads the soul directly to judgment. Bad people stay in Sheol for punishment. Good people go to Paradise, which is like the Garden of Eden. Paradise is also called "the lap (or bosom) of Abraham."

3) Some believed in <u>Resurrection</u>: Some rabbis taught that the soul would be brought back into the body. Some people would be raised to reward and some to punishment. Most ordinary Jews believed this.

Jesus used the Jews' belief of Sheol and Paradise (the lap of Abraham) in His word picture in the following story.

Lazarus and the Rich Man
Luke 16:14-15, 19-31

Jesus told the leaders of God's people, "You try to make people think you're always right. But God knows what's in your hearts. . . . Then Jesus told this story:

Once there was a rich man who wore fine purple clothes. He had everything he wanted.

A beggar named Lazarus sat at the rich man's gate. Lazarus had hurt places all over his body. . . . Lazarus was hungry, too. He would have loved to eat the bits of food that fell from the rich man's table.

One day, Lazarus died. Angels took him to sit by Abraham.

Sometime later, the rich man died. But he went to hell. He felt terrible. He hurt all over. He rich man looked up and saw Abraham far away. Lazarus was sitting beside him. So the rich man called, "Father Abraham! Be kind to me. Tell Lazarus to dip the tip of his finger in water. Send him here to cool my mouth with the water. All this fire is too much for me!"

But Abraham said, "Remember the way you lived? You got your good things on earth. Lazarus got bad things. But now he is feeling good and you're not. Even if Lazarus wanted to come, he couldn't. There is a big space between us and you. Nobody can cross from us to you. And nobody can cross from you to us."

The rich man begged. "Then please send Lazarus to my brothers. There are five of them. Ask Lazarus to tell them what happened to me. Maybe then they won't have to come to this fearful place!"

Abraham answered, "They know the Law. They know what the prophets said. So they should already know how to live."

The rich man said, "They don't listen to the Law. But they know Lazarus is dead. If he went to see them, they would change."

Abraham told the rich man, "Your brothers don't listen to the Law. They don't listen to the prophets. So they won't believe anyone, even if that person comes alive again."

 Friday

Scavenger Birds

Several kinds of large birds lived in the area of ancient Palestine. There were eagles and hawks, which hunted and killed living prey. Then there were scavenger birds like ravens and vultures, which fed on animals that were already dead. There was a common saying in those days: "Where the body is, there the vultures will gather." It means, "It will happen when the time is right." Jesus used that ancient saying in the following story.

Like Lightning
Luke 17:20-37

Some Jewish leaders asked Jesus when the kingdom of God would come.

"Watching for God's kingdom won't make it come," said Jesus. "People won't say, 'Here it is!' They won't say, 'There it is!' That's because God's kingdom is inside people."

Then Jesus talked to his followers. "One of these days, you'll wish I were with you. But you won't see me. People may say, 'There he is!' They may say, 'Here he is!' But don't follow them.

"I'll come back like a flash of lightning," said Jesus. "I'll light up the whole sky. Before that, I'll go through a lot of pain. People won't believe me. It will be like the time when Noah lived.

People ate and drank while Noah went into the ark. They thought it was a day like any other day. Then the flood came. It got rid of them all.

"The same thing happened when Lot lived," said Jesus. "People ate and drank. They bought things. They sold things. They planted fields. They built buildings. But when Lot left the city of Sodom, fire came down from heaven. It got rid of them all.

"When I come back, people will be living the way they always do," said Jesus. "What if a man is up on his roof when I come? All his things are inside his house. He shouldn't try to run inside to get his things. People may be at work in their fields. They shouldn't try to go home to get things. Remember Lot's wife? People trying to hold on to life will give up real life. People who give up life for me will have real life.

"When I come, two people may be in one bed," said Jesus. "One will go with me. The other will be left behind. Two women may be making grain into flour. One will go with me. The other will be left behind."

"Where will this happen?" asked Jesus' friends.

"Think about it," said Jesus. "The wild birds come wherever there is something dead."

WEEK 25

 Monday

Judges

The great high court for the Jews was in Jerusalem. It was made of 70 men called the Sanhedrin. They judged criminal cases, the hardest cases of lawbreaking. Courts in smaller towns had three judges. They could judge cases about people not treating each other fairly. But the woman in the following story went to only one judge. So she must have lived in a very small town or out in the country. In those places, they had only one judge.

In a court of law, only healthy men were considered to be reliable witnesses. Women, children, slaves, the deaf, mute, and blind were not allowed to be witnesses. The leaders said these people were not good witnesses, because they lied too easily. They were thought to be irresponsible.

The Judge
Luke 18:1-8

Jesus wanted his followers to see that they should always pray. He wanted them to know they should never give up. So he told them a story:

Once there was a judge. He didn't worship God. He didn't care about people.

There was a lady who lived in his town. Her husband had died. The lady kept coming to see the judge. "My enemies aren't treating me right," she would say. "Help me, please."

Time after time she came. But the judge wouldn't listen to her.

At last the judge thought, "I don't worship God. I don't care about people. But this lady keeps bothering me. So I'll make sure she is treated fairly. Then she won't wear me out by coming so much."

"Listen," said Jesus. "Won't God help his people? They call him night and day. Will he send them away? No. He will make sure they are treated right. He will be fast about it. But I wonder. Will I find people who believe in me when I come back?"

 Tuesday

Fasting and Prayer

In Jesus' time, people believed that the person who did good deeds was right with God. These good deeds included offering sacrifices and praying. Good Jews prayed three times a day. Prayers made at the temple were thought to be better at getting God's attention and His answer. Going without eating (called fasting) was supposed to help your prayers too.

According to Jewish law and tradition, there was really only one day when people were supposed to go without food: the Day of Atonement. But many of the Jewish leaders thought they could score extra points with God by fasting two days a week. The days they usually chose were Monday and Thursday. On those days, country people came to market in the city, and the streets were crowded. These men who were fasting would walk the streets dressed in ragged clothes with their faces sad and hungry-looking. They wanted people to see them and talk about how good they were. The leader in Jesus' story was like one of those men.

The Proud Prayer
Luke 18:9-14

Some people were sure they did what was right. They were proud of it. They thought they were more important than anyone else. So Jesus told them a story:

Once there were two men. They went to the worship house to pray. One man was a leader of God's people. The other man was a tax man.

The leader stood up tall. He prayed about himself. "God, thank you that I'm not like other men. I'm not a robber. I don't sin. I'm not like this tax man. I go without food to worship God two times a week. I give God one out of every 10 pieces of money I earn."

The tax man stood a little way off. He wouldn't even look up. He pounded his chest. "God, be kind to me," he said. "I'm a sinful person."

"God forgave the tax man," said Jesus. "It was just as if he'd never sinned. But God didn't forgive the leader. Some people think they're great. God will make those people feel like they're not important. Some people don't act like they're important. God will make those people feel great."

Wednesday

Workers and Jobs

In Jesus' time, people who did the same kinds of jobs often lived and worked in the same town. Sepphoris was a town where lots of weavers lived, because flax for making cloth grew in the countryside there. Fish-salters lived near Lake Galilee. Good clay was found near Hebron, so potters lived there.

In a big city like Jerusalem, people who did the same kinds of jobs often lived and worked in the same neighborhood. Tradesmen would live in or near their workshops. So certain sections of the city, or certain streets, were named after what the workers on that street did. Like the Street of Bakers, or the Street of Sandalmakers.

If you lived in a town where Roman soldiers were stationed, you would see a garrison in one part of town. A garrison was a fort-like building where the soldiers lived. In some towns, there was also a day workers' corner where men came to stand to show they needed work. It was usually near the market. Farmers and vineyard owners came into town to hire day workers.

Workers Who Fussed
Matthew 20:1-16

"Here's what the kingdom of heaven is like," said Jesus. "It's like a farmer who had a grape field." Jesus told this story:

The farmer went to town early in the morning. He got men to come and work in his field. He told them what he'd pay them for the day. Then he sent them out to work in his field.

At nine o'clock that morning, the farmer went back to town. He saw more people standing there. They were in the market place, but they were not doing anything. So the farmer took them with him. "You can work in my field too," he said. "I'll pay you whatever is right." So they went to work.

The farmer got more workers at noon. He got more workers at three o'clock in the afternoon. At five o'clock, the farmer still found people standing around. He asked them, "Why did you stand around all day doing nothing?"

They said, "Nobody asked us to work."

The farmer said, "You can work in my field." So they did.

It wasn't long until evening came. "Call the workers," said the farmer to the head servant. "Pay them. Start with the last men who came to work. Then go on to the first men."

The workers who went to work at five o'clock came. Each one got paid for a whole day's work. Then the early morning workers came. They thought they would get more money. But the farmer paid each worker for one day's work.

The workers who had worked all day started fussing. "You gave the same pay to the men who worked only one hour," they said. "You treated them just like us. We worked all day long in the hot sun."

The farmer said, "I'm being fair to you. I asked you to work for me. I told you what I would pay you. You said you would work for that much. Take your money and go. I want to give the others what I gave you. It's my money. Can't I do what I want with it? Or are you mad because I'm being kind to them?"

"The last will be first," said Jesus. "The first will be last."

Burial in Ancient Palestine

When someone died in Jesus' time, family or friends would wash the body with oil or perfumes and spices. Then they wrapped the body in linen strips. They also veiled the face with a cloth. They buried the dead within a day after the person had died. After the burial, the family had a funeral meal. Then friends came and visited to mourn with the family.

After Jesus heard Lazarus was sick, He waited two days to go see him. By the time Jesus got to Mary and Martha's house, they had already washed Lazarus' body, wrapped it, and veiled his face. They had already buried Lazarus and had the funeral meal. Jesus arrived at the time when friends were visiting. Lazarus had already been in the grave four days.

A Trip to Bethany
John 11:1-17

Mary and Martha were from a town called Bethany. They had a brother named Lazarus. One day, Lazarus got sick. Mary and Martha sent a message to Jesus. "Lord, Lazarus is sick."

Jesus got the message. "This sickness won't end in death. It's to show God's great power," he said.

Jesus loved Mary and Martha and Lazarus. But he didn't go see them right away. He stayed where he was for two more days. Then he said to his friends, "Let's go to Judea."

"But the Jewish leaders tried to throw rocks at you there. Are you going back?" his friends asked.

"The light shines for twelve hours each day. Right?" said Jesus. "People won't fall down if they walk in the daytime. They see the world's light. But they fall when they walk at night. They have no light then. Our friend Lazarus is sleeping. I'm going to wake him up."

"If he is sleeping, he will get better," said Jesus' friends.

Jesus meant that Lazarus had died. But Jesus' friends thought he meant Lazarus was really asleep. So then Jesus made it clear. "Lazarus is dead," he said. "When I think of you, I'm glad I wasn't there. Now you'll believe in me. But we need to go to Bethany."

Sometime later, Jesus got to Bethany. Lazarus was dead. His body had been in the grave for four days.

More About Burial

In ancient Palestine, among the Jews, there were no official cemeteries except for the poor and strangers. If you were not poor, you would buy a piece of land for burying family, or you would make graves on your own land. The typical tomb was a cave or a cave of rooms cut into a rocky cliff. Usually the body would not be buried in a coffin. Instead, you would carry the body to the grave on a stretcher and lay on a bench cut in the rock.

The tombs of poorer people would be walled-up after the body was placed inside. But richer people, like Mary and Martha, used a large stone for a door. They rolled the stone into place in a large groove in the ground. Or they might pile up several stones to make a wall. Blocking the doorway with a stone or wall kept wild animals from prowling into the cave and getting the body.

Deep Sadness
John 11:18-41

The town of Bethany was only about two miles from Jerusalem. So lots of people went to see Mary and Martha. The people hoped they could make the two sisters feel better. Someone said that Jesus was coming. Martha went to meet him, but Mary stayed home.

"Lord!" Martha said. "If you had been here, Lazarus would not have died. But I know God gives you whatever you ask for. He will give it even now."

"Your brother will come to life again," said Jesus.

"I know," said Martha. "He will come back to life at the end of time."

"I hold the power of life," said Jesus. "I am new life. People who believe in me will live even after they die. People who live and believe in me will never really die. Do you believe what I'm saying?"

"Yes, Lord," said Martha. "I believe that you are the one God promised to send. You are God's Son."

Then Martha went back home. She told Mary, "Jesus is here. He wants to see you."

Mary got up quickly. She went to see Jesus. He had not come into town yet. He was still at the place where Martha had seen him.

People at Mary's house were trying to cheer her up. But they saw how fast she got up. They thought she was going to Lazarus' grave to cry. So they followed her.

Mary went to the place where Jesus was. She bowed down at Jesus' feet. "Lord," she said. "If you had been here, Lazarus would not have died." Mary began to cry. The people who had followed Mary began to cry too.

Jesus felt their deep sadness. "Where is the grave?" he asked.

"We'll show you," they said.

Then Jesus cried too.

"Look at how much Jesus loved Lazarus," said the people.

Others said, "He made people's eyes well. Couldn't he have kept Lazarus from dying?"

Soon Jesus came to the grave. He felt the deep sadness again. The grave was a cave. A big stone blocked the opening. "Take the stone away," Jesus said.

"But, Lord!" said Martha. "He has been dead four days! It will smell bad in there."

"Remember what I told you," said Jesus. "If you believe in me, you'll see God's power."

So they took the stone away.

WEEK 26

 Monday

The Dead

Because a dead body would soon begin to smell bad, spices were placed in the strips of cloth as the body was wrapped. The spices were gummy and sticky and helped hold the strips of cloth together as they were drawn around the body. Spices were also a way of showing respect to the dead.

In Jesus' time, the Jews believed that the dead person's spirit stayed around for three days after the person died, and after that, the person's spirit left. By the time Jesus got to Mary and Martha's house, Lazarus had been dead four days. There was no way that people would have thought Lazarus' spirit was still hanging around, ready to be brought back. They believed Lazarus' spirit was long gone. He was really dead. So when Jesus brought Lazarus back to life, the people believed that Lazarus definitely had come back from the dead.

Out of the Grave
John 11:41-54

Jesus looked up. "Father," he said, "thank you for hearing me. I know you always hear me. But saying this will help people believe you sent me." Then Jesus called loudly, "Lazarus, come out!"

Lazarus came out! Cloth covered his hands and feet. There was a cloth around his face.

"Help him out of his grave clothes," said Jesus.

Many people who saw this chose to believe in Jesus. But some of them went to the Jewish leaders. They told the leaders what Jesus had done.

These leaders of God's people called a meeting. "What good are we doing?" they asked. "Here is this man, doing lots of wonders. What if everybody starts believing in him? Then the Romans will come. They'll take away our nation! They'll take over our worship house!"

One of the leaders was the high priest that year. He said, "You don't know anything. It's good for one man to die for the people. It's better than the whole nation dying."

Now he didn't think about saying this himself. His words were a message from God. Jesus would die for the whole nation. He would die for all people. That way, they could be God's children.

From then on, the leaders made plans to kill Jesus. So Jesus did not go where he could be seen in public anymore.

Parents and Children

It was up to the father of the family to make sure everyone knew and followed the laws of the Jewish community. He would attend the synagogue services at the required times. But he would also work at the job he had learned from his own father, whether it was carpentry, pottery, farming, metal working or any other skill. He was to train his own sons to do the same.

Mothers were expected to supervise their young children, spin and weave cloth, make bread (which included grinding the grain), and make meals. They had to milk the goats, make the cheese, fetch the water at the well, and make sure the family had enough olive oil to fill their lamps. Depending on the family's needs, the mother might also work in the fields or help with other chores. She was to train her daughters to do the same.

Because there was so much physical work to do to make a living and keep the family going, it was important to have a big family. The more sons a father had, the more help he had in the fields or in the shop. The more daughters, the more the work of housekeeping could be spread out between them so the work was easier on everyone. So families were usually large.

Like a Child
Matthew 19:13-26; Mark 10:13-27; Luke 18:15-27

People started bringing little children to Jesus. They wanted Jesus to touch the children and pray for them. But Jesus' friends got mad at the people.

Jesus saw this, and he was upset. He said, "Let the little children come to me. Don't stop them. God's kingdom belongs to those who are like these children. People must welcome God's kingdom like a child does. If they don't, they won't get to go into God's kingdom."

Then Jesus picked up the children. He held them in his arms. He touched them. He prayed that God would bring good things to them.

As Jesus left, a man ran up to him. The man bowed down in front of Jesus. "Good Teacher," said the man. "What do I need to do to live forever?"

"Why are you calling me good?" Jesus asked. "God is the only one who is good. Are you calling me God?

"But to answer your question, you know the laws," said Jesus. "Don't kill. Stay with the one you marry. Don't take things that belong to someone else. Don't lie. Be kind to your father and mother."

"I've done all those things," said the man. "I've done them since I was a boy."

Jesus took a good look at the man and loved him. "There is one more thing for you to do," said Jesus. "Go and sell everything you have. Take the money you get and give it to the poor. Your riches will be in heaven. Then come and follow me."

When Jesus said this, the man grew sad. That's because he was very rich.

Jesus turned to his followers. "It's hard for rich people to come into God's kingdom. It's harder than a camel going through the hole in a needle."

Jesus' followers were surprised. "Who can be saved?" they asked.

"It's impossible for people," said Jesus. "But anything is possible with God."

Expecting a Messiah

The Jews had been expecting a Messiah, God's chosen man, who would set their nation free. They said this leader Messiah would crush the heads of the enemies, pile up the enemies' bodies, strike arrows into the enemies' hearts. Then he would rule in a time of perfect happiness. Jerusalem would be the center of the world, and all nations would serve the Jews.

Some people said, "When the Messiah comes, we won't have to harvest grain or grapes, but we will still have plenty of wheat and wine." Other people thought that sounded crazy. They did not think the idea of a real Messiah was true. "That will happen when the Messiah comes" was a popular saying. It meant something like our expression, "That will happen when pigs fly."

When we read about Jesus, we can see how careful He was not to advertise being the Messiah. He probably did not want to raise people's hopes that He would lead a revolt against Rome. He was a different kind of Messiah than they were expecting. Instead of leading a fight against the enemy, He said, "Love your enemies."

In the following story, James and John's mother probably expected Jesus to set up an earthly kingdom.

To Sit at Your Right Hand
Matthew 20:17-28; Mark 10:32-45; Luke 18:31-34

Jesus headed for Jerusalem. His twelve closest friends and other followers went with him. His closest friends were surprised to see him going to Jerusalem. His other followers were afraid.

Jesus told his closest friends what was about to happen. "We're on our way to Jerusalem," he said. "One of my friends will turn against me. He will tell the leaders at the worship house where I am. They will take me away and blame me. They will say I should die. Then they will send me to the Romans. The Romans will make fun of me and beat me. Then they will kill me. But on the third day, I will come back to life."

Jesus' friends didn't understand. They didn't know what Jesus was talking about.

Then James and John's mother brought them to Jesus. She bowed down.

"What do you want?" Jesus asked.

"Someday you'll be the king," she said. "Let one of my sons sit at your right side. Let my other son sit at your left side."

"You really don't know what you're asking," said Jesus. "Can you do what I'm about to do?"

"We can," said James and John.

"You will," said Jesus. "But I'm not the one to say who will sit at my right or left."

Jesus' other friends heard what James and John wanted. They got angry at James and John. So Jesus called them all together. He said, "You know, the world's rulers boss everyone around. They tell everyone what to do. But you're not supposed to act like that. Instead, if you want to be great, serve people. Anyone wanting to be first has to be a servant. Even I didn't come to earth to be served. I came to serve. I came to give up my life. Then I can set people free from sin."

  Thursday

Tax Collectors

In Jesus' time, tax collectors bought their jobs from the government by agreeing to give the Roman government a certain amount of money each year from taxes. The Romans didn't care how much the tax collector charged as long as Rome got the agreed-upon amount. Whatever money a tax collector collected that was *more* than Rome's amount, they got to keep. So many tax collectors got rich by charging a lot more than the real tax.

Because of this, nobody liked tax collectors. They were accused of being cheaters and thieves. In lots of places, people would not even let tax collectors into the synagogue, because they said tax collectors were "unclean."

People used only coins, not paper money in Jesus' time. The coins could be very valuable, some made of pure silver or gold. Since people did not have pockets, they tucked their coins into the fold of their belt, or sewed them into the hem of their robe. Or they carried a small pouch, which they called a "purse" or "wallet." Tax collectors always had full purses.

Up in a Tree
Luke 19:1-10

Jesus came to the town of Jericho. A man named Zacchaeus lived there. He was a tax man. He was very rich.

Zacchaeus heard that Jesus was coming. He wanted to see who Jesus was. But Zacchaeus was a short man. He couldn't see around the crowd. Zacchaeus knew which way Jesus was going. So he ran ahead of the crowd and climbed into a tree. He wanted to make sure he could see Jesus.

Jesus did come that way. When he got to the tree, he stopped and looked up. "Zacchaeus!" he called. "Come down right away. I need to stay at your house today."

So Zacchaeus came down. He was glad to welcome Jesus into his house.

The other people began to fuss. "Jesus has gone to stay with a sinner!" they said.

But Zacchaeus was making things right. "Look, Lord," he said to Jesus. "I'll give half of everything I own to poor people. Did I trick people into giving me too much? Then I'll pay them back. I'll pay four times what I took!"

"Someone has been saved today at this house!" said Jesus. "This is why I came. I came to look for people who lost their way. I came to save them!"

The Poor

Lots of people in Jesus' time worked hard but didn't earn much money. Others wanted to work, but didn't have steady jobs. They would stand in the marketplace every morning, hoping someone would come and hire them for the day. If they didn't get hired, they earned nothing that day. Then there were servants whose masters paid them hardly anything. Last of all were the beggars. Most of them were crippled or blind and couldn't work, so they had to beg for money or food.

Beggars were common, because there were no jobs for people who were blind or lame or had other kinds of disability. There were no jobs for women whose husbands had died. There were no hospitals or nursing homes to take care of people who couldn't care for themselves. So those people sat by the road, or in the marketplace, or near gates to the city or the temple, calling out for people to give them food or money. And people did. This giving was called "alms."

By the Side of the Road
Matthew 20:29-34; Mark 10:46-52; Luke 18:35-43

Jesus and his friends were leaving Jericho. A big crowd of people followed them.

A man was sitting by the side of the road. He could not see. His name was Bartimaeus. He was begging for money. Bartimaeus heard people say that Jesus was coming. So he started shouting, "Jesus! Be kind to me!"

People got mad at Bartimaeus. They told him to be quiet.

Bartimaeus just shouted louder. "Jesus!" he called. "Be kind to me!"

Jesus stopped walking. "Tell that man to come here," he said.

"Stand up!" the people told Bartimaeus. "You can cheer up now! Jesus is calling you!"

Bartimaeus threw off his coat. He jumped up and went over to Jesus.

"What do you want me to do?" Jesus asked.

"I want to see!" said Bartimaeus.

"All right," said Jesus. "You are well because you believe in me!"

Right away, Bartimaeus could see. He followed Jesus, cheering for God.

All the people saw it. They cheered for God too.

WEEK 27

 Monday

Bankers and Merchants

Bankers were also called "money-changers." They traded one type of coin for another kind for people. They also loaned money to borrowers and invested money into businesses. Rich people often put their money into the care of bankers, who were thought to be quite smart and wise in the ways of business. To make money, bankers loaned that money and made business deals with other bankers and businessmen (who were often their relatives) in Palestine and in other countries as well. Bankers also made deals with non-Jews.

Traders and merchants were some of the people who borrowed money from bankers. It was not unusual for a trader from Palestine to go to live in another country for a year. Babylon, Damascus, Alexandria, and Rome were some of the popular big cities to live in. There the merchants would sell goods they had brought from Palestine. Then they would buy things in the other city to take back. Sometimes, people in other countries would place orders with the merchant, asking him to buy things they wanted or needed (usually wheat, oil, salt fish, dried fruit, balsam and other scented products). When the merchant returned home to Palestine, he would sell the things he had bought or traded for.

Traveling merchants or peddlers would go from town to town and village to village with donkeys loaded with their goods: new robes and linen, gold jewelry, even carpets. At holiday times, they would come to the big cities to sell their wares. Of course, the big cities always had their marketplaces or "souks," where merchants could sell from shops, calling out for people to come and buy.

The Servants and the Money
Luke 19:11-15

Jesus and his followers were getting close to Jerusalem. His followers thought about God's kingdom coming. They thought it would show up right away. So Jesus told them a story:

Once there was an important man. He had to go to a land far away. He was going to have the people there make him their king. Then he would come back home as a king.

So the man called ten servants. He gave each of them some money. "Use this money to get more money," he said. "See how well you can use it until I come back."

Now some of the people hated this man. Some of them followed him to the land far away. They said, "We don't want this man to be king."

But the man was made king anyway. Then he came home. He sent for the servants who had the money he had given them. He wanted to find out what they had done with it.

True To Herod's Story

The story that Jesus tells about the man who gave coins to his servants has a second part: the part about the man being made king. That part seems very strange. But if we look at real history, maybe it's not so strange at all.

Herod the Great ruled when Jesus was born. He was the king the Wise Men went to see, He was also a cruel and violent king. When Jesus was a boy, Herod the Great died. Soon after his death, one of his sons traveled to Rome to make sure he was chosen king after his father. But a group of Jewish leaders followed Herod's son to Rome. They spoke against him, hoping he would not be made king. They did not succeed. When Herod's son came back as king, he had all those leaders killed. This kind of thing happened all the time in the ancient world as rulers came and went. So Jesus sets his story in a true-to-life world, the world the people knew.

The King
Luke 19:16-27

The first servant said, "Sir, I made more money for you. You gave me one coin, and I got ten more."

"Well done!" said the king. "You are a good servant! I see I could trust you with a little bit. Now you may be in charge of ten cities."

The second servant said, "Sir, I made more money for you. You gave me one coin, and I got five more."

"Well done!' said the king. "You may be in charge of five cities!"

Another servant said, "Sir, here's the coin you gave me. I hid it in a piece of cloth. I was afraid, because you are a hard man to work for. You take what doesn't belong to you. You bring in crops you didn't plant."

The king said, "I see! You know I'm a hard man to work for. So why didn't you put my money into the bank? I could have made more money in the bank."

Other people were standing nearby. The king said, "Take the money away from this man. Give it to the servant who has ten coins."

"But that man already has ten," said the people.

The king answered, "Everyone who has something from me will get more. Unless it means nothing to him. Then even what I gave him will be taken away."

Then the king looked for his enemies. They were the ones who didn't want him to be king. He told his men to bring the enemies to him and kill them.

 Wednesday

Perfume

Perfume-making was an important business in Jesus' time. People did not have deodorant. So if they could afford perfume, they might wear it or set it out at home to cover smells they wanted to hide. Perfume was made in three different ways:
1. Drop flower seeds and petals into hot oil, then strain the seeds and petals out before the oil cools.
2. Spread fresh flower petals on a layer of animal fat. The fat absorbs the fragrance.
3. Put flower petals into a fabric bag. Wring the bag tight to squeeze out the flower oils.

Some of the most common scents were aloe, balsam, sweet cane (calamus), cassia, frankincense, henna, myrrh, and saffron. The perfume Mary poured on Jesus' feet was called nard or spikenard. It was very expensive. It may have been part of her "dowry," the things girls saved for when they got married.

A Jar of Perfume
Matthew 26:6-13; Mark 14:1-11; Luke 19:28; John 11:55–12:11

Jesus kept traveling toward Jerusalem. It was almost time for the Passover holiday. So lots of people were coming to Jerusalem. They were getting ready for the holiday. They were also looking for Jesus. People stood around the worship house, asking each other, "What do you think? Do you think Jesus will come for the holiday?"

But the leaders at the worship house sent word to the people: Anyone who knew where Jesus was, had to tell the leaders. They were looking for a way to catch Jesus.

Six days before the Passover holiday, Jesus went to Bethany. That was where Mary, Martha, and Lazarus lived. Lazarus was the man who had been brought back to life by Jesus.

A man named Simon also lived in Bethany. He had a dinner party for Jesus. Martha served the food. Lazarus ate at the table with Jesus.

But Mary took out a jar of nard. It was perfume that cost a lot of money. She tipped the jar over. She let perfume flow out onto Jesus' feet. Then she wiped his feet with her hair. The air was filled with the sweet perfume smell.

Judas, one of Jesus' closest helpers, said, "Why didn't Mary sell this perfume? Think of the money she could have made! It would have been enough to pay a working person for a year. She could have given the money to poor people!"

Now Judas didn't really care about poor people. He was a robber. He kept the money bag for Jesus and his friends. He would take out whatever he wanted for himself. Judas was the one who would turn against Jesus.

"Leave Mary alone," said Jesus. "It was right for Mary to save this perfume. She got my body ready for the grave. Poor people will always be around you. But I won't always be here. I'm going to die. The news about me will be shared all over the world. Then people will hear what Mary did tonight," said Jesus.

Many people found out that Jesus was in Bethany. So they went to Bethany. They didn't go just to see Jesus. They went to see Lazarus, too. They wanted to see someone Jesus had brought back to life. So the leaders at the worship house made plans to kill Jesus and Lazarus. They were angry about Lazarus. Many people had seen him alive again. They believed in Jesus because of Lazarus.

A King on a Donkey

"He who comes" was the way many Jews referred to the coming Messiah. Zechariah 9:9 says, "Rejoice greatly, O people of Zion! Shout in triumph, O people of Jerusalem! Look, your king is coming to you. He is righteous and victorious, yet he is humble, riding on a donkey – even on a donkey's colt." All Jews knew this scripture. So when Jesus chose to ride into Jerusalem on a donkey, they knew He was claiming to be the Messiah.

In addition, the people were shouting "Hosanna," which means "save now." They were asking God to save His people through this Messiah. The people expected their Messiah to be a war-leader. But Jesus was giving them a very clear message that He did not come to be a war-leader. The message came through the animal He chose to ride. A king who planned to wage war rode in on a horse. But Jesus came on a donkey. Donkeys were not considered lowly animals, as we think of them today. Kings often rode donkeys. But when they did, it meant they came in peace.

A Colt
Matthew 21:1-9; Mark 11:1-10; Luke 19:29-40; John 12:12-16

Now Jesus came to Olive Mountain. He asked two of his friends to go into the next town. "You'll see a donkey with her colt just as you go into town," said Jesus. "Nobody has ever ridden the colt before. It will be tied up there. Untie it, and bring it to me. I anyone asks what you're doing, tell them the Lord needs it."

Jesus' two friends went to town. They found the colt. It was in the street, tied by a door. They untied it.

Some people were standing there, watching. They said, "What are you doing? Why are you untying that colt?"

Jesus' friends told them just what Jesus had said. Then the people let them take the colt. Jesus' friends took the colt to Jesus. They put their coats on the little donkey's back. Then Jesus got on. Down the road they went.

That made the words of the prophet Zechariah come true. He wrote to Jerusalem, "See? Your king is coming to you. He is kind and good. He rides on a donkey. It's a colt, a donkey's baby."

Jesus' friends did not understand why he wanted a colt. They understood later, after Jesus died and came to life again. Then they knew that the prophet had written about him. They saw that they had helped these words come true.

Lots of people were in Jerusalem for the Pass Over holiday. They heard that Jesus was on his way to Jerusalem. So they got big branches from palm trees and ran to meet him.

"God save us!" the people shouted. "May good things come to the King of God's people! May good things come! He comes in the Lord's name!" They began to follow him.

Some leaders of God's people were in the crowd. They said to Jesus, "Tell your followers to be quiet!"

"If they are quiet, the stones will shout!" said Jesus.

A Fig Tree

The fig tree was one of the most important trees in ancient Palestine. It usually gave two crops of figs each year. The main harvest was in the fall, but fig trees also bore their fruit in the spring. The day after Passover, people began looking for early figs.

A fig tree could be trimmed to make a sort of umbrella so people could sit in its shade in their yard or out in the fields. It became a symbol of home. To be "in the shade of your fig tree" meant to be happy and relaxed.

What Jesus says about the fig tree in this next story sounds strange. But some people believe Jesus was giving a real-life word picture, an object lesson, that compared this particular fig tree with the Jewish leaders. The fig tree was supposed to bear figs, but there were none. The Jewish leaders were supposed to represent God, but they didn't show God's love.

A Fig Tree
Matthew 21:10-11, 18-22; Mark 11:11-14, 20-33; John 12:17-19

Jesus went into Jerusalem. Everyone in the city was talking about him. "Who is this?" they asked.

"This is Jesus," said the people who had followed him. "He is the prophet from Nazareth." People told how Lazarus had come back to life. Lots of people who heard about it went to see Jesus.

"Look how everybody in the world follows him," said the Jewish leaders. "This isn't getting us anywhere."

Jesus went to the worship house. He looked around. But it was late. So Jesus and his friends went back to Bethany. They spent the night there.

The next day, they headed for Jerusalem again. Jesus was hungry. He saw a fig tree ahead. It had leaves on it. So Jesus went to see if it had any fruit. But when he got there, he found only leaves. It wasn't the season for figs to grow yet.

Jesus spoke to the tree. "No one will ever get fruit from you again."

Some time later, Jesus and his friends headed back to Jerusalem. They passed the fig tree Jesus had talked to. It had dried up.

Peter remembered what Jesus had said to the fig tree. "Look!" said Peter. "You talked to the fig tree. You said no one would get fruit from it. It dried up!"

Jesus' friends were surprised. "How did it dry up so fast?" they asked.

"You can do the same thing if you have faith," said Jesus. "You can tell a mountain to jump into the sea. It will. Believe in God. Then you'll get whatever you ask for when you pray. But when you pray, ask yourself if you are angry at someone. Forgive that person. Then your Father in heaven will forgive you."

WEEK 28

 Monday

Kinds of Priests

Jesus saw all these different kinds of priests at the temple.

High Priest
There was only one of these. He:
>was head of the Jews' high court
>was the most powerful of the Jews
>wore special robes
>lived in a palace in Jerusalem
>served barefoot

Chief Priests
There were about 200 of these. They:
>included the captain of the temple
>were in charge of temple activities
>(some) were in charge of daily services
>were upper class rich, from Jerusalem
>served barefoot

Ordinary Priests
There were about 7,200 of these. They:
>usually lived away from Jerusalem
>served one week at at time
>lit altar fires
>offered incense on the altars
>killed the sacrifice animals
>served barefoot
>**Levites**

There were about 9,600 of these. They:
>   served one week at a time
>   (some) were temple guards (policemen)
>   (some) were doorkeepers and servants
>   (some) were singers, musicians
>   were not allowed to go near the altar
>   served barefoot

A Hiding Place for Robbers
Matthew 21:12-16; Mark 11:15-18; Luke 19:45-48

When he got to Jerusalem, Jesus went to the worship house. People were buying and selling animals there. Others were trading money that people brought from different places. They traded it for money that people could use to buy things. Jesus started chasing those people out. He turned over tables where men traded money from other places for money people could use. Jesus turned over the seats of the people selling doves. He wouldn't even let people carry things across the yards at the worship house.

"My house is supposed to be a house of prayer for all people," said Jesus. "You turned it into a hiding place for robbers!"

The leaders at the worship house heard this. They wanted to kill Jesus. They were afraid of him.

But there were crowds of people around Jesus. People were listening to what he said. People who couldn't see came. People who couldn't walk came. Jesus made them well. So it was hard for the leaders to catch him.

The leaders saw the wonderful things Jesus was doing. They saw children shouting. "Cheer for the King!" called the children. The worship-house leaders were upset. They talked to Jesus about it. "Do you hear what these children are saying?" they asked.

"Yes," said Jesus. "Haven't you read from the psalm? It says that God planned for children and babies to praise him."

Making Sense of a Strange Answer

Jews who lived in other lands dreamed of going to Jerusalem at least once in their lifetime. There were only synagogues where they lived, and they wanted to worship at the one and only temple. So when a holiday came around, Jews from everywhere gathered in Jerusalem to celebrate. The following story tells about some men who came from Greece. They had heard about Jesus and told Philip and Andrew they wanted to meet Him. When Philip and Andrew told Jesus, He said, "The time has come for me to enter into my glory." That sounds like a strange answer. In fact, it sounds like Jesus didn't answer them at all.

If we understand what "glory" is, we can understand Jesus' answer. "Glory" is showing who God is in all His life-giving love. So the Greeks say, "We want to see Jesus," and Jesus' answer means, "They will. It's time. God is getting ready to show all His life-giving love in me." Maybe Jesus saw in the Greeks that His message was spreading far beyond Palestine. Maybe that led Him to the thought that the growth of God's message into all the world would be possible only through His death He expressed that thought in His word picture about a seed.

A Seed
John 12:20-36

Some people from the land of Greece came to Jerusalem to worship. They found Philip and said, "Sir, we want to see Jesus."

Philip went to tell Andrew. Then Andrew and Philip went to tell Jesus.

Jesus talked to Andrew and Philip. "It's time for God to show his greatness in me. It's time for the whole world to see who I am. A wheat seed falls to the ground. It dies. It's just a little seed. But it will make many other seeds. It will send out roots and grow. It will live again.

"Some people want to serve me," said Jesus. "To serve me, they will have to follow me. Then they will be where I am. If someone serves me, my Father will make that person feel special.

"Right now I feel troubled," said Jesus. "What can I say? 'Father, save me from what's going to happen'? No. I came into the world because of what's going to happen. So I say, 'Father, show how great you are in me. Let the world see you.' "

Just then a voice came from heaven. "I have shown how great I am. And I will show how great I am again."

People heard the voice. Some of them said it was just thunder. Others said it was an angel talking.

"This voice was for you, not for me," said Jesus. "It's time for the world to be judged now. It's time to chase away Satan, the world's sinful prince. I'll be lifted up from the earth. Then I'll draw all people to me." Jesus was talking about how he would die.

"The Promised One will stay with us forever," people said. "So how can you talk about being lifted up?"

"You have the light just a little while longer," said Jesus. "Walk while you have the light. The dark is going to come. People in the dark don't know where they're going. Trust in the light while it's here. Then you can be children of light."

Then Jesus left Jerusalem. The people didn't know where he went.

A Word Picture

Jesus gave another word picture to describe the Jewish leaders: a son who said he would do his chores, but didn't; and a son who said he would not do his chores, but did. The Jewish leaders were like the son who said he would take his responsibility, but didn't. The Jewish leaders had a responsibility to follow God's way. But they didn't. They bragged about following God's ways. They thought God accepted them because they said long prayers, gave lots of money, wore the right clothes, and washed their hands the right way. They thought they had nothing to apologize for. But God's way is the way of perfect love: loving your enemy, loving your neighbor as yourself. The leaders did not follow the way of love.

Meanwhile, other people did not claim to follow God's ways perfectly. Yet they were sorry for doing wrong. Many of them showed more of God's love than the leaders did. That's why Jesus told the leaders that tax men and sinners would get into God's kingdom before the leaders would.

Two Sons and a Grape Garden
Matthew 21:23-32; Luke 20:1-8

In Jerusalem, Jesus went to the worship house again. The leaders came to him and asked, "Who gave you the right to do the things you do?"

"Let me ask you a question," said Jesus. "If you answer me, then I'll answer you. Tell me. John baptized people. Was that his idea? Or did God tell him to do that?"

The worship-house leaders talked to each other. "If we say it was God's idea, he will say, 'Why didn't you believe John?' If we say it was John's idea, we're in trouble with the people." They were afraid of the many people who said John really was a prophet. At last the leaders answered, "We don't know."

"Then I won't answer your question," Jesus said. Then he told this story:

There once was a man who had two sons. The man talked to his first son. "Go work in the grape garden today," he said.

His first son said no. Later, he changed his mind. He did go.

The man talked to his other son. "Go work in the grape garden today," he said.

His other son said, "Yes, sir. I will." But he didn't go.

"Which son did what his father wanted?" asked Jesus.

"The first one," they said.

"John came to show you the right way to live," said Jesus. "Tax men and sinners believed John. They will get into God's kingdom. But you would not believe John. You would not be sorry for the wrong things you did. So tax men and sinners will get into God's kingdom before you."

Thursday

Landlords and Stewards

In ancient Palestine, some rich men owned lots of land but didn't work on it themselves. They hired a steward to farm the land for them. The rich men were called landlords. What they really wanted was to collect the rent on the land. The rent might be money or it might be part of the crop that the steward grew. The steward lived on the land, hired the workers, bought the seeds, planted and tended the crops, and harvested them when the time came. After that, the steward owed the landlord either money or part of the crop.

If the land was a vineyard, as it is in the following story, there would probably be a thick, thorny hedge all around. The hedge would keep out wild boars, foxes, and thieves. A tall tower stood in one part of the vineyard. The vineyard workers would live in the tower, and from the top, a watchman would keep an eye out for robbers. The vineyard would probably have a wine-press, too. A winepress was two troughs of rock or brick. One trough was higher than the other. The grapes were mashed in the higher trough, and the juice would run into the lower trough.

Jesus used the common scene of the landlord and stewards as a word picture. He showed God as the landlord and the Jewish leaders as the stewards of God's people and God's way of love.

The Farmers and the Grape Garden
Matthew 21:33-46; Mark 12:1-12; Luke 20:9-19

"Once a man planted a garden of grape vines," said Jesus.

The man built a wall around his field. He built a tall tower for watching over the field. Then he let some farmers rent the field. He went away on a long trip.

In time, the grapes were ready to be picked. So the man sent a servant to get some. But the farmers caught the servant. They beat him up. They sent him away without any fruit.

The man sent another servant to the farmers. But the farmers hit him on the head. They were very mean to him.

The man sent another servant. But the farmers killed him.

The man sent lots of other servants. The farmers beat up some of them. They killed others.

At last, there was only one person left to send. It was the man's son. He loved his son very much. "They will listen to my son," he said. So he sent his son to them.

But the farmers said, "Aha! This is his son! Come on! Let's kill him! Then the field will be ours!" So they killed the son. They threw him out of the field.

"What will the owner of the field do?" asked Jesus. "He will come and kill those farmers. He will give his field to somebody else."

"We hope this never happens," said the people.

Jesus said, "Have you read this psalm? 'There was a stone that the builders didn't want. Now that stone holds up the whole building. God made this happen. We think it's wonderful!' God is going to take his kingdom away from you. He will give it to people who will follow him. They will obey him."

The leaders at the worship house heard this story. They knew Jesus was talking about them. So they looked for a way to catch him. But they couldn't, because the people said Jesus was a prophet. The leaders were afraid of the crowd.

Sadducees

The men trying to trick Jesus in the following story were all Jews, but some were Pharisees (the ones who had lots of picky laws) and some were Sadducees. Most rich Jews were Sadducees. The priests were Sadducees. The High Priest was a Sadducee. They believed in only the first five books of the Torah, our Old Testament. But they were very strict about following the Torah. They also wanted to keep peace with the Romans. They were afraid Jesus would lead a rebellion and upset the peace. That's why they tried to trick Him into saying something they could arrest Him for.

Notice how Jesus does something very tricky himself. Remember that good Jews were not supposed to make or have anything that had the image of a person on it. When Jesus asks the leaders to show Him a coin, what did they have? A coin with an image on it.

Tricks
Matthew 22:15-32; Mark 12:13-25; Luke 20:20-40

Some Jewish leaders tried to think of ways to trick Jesus. They wanted to make him say the wrong thing. Then they could blame him and the Roman leaders would put him in jail.

So the Jewish leaders sent some people to trick Jesus. They said, "We know you tell the truth. You teach about God. You don't follow people's ideas. So tell us something. Should we pay taxes to the king?"

Jesus said, "Why are you trying to trick me? Show me the money you pay your taxes with."

They showed him the money.

"Whose picture is on it?" asked Jesus. "Whose name is on it?"

"The king's," they said.

"Then give the king what belongs to him," said Jesus. "And give God what belongs to God."

The people were surprised by what Jesus said. They couldn't think of anything else to say.

The same day, some other leaders of God's people came to see Jesus. These leaders did not believe that people go to heaven after they die. So they tried to trick Jesus too. They said, "Here's a problem. Moses told what should happen if a man dies. His brother has to marry his wife and have children for him. Now there were seven brothers. The first brother got married and then died. But he didn't have any children. So the second brother married his wife.

"But the second brother died. He didn't have any children. So the third brother married his wife. Then this brother died. He didn't have any children. So the fourth brother married her. Then he died. And the fifth brother married her. But the same thing kept happening. All seven brothers married the woman. All died. There were no children. At last, the woman died.

"Now, what if people live again?" said the leaders. "What if they go to heaven? Whose wife will the woman be? She married all seven brothers."

"You are thinking the wrong way," said Jesus. "You don't understand what God says. You don't know God's power. People will come back to life. But they won't marry. And they won't die. They'll be like the angels in heaven."

WEEK 29

 Monday

Jewish Laws

All good Jews in Jesus' time knew the Ten Commandments. Of course, there were other laws, too. As we have seen, the Jewish rabbis and leaders had made hundreds of picky laws over the years, laws that are not in the Bible, including some we learned earlier about the Sabbath. Here are some laws we find in the Old Testament. Some of them are in the Ten Commandments.

> Don't make idols or say bad things about God.
> Don't steal or lie or copy others who are doing wrong.
> Show your joy for what God has given you.
> Be fair to people from other lands and to children who have no fathers.
> A robber must pay back whatever he stole.
> Do right for the people who work for you.
> Don't make a person pay back more than he borrowed.
> Don't eat eagles, vultures, ravens, owls, gulls, or hawks.
> Don't eat storks, herons, bats, weasels, rats, or lizards.
> Don't eat anything you find that is already dead.
> Be kind to your father and mother.
> Don't tell bad things about other people.
> Don't try to get back at someone who has done you wrong.

But none of these is the most important law, according to Jesus. When He said what was most important, He did not make a new law. Instead, He quoted two scriptures from the Torah, (part of our Old Testament): "Love the Lord your God with all your heart, all your soul, and all your strength" (Deuteronomy 6:5) and "Love your neighbor as yourself" (Leviticus 19:18).

What's Most Important?
Matthew 22:34-46; Mark 12:28-37; Luke 20:41-44

One teacher of God's laws saw that Jesus had given a good answer. So he said, "There are many rules. Which one is the most important?"

"The most important rule is this one," said Jesus. "The Lord is the only God. Love the Lord with all your heart. Love him with all your soul. Love him with all your mind. Love him with all your strength. The next important rule is to love your neighbor like you love yourself. No other rule is greater than these."

"You answered that very well," said the teacher. "You're right to say there is only one God. It's important to love him with all our heart. We must love him with all our soul, mind, and strength. It's important to love our neighbor, too. All of this is more important than any gift we could give God."

Jesus could see this man was wise. "You're not very far from God's kingdom," he said.

The Jewish leaders were standing there together. So Jesus asked, "What do you think about the Promised One? Whose son is he?"

"He is King David's son," they said.

"Then how could David call him his Lord?" asked Jesus. "Remember what David wrote in the psalm? David called the Promised One 'Lord.' So how could he be David's son?"

Nobody could answer Jesus. After that, nobody dared to ask any more questions.

 Tuesday

Temple Giving

Every Jew was supposed to give three ways.

1. Alms. Alms were given to beggars and other needy people.

2. The Temple tax. This money helped pay for keeping the Temple clean and in good repair. It also paid for the needs of the priests. Whether you were rich or poor, if you were older than thirteen, you had to pay this tax.

3. Tithes. A tithe was one-tenth of everything you grew. Some farmers would load their carts with a tenth of their harvest and bring it to the temple in a mood of celebrating. Other farmers gave their tithes to Levites (men from the families of priests) who were sent out to collect them. The rabbis said that anything a farmer grew and did not tithe was unclean. They also said that anyone who ate from an untithed harvest was sinning.

The money brought to the temple was collected in boxes that stood in the court of women. There were thirteen of these boxes. They were called "the trumpets" because of their shape, wide at the bottom and narrow at the top. Each box was for money given for something different. One was for money to buy grain. Another was for money for oil. There was one for wine, another for wood, one for incense, and another for keeping the golden bowls and cups clean and shiny.

The coins the widow put into one of "the trumpets" were leptons. Lepton means "thin one." It was the smallest of all coins and was worth only part of a penny.

The Most Money
Mark 12:41-44; Luke 21:1-4

Jesus sat down at the worship house. He was across from the place where people gave money. He watched people put money into the offering box.

Lots of rich people came by. They threw in lots of money. Then a poor woman walked up. Her husband had died. She dropped in two small pennies.

"Look!" Jesus told his friends. "This woman put the most money into the offering box. It's more than what the rich people put in! The other people gave only part of their riches. This poor woman gave all the money she had."

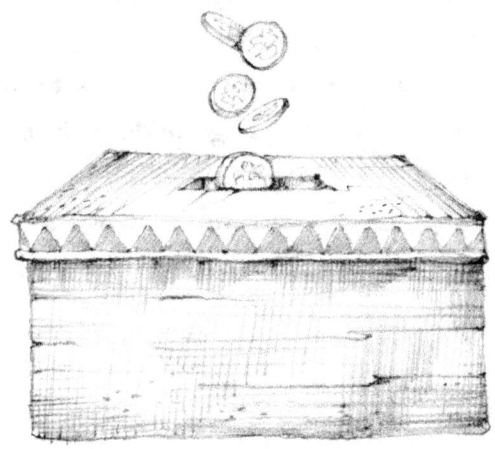

Herod's Temple

The temple that Jesus went to in Jerusalem was not the original temple that King Solomon had built, although it stood on the same spot. Solomon's temple had been burned down almost 600 years before Jesus was born. It had been rebuilt, but in Jesus' time, it was over 500 years old. Herod the Great started cleaning it up and remodeling it about 15 years before Jesus was born. All through Jesus' life, the temple was still being remodeled. It wasn't finished until about 34 years after Jesus died.

In the following story, Jesus' friends point out how wonderful the temple looks. It truly was an amazing building. Built on a raised area of land, it was made of white marble covered with gold. People said that when the sun shone on the temple, it was so bright you could hardly look at it.

When Will This Happen?
Matthew 24:1-14; Mark 13:1-13; Luke 21:5-19

Jesus and his helpers left the worship house.

"Look!" said one of his friends. "Look how big the stones in the worship house are! What wonderful buildings!"

"Yes, look at all these big buildings," said Jesus. "Someday they will be torn down. Not one stone will be left on top of another." Jesus walked up Olive Mountain. He sat down. From there, he could see the city across the valley. He could see the worship house.

Peter, James, John, and Andrew came up to Jesus. They said, "When will that happen? And what will happen to let us know you're coming again? How will we know when the end of time is coming?"

"Be careful," said Jesus. "Don't let anyone trick you. You'll hear people say, 'I am the one God promised to send.' They'll fool lots of people. You'll also hear about wars. Don't be scared. This has to happen. That doesn't mean the end of time has come yet. Nations will fight each other. Kingdoms will fight each other. Sometimes there won't be enough food. The ground will shake in different places. This is just the beginning.

"You'll have to be careful," said Jesus. "People will send you to judges. They'll beat you because of me. But you will tell rulers and kings about me. I'll help you know what to say. There will be more and more sin. Most people's love will grow cold. People will hate you because you belong to me. But keep loving me, and you will be saved. The Good News of the kingdom will be told all over the world. All nations will hear it. Then the end will come."

  Thursday

The First-Century Destruction of Jerusalem

As beautiful as the temple was, Jesus talked about a time to come when the temple would be attacked and torn down. About 40 years after Jesus died (only six years after the remodeling was finished), that really happened. Rome finally got tired of the trouble the Jews were giving them. Since Jerusalem had a strong wall around it, the Romans decided to surround the city and not let any food get in. They starved the people until most of them died and the rest were too weak to defend the city. Then the Romans entered. About 97,000 people were captured and made slaves. Another one million died. The Romans destroyed the whole city, including the temple.

Days to Come
Matthew 24:15-27; Mark 13:14-23; Luke 21:5-19

"One day, you will see armies all around Jerusalem. Then you'll know bad times are coming for Jerusalem. People living nearby will need to run to the mountains. People in the city should get out. People in the country should not go back to the city. This will pay God's people back for their sins.

"Pray that you won't have to leave in winter," said Jesus. "Pray that you won't have to leave on a worship day. There will be lots of trouble. Things will be worse than they have been since time began. Things will never be that bad again. Some people will be killed. Others will be taken to live in other lands. People who are not Jewish will control Jerusalem for a while. This won't last long. If it did, no one would live through it. The time will be short because of God's people.

"Someone might say, 'Look! Here's Jesus!' They might say, 'There he is!' Don't believe them. Fake promised ones and fake prophets will come. They'll even do great wonders. They'll try to fool God's people if they can.

"See?" said Jesus. "I've told you all this before it happens. Someone might say, 'There is Jesus. He is out in the desert!' Don't go there. They might say, 'Here he is. He is in one of the rooms in this building!' Don't believe it. When I come, it will be like lightning. You can see it when you're in the east. You can see it when you're in the west."

Friday

Pictures of the Future

The Jews of Jesus' day thought of time as being divided into two parts: this present age and the age to come. In between these two, they expected what they called "the Day of the Lord." That was the day God would change this bad present age into the good age to come. They described the Day of the Lord with all kinds of word pictures in which everything goes haywire. The whole world is shaken. The sun shines at night, the moon in the daytime. Stones have voices. Fresh water has salt in it. Planted fields look as if they've not been planted. Barns that were full are now empty. Wells are stopped up.

Several prophets of the Old Testament wrote about the Day of the Lord, about stars not giving light, signs on earth and in the sky, the sun turning dark. Many of the same things were written in other Jewish books (the Apocrypha) that were popular at the time of Jesus. These books are dreams, word pictures that point to God breaking into human history. So when Jesus talked about the sun and moon not shining and the stars falling, He was using the Jews' own language to talk about another time to come. And He was making one very important point: No matter what happens, God will not leave us.

No One Knows
Matthew 24:29-36; Mark 13:24-37; Luke 21:25-36

"Right after the hard times, the sun will turn dark," said Jesus. "The moon will not shine its light. Stars will fall from the sky. Then my sign will show up in the sky. Nations will cry. They will see me coming through the sky on clouds. I'll come with power. I'll send my angels out with a loud call from a horn. The angels will bring my people together. They'll come from one end of the sky to the other. There will be signs in the sun. There will be signs in the moon. There will be signs in the stars. The sea will roar and toss. People will wonder and be afraid of what's coming.

"Look up when this starts happening. Watch!" said Jesus. "That means it's time for you to be saved. Learn a lesson from the fig tree. You see its leaves coming out. So you know summer will soon be here. You may see these things I've talked about. Then you'll know the time is coming soon. One day there will be an end to the sky. There will be an end to the earth. But there will never be an end to my words.

"No one knows when this will happen," said Jesus. "Even the angels in heaven don't know. Even I, the Son, don't know. Only the Father knows. I tell everyone the same thing. Watch!"

WEEK 30

 Monday

Weddings

In Jesus' time, it would have been very strange for a woman to never marry. All women were expected to get married. In fact, parents chose who you were going to marry. Sometimes they chose while you were still a child. Most girls got married when they were thirteen or fourteen.

On the evening of the wedding, the bride would dress in her fancy wedding clothes. With her girl friends, she would wait for the groom to come to her house and get her. To show the groom that he was at the right house, the girls often held up little oil lamps. It was not unusual for them to also carry extra oil in small bottles that swung on cords from their fingers.

Meanwhile, the groom left his house with his friends. They carried torches and walked through the street to the bride's house. There the bride and her friends would join the groom, and they would all walk back to his house, where they would have a great feast with music and dancing. The celebration might go on for as long as a week.

Ten Lamps
Matthew 25:1-13

Jesus told a story about the time when he will come back:

The kingdom of heaven will be like ten young people. They were going to a wedding party. They were going to be with the groom.

All the young people brought their lamps with them. Five of these young people were foolish. They didn't bring any oil to keep their lamps lit. Five were wise. They brought oil in jars.

It took a long time for the groom to come. All the young people got sleepy. In fact, they went to sleep.

In the middle of the night, a voice called out. "Here comes the groom! Come and meet him!"

All the young people woke up. They lit their lamps. But the foolish ones had run out of oil. They said, "Our lamps! They're going out! Give us some of your oil!"

The wise ones said, "No. We don't have enough for us and for you, too! You'll have to go to the store. Buy your own oil."

So the foolish people went to the store. While they were gone, the groom came. The young people who were there went with him to the wedding party. The door closed behind them.

Sometime later, the other young people came back. They called, "Open the door. Let us in."

But the groom said, "I don't know you."

"So watch. You don't know when I'll come," said Jesus.

 Tuesday

Sheep vs. Goats

Big herds of sheep and goats grazed in the hills all around ancient Palestine. Sheep were prized for their wool and their meat. Goats were valued too. People drank tangy goats' milk and made cheese from it. Goat skin was used to make clothes, water bottles, and musical instruments. Goat hair was woven to make a fabric often used to make tents. Both sheepskin and goatskin were used as scrolls to write on.

The goat is no less valuable to the shepherd than the sheep. They often roamed the same pastures. But sometimes goats had to be separated from sheep, because male goats could start acting mean to the sheep. Goats eat almost any kind of plant. As they graze, they tear the plants out of the ground, so they tend to ruin the land they graze on. Sometimes they even prop their front feet on a tree trunk and nibble on the lower leaves if they can reach them. So they can totally ruin a field if they are not controlled. But sheep can damage a field too. Because they bite off grass close to the ground, too many sheep grazing the same area can be bad for the land.

Both sheep and goats were used as temple sacrifices. The goat had a special job on the Day of Atonement. The high priest placed his hands on the goat as if placing the sins of God's people on the animal. Then the goat, carrying those sins, was sent out into the desert. This was an object lesson, a living word picture. It showed God forgiving the people, separating them from their sins. That's what the word "judge" means. It means to separate or select.

Sheep and Goats
Matthew 25:31-45

"I'll come back," said Jesus. "All the angels will come. All the nations will come together and see me as the king of my kingdom. Then I'll put the people into different groups.

"A shepherd puts his sheep into one group," said Jesus. "He puts the goats into another group. I'll put people who are my sheep into one group. They'll be on my right. I'll put people who are like goats on my left. Then I'll talk to the people on my right. I'll say, 'Come! My Father has good things for you. . . .'

"I'll say, 'I was hungry, and you gave me food. I was thirsty, and you gave me a drink. I needed a place to stay, and you asked me to come in. I needed clothes, and you gave me clothes. I was sick, and you took care of me. I was in jail, and you came to see me.'

"The people who did what's right will wonder. They'll say, 'Lord, when did we see you hungry? When did we give you food? When did we give you a drink? When did you need a place to stay? When did we ask you to come in? When did we give clothes to you? When were you sick? When were you in jail? When did we come to see you?'

"Then I'll say, 'You did these things for people who don't seem important at all. That's when you did them for me.'

"Then I'll talk to the people on my left. 'Go away from me,' I'll say. 'Go into the fire that burns forever. It's been made ready for the devil and his helpers.'

"I'll say, 'I was hungry. But you didn't give me any food. I was thirsty. But you didn't give me anything to drink. I needed a place to stay. But you left me outside. I needed clothes. But you didn't give me any. I was sick. I was in jail. But you didn't take care of me.'

"They will say, 'Lord, when did we see you hungry or thirsty? When did you need clothes, or a place to stay? When were you sick or in jail?'

"Then I'll say, 'You never did these things for people who don't seem important. So you left me out too.'"

Thirty Coins

Two sides came together to make a deal in the following story. First there were the Jewish leaders. They were afraid of Jesus. Some were afraid their own followers would stop listening to them and would follow Jesus instead. Others were afraid Jesus would start a revolt or stir up attacks on the Romans. If that happened, the Roman army would come into the city and there would be fighting. The Romans would take away some of the leaders' privileges.

Then there was Judas. We don't know why he betrayed Jesus. Maybe Judas was greedy for money. Maybe he was disappointed that Jesus was not the war-leader, the kind of Messiah he wanted to serve. Maybe he thought if the guards came out to arrest Jesus, it would force Jesus to fight like the great war-leader Judas hoped He would be. At any rate, Judas made a deal with the leaders: He would show them where Jesus was if they would give him 30 silver coins.

Thirty silver coins would have bought Judas a new cloak or an ox. But the saddest thing is that 30 pieces of silver was the usual price for a slave. Judas sold Jesus as if Jesus were a slave.

Thirty Silver Coins
Matthew 26:3-5, 14-16; Mark 14:1-2, 10-11; Luke 21:37–22:6;
John 12:37-47

The leaders of God's people got together at the high priest's palace. They made plans to catch Jesus by some trick. Then they would kill him. They planned carefully. "We won't do it while the Passover holiday is going on. If we do, the people might fight us," they said.

Judas was one of Jesus' closest friends. But Satan took control of Judas now. He went to the leaders at the worship house. He told them he could show them where Jesus was. "What will you give me if I do?" he asked.

The leaders counted out 30 silver coins for Judas. He took the money. Then he waited and watched. He looked for a time when no crowds were around.

Every day, Jesus went to the worship house to teach. People came early in the morning to hear him. At the end of every day, he left the city. He spent the night on Olive Mountain.

People had seen Jesus do many wonders. But many people still would not believe in him. So Isaiah's words came true: "Who believed our news? Who did God show himself to?" Isaiah also said, "Their eyes can't see. Their hearts are dead. They don't see or understand. If they did, I would make them well." When Isaiah said this, he was talking about Jesus.

Many of the Jewish leaders did believe in Jesus. But they didn't talk about it. They were afraid of the leaders who didn't believe. Because of those leaders, they might not get into the towns' worship houses. They really loved cheers from people more than cheers from God.

"People who believe in me also believe in my Father," said Jesus. "When you look at me, you see God. I came to be a light to the world. People who believe me don't stay in darkness. But I'm not here to blame people who hear what I say but don't do it. I came to save them."

 Thursday

Passover

The Passover holiday was celebrated every spring. It was the most popular festival of the year. Crowds of people, most of them walking, came to Jerusalem to celebrate. Most people formed groups of family and friends. They would bring lambs for their group to give as their Passover sacrifice. The lambs had to be at least eight days old, but no more than one year old. The men of the group would carry their lamb or lambs to the temple. All afternoon, the priests would kill the lambs. They would sprinkle the blood on the base of the altar. This was a reminder of the blood that God's people painted on their door frames the last night they were in Egypt so the death angel would "pass over." After the blood was sprinkled on the altar, the lambs' bodies were given back to the group. They would take it to wherever their group was staying. There they would roast the meat for supper.

The special supper, known as the seder, celebrated God saving His people from Egypt in the days of Moses. For the Passover meal, the men and boys would sit or recline on straw mats around a low table. They would eat bread made without yeast, because God's people did not have time to let their bread rise as they got ready to escape from Egypt. They also ate lamb meat, which was what they ate in Egypt the night before they left. Other foods they ate were bitter herbs (endives and chicory probably) and haroset (charoseth), a mixture of fruit and nuts. Haroset is meant to look like the mortar the Israelites put between the bricks when they served as slaves of the Pharaohs in Egypt. Now and then during the meal, the men would say certain scriptures about God saving His people, and they would drink cups of wine.

The Room Upstairs
Matthew 26:17-20, 26-29; Mark 14:12-17, 22-25; Luke 22:7-20; John 13:1

At last, the Passover day came. Jesus sent Peter and John into the city. "Go find a place to eat the Passover dinner," he said. "Get everything ready."

"Where?" they asked.

"Go into the city," said Jesus. "You'll see a man carrying a jar of water. Follow him. He will go into a house. Find the owner of the house. Tell him, 'Jesus wants to know where he can eat the Passover dinner.' That man will show you a big room upstairs. It has a table and seats in it. That's where you'll get dinner ready."

So Peter and John left. Things happened just the way Jesus said. They got dinner ready.

At dinner time, Jesus and his closest friends gathered around the table. "I wanted to eat Passover dinner with you," said Jesus. "A time of pain is coming for me. I won't eat this Passover dinner again until it has a new meaning in the kingdom of God."

Jesus held up a cup of wine. He thanked God. "Take this," he told his friends. "Share it with each other. I won't drink wine again until God's kingdom comes."

Then Jesus picked up the flat bread. He thanked God. He broke some off to give to his friends. "This will help you remember my body," he said. "I'm giving my body for you. Eat this to remember me."

They finished dinner. Then Jesus picked up the cup of wine. "This shows God's new special promise," he said. "It's a promise made with my blood. I will give my blood for you."

Jesus knew it was time to leave the world. It was time for him to go to his Father. He loved his friends very much. They were his own people here in the world. He was about to show how much he loved them.

 Friday

Foot Washing

Almost everyone wore sandals in Jesus' time, even on cold days. That meant your feet would get dirty and dusty from walking on the dirt streets and floors. So you would wash your feet as soon as you came into a house. Unless you were very poor, you would have a foot-washing bowl or basin just inside your front door. In wealthier homes, a servant would wash your feet when you arrived. It was an important way to welcome a guest.

If your feet were being washed, you would rest your feet on a raised part in the middle of a large bowl made of clay pottery. Water would be poured over your feet, Then your feet would be scrubbed. In the following story, it is Jesus who washes His friends' feet. They had just been arguing over who was the greatest. Maybe no one wanted to lower himself to the place of a servant. So no one stepped up to do the foot washing – no one except Jesus.

Clean Feet
John 13:3-17

Jesus knew God had given him power over all things. He knew he had come from God. He knew he was going back to God. Jesus got up from the table. He took a long cloth. He tied it around himself like a belt. Then he got a big bowl of water. He started washing his friends' feet. He dried their feet with the long cloth.

Soon it was Peter's turn. But Peter said, "Lord, are you going to wash my feet?"

"I know you don't understand now," said Jesus. "But someday you'll understand."

"No," said Peter. "I can never let you wash my feet."

"That means you won't belong to me," said Jesus. "You won't be part of what I'm doing."

"Then don't just wash my feet, Lord," said Peter. "Wash my hands and my head, too!"

Jesus said, "People who had a bath only need to wash their feet. The rest of their body is already clean. So you're clean now. But not all of you are clean." Jesus knew which friend had turned against him. He was talking about this person's heart.

Jesus finished washing his friends' feet. Then he went back to his place. "Do you understand what I just did?" he asked. "You call me Teacher. You call me Lord. That's right. That's what I am. Your Lord and Teacher just washed your feet. So you need to wash each other's feet. I'm showing you the way to treat others. The master is always greater than the servant. The person who sends a message is greater than the one who takes the message. Look at what you know now. God will bring good to you if you do what you know."

WEEK 31

 Monday

Dipping Into a Dish

Another interesting thing happens in the following story. When Jesus is talking about who is going to betray Him, He says it's the one who ate from the bowl with Him. One of the superstitions of the ancient Jews was that during supper, putting your hand into a dish at the same time as another person would bring bad luck. Jesus may have been hinting at the fact that things were going to turn bad very soon.

Lord, Who Is It?
Matthew 26:21-25; Mark 14:18-21; Luke 22:21-23; John 13:18-30

Then Jesus became sad. "One of you has turned against me," he said. "This will make David's psalm come true. 'The person who shares my bread has turned against me.' I'm telling you about this before it happens. Then when it happens, you'll believe that I'm God's Son."

Jesus' friends were sad. One after another they said, "I'm sure it's not me."

"It's the one who ate from the bowl with me," said Jesus. "He is the one who has turned against me. How sad it is for him. It would be better if he had never been born."

Jesus' friends looked at each other. They didn't know what he was talking about. Peter whispered to John, "Ask Jesus who he is talking about."

John moved close to Jesus. "Lord, who is it?" he asked.

"I'll dip my bread in the dish," said Jesus. "Then I'll give it to someone. He is the one I'm talking about."

Jesus dipped his bread in the dish. He gave it to Judas.

Judas took the bread. Right away, Satan took control of him. Judas said, "I'm sure I'm not the one."

"Yes, you are," said Jesus. "Do what you planned. Do it now."

No one understood why Jesus said that to Judas. But Judas was in charge of the money. So some of them thought Jesus sent Judas out to buy something. Some thought Jesus sent him to give money to poor people.

Right after Judas took the bread, he left. It was night.

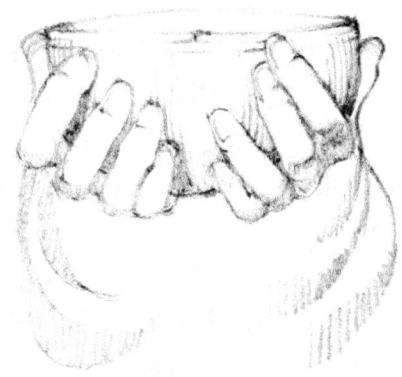

Tuesday

"My Father's House"

The father was the unquestioned authority of the family. The whole family was supposed to go along with whatever the father decided. He was the head of the household in daily matters and spiritual matters. The Greek word for the household, *oikia*, meant not only the family members, but their house, their possessions, and even the servants or slaves they might have. 'My father's house' was a common expression that meant 'my family.'

Where Are You Going?
Matthew 26:34-35; Mark 14:29-31; Luke 22:31-34; John 13:31–14:14

Judas was gone. Jesus said, "Now God is going to show his greatness in me. I'll be here a little longer. You'll look for me. But you can't come where I am going. Here's a new rule for you. Love each other like I love you. Everyone will know you're my friends if you love each other."

"Lord, where are you going?" asked Peter.

"You can't follow me," said Jesus. "You'll come later."

"Why can't I follow you?" asked Peter. "I'll even die for you."

"Peter!" said Jesus. "Satan wants to toss you around like bits of wheat. But I prayed for you, Peter. I prayed that you'll keep believing in me. Then you can help others to be strong."

"Lord, I would go to jail for you," said Peter. "I would even die for you!"

But Jesus said, "Peter, something will happen before the rooster crows today. You will say you don't know me. You'll say it three times."

"Don't worry," said Jesus to his friends. "Trust me. Trust God. There are many rooms in my Father's house. I wouldn't say that unless it was true. I'm going there to get a place ready for you. So you can be sure I'll come back for you. I'll take you with me. You know the way to the place where I'm going."

"We don't know where you're going," said Thomas. "How can we know the way?"

"I'm the way," said Jesus. "I'm the truth. I'm the life. I'm the only way to get to the Father. You know me. So you know the Father. You've seen him."

"Show us the Father," said Philip. "That will be enough for us."

"Don't you know me yet, Philip?" asked Jesus. "I've been with you such a long time. Anyone who has seen me has seen the Father. How can you say, 'Show us the Father'? Don't you believe that I'm in the Father? Don't you believe that the Father is in me? This isn't just my idea. The Father lives in me. So he gives me his ideas and words.

"You can believe me because of what I say," said Jesus. "Or you can believe because of the wonders I do. But all people who believe in me will do what I've been doing. In fact, they'll do even greater things. That's because I'm going to the Father. I'll do whatever you ask in my name. That way, I can show how great God is."

The Holy Spirit

In Hebrew and Greek, languages the Bible was written in, the word for "spirit" is the same as the word for "breath" and "wind." The word is used for our life energy, because when we are breathing air, we are alive. Breathing air into your lungs is called "in-spir-ation." So *spirit* is connected with the another meaning of inspiration: something that motivates or encourages us.

The ancient Jews saw God's Spirit as the breath of life, the breath of judgment, and the breath of grace. They believed that God's Spirit represented God in the world and brought wisdom and understanding. The Spirit could inspire prophets and writers of scripture. The Spirit was seen as a gift to people who were right with God. So people who were righteous had this special link to God through His Spirit.

In the following story, when Jesus talks about God's Spirit, He calls the Spirit "another *parakletos*." Some people say the Greek word *parakletos* means Helper. Some say Counselor. Some say Advocate. Some say Comforter. That's because the word is used in all these ways in different Greek writings. It can mean simply "someone called in to help." Or it can be used in court. The parakletos comes in to defend or support the person accused of a crime. In this sense, the parakletos is what we might call an Advocate (related to a word that means lawyer), someone who can teach, advise, and counsel.

The rabbis often said that a person's good works were his advocate before God. But the picture Jesus gives is the Holy Spirit coming from God as an advocate who lives for us and with us and in us.

Never Alone
Luke 22:35-38; John 14:15-21, 26-31

"You'll obey me if you love me," said Jesus. "I'm going to ask the Father to give you another Helper. He will be with you forever. He is God's Spirit of truth. The world can't believe that this Spirit is real. They don't see the Spirit. They don't know the Spirit. But you know the Spirit. He lives with you, and he will be in you."

Then Jesus said, "I won't leave you by yourselves. I'll come to you. In a little while, the world won't see me. But you'll see me. Because I'm alive, you'll be alive too. That's when you'll know that I'm in the Father. You're in me, and I'm in you. Know my rules. Obey me. Then I'll know you love me. The Father will love whoever loves me. I'll love them too. I'll show myself to them.

"My Father will send the Holy Spirit in my name," said Jesus. "He will help you. He will teach you everything. He will help you remember everything I've told you. I'm giving you my peace. Don't worry. Don't be afraid. I've told you what's going to happen before it happens. Then you can believe when it really does happen.

"I won't talk to you much longer," said Jesus. "Satan, the world's sinful prince, is coming. He can't hold on to me. The world has to learn that I love the Father. They have to know I'll do whatever he tells me."

Then Jesus said, "Remember when I sent you out two by two? Remember when I sent you to teach? I told you not to take a bag or shoes. Did you need anything?"

"No," they said.

"Now take a bag with you," said Jesus. "You should get a sword, too. Isaiah said, 'They treated him like a sinner.' This is coming true about me."

"We have two swords here," said Jesus' friends.

"That will be enough," said Jesus. "Let's leave now."

Gardens and Vines

In ancient times, there were not many gardens in a city. There was not enough room for gardens, except in palaces. But out in the country, everyone had a garden. These were usually plots of ground surrounded by walls or hedges. An orchard or small vineyard or olive grove might also be called a garden. The garden might grow food for a family or group, or it might be kept as a peaceful place to pray or meditate. Sometimes gardens were grown around places where graves were kept for a family. A gardener could be the owner of the garden or a person hired to plant, weed, water, and harvest.

The vine was a symbol of Israel, the Jewish people. Vines were even pictured on some of the coins before Jesus' time. In a vineyard, vines might climb into fig and other fruit trees. They also trailed along the ground. After the vine flowered, the gardener might trim it. Trimming made the branches stronger so the vine would produce more fruit. Even so, some branches on a grape vine held fruit, some did not. The branches that didn't bear fruit were clipped off so all the nourishment would go to the grapes on the other branches.

The woody vine that was trimmed off was too soft to be used for anything. In fact, people were supposed to bring wood to the temple at certain times of the year for the offerings on the altar. But they were not allowed to bring the soft wood from a vine. Vine wood was good for nothing except to be thrown away.

The Vine
Matthew 26:30; Mark 14:26; Luke 22:39; John 15:1-11

Jesus and his friends sang a song. Then they headed for Olive Mountain.

"I'm like a vine," said Jesus. "You are like the branches. My Father is the one who takes care of the garden. He cuts off the branches that don't grow fruit. He trims the branches that do grow fruit. That way they will grow even more fruit.

"So stay in me," said Jesus. "Then I will stay in you. Branches can't grow fruit by themselves. They have to stay on the vine. You'll grow a lot of fruit if you stay in me. You can't do anything without me. So what happens if you don't stay in me? You're like a broken branch. It dries up and gets thrown away. Then it gets burned up in the fire. Stay in me, and let my words stay in you. If you do that, you can ask for anything you want. And it will be given to you.

"Be like a branch that grows lots of fruit," said Jesus. "Show everyone that you are my followers. Then people will see what my Father is like. They will see how great my Father is. I love you the way my Father loves me. Stay in my love. You do this by obeying me. That's how it is with my Father and me. I obey my Father's rules. I stay in his love. I've told you this so you can have joy. The joy that I have will be in you, too."

 Friday

Trouble in the Ancient World

Jesus was very honest with His followers. He said they would have trouble in this world. But what kind of trouble would Jesus' followers have run into in His ancient world? Put yourself in their place.

1. Silversmiths earn lots of money by making and selling silver idols. But now that you and your friends are Christians, you don't buy silver idols anymore. The silversmiths are angry, because they are losing money. They are out to get you.

2. The Roman emperor sees himself as the highest power, the Lord. The common way to praise him is to say, "Caesar is Lord." But now you and your Christian friends are telling everyone, "Jesus is Lord." It sounds like you are against the emperor.

3. When a leader of a rebel group is caught and killed, his followers are usually tracked down and killed too. Jesus was crucified. You are one of his followers.

4. Your Roman family worships many gods. But you believe in Jesus. Your family thinks you are crazy. Your father will lose his job working for the governor if it is known that you claim Jesus, not the emperor, to be Lord. So your family disowns you.

The Rule
John 15:12-16; 16:7-8, 20-33

"This is my rule," said Jesus. "Love each other like I love you. There is one thing that shows the greatest love. It's giving up your life for your friends. You're my friends if you do what I say. I'm not calling you servants anymore. I'm calling you friends. I've told you everything I learned from my Father.

"I chose you. You didn't choose me. I chose you to go out and be like a tree that grows fruit. Grow fruit for God by doing things for him that will last.

"I'm going away," said Jesus. "That's really the best thing for you. Then I can send the Helper to you. He will show the people of the world that they've sinned. He will show what it's like to be right with God.

"You'll cry while the world is happy," said Jesus. "You'll cry, but your crying will turn into joy. It's like a woman who's going to have a baby. It hurts when it's time for the baby to be born. But then the baby comes. She forgets the hurting. She is so happy that the baby is born. So now is your time to cry. But I will see you again. Then you'll be happy. No one will be able to take your joy away.

"I've been talking in stories," said Jesus. "But someday I'll tell you clearly about my Father. I came from him. Now I'm going back to him."

"You are talking clearly," said Jesus' friends. "We believe that you come from God."

"At last you believe!" said Jesus. "Soon each of you will go back home. You'll leave me all alone. But I won't really be alone. My Father is with me.

"You'll have trouble in this world," said Jesus. "But be happy! The world has lost. I have won."

WEEK 32

 Monday

More Trouble

Here are some other kinds of trouble Jesus' followers had. Put yourself in their place.

1. You are Greek. You have never been a Jew. When you became a Christian, many of the Jews who were Christians insist that you must follow Jewish traditions and live the way Jews live if you want to be a Christian. But you ask: why live like a Jew if you are not a Jew? This causes trouble between you and Jewish Christians.

2. You live near the Black Sea. There the Romans have forbidden any kind of gatherings. No clubs. No groups meeting together. Not even fire fighters can gather together. But Christians meet together anyway. If you are found out, you will be in big trouble.

3. People are spreading a rumor that Christians are superstitious. They have heard that when you eat bread, you think of Jesus' body. You drink wine and remember Jesus' blood. People begin to say that Christians are cannibals, eating bodies and drinking blood. They don't even give you a chance to explain.

4. You do not honor Rome's many gods. Now when bad things happen, the Romans think it's your fault. They think the gods are angry because Christians do not honor them. They tell you that you must honor all the gods so Rome will be blessed once more. But you will not turn away from your faith in Jesus.

5. You are used to meeting in synagogues with your Jewish friends. There are no church buildings yet. You want to gather with your old friends on holidays and Sabbaths just like you used to do. But because you believe in Jesus, they will not allow you to go into the synagogue.

Out of the World
John 17

Then Jesus looked up toward heaven. He prayed, "Father, it's time now. Show your greatness in me. Show who I am so I can show who you are. You put me in charge of all people so I could give life that lasts forever. I can give it to everyone you gave me. This life comes from knowing you and me. You are the only real God. And I'm the one you sent.

"I've shown your greatness," said Jesus. "I've done the work you sent me to do. So now, Father, show who I am. Give me the place I had with you before the world started. I've shown you to the people you gave me. They were yours. You gave them to me. They obey your word. I told them the words you told me, and they believed that you sent me. I'm praying for them.

"They're still in the world," said Jesus. "But I'm coming to you. Father, keep them safe by the power of your name. I kept them safe. Only one of them turned away. I'm not asking you to take them out of the world. I'm asking you to keep them safe from Satan.

"My prayer isn't just for them," said Jesus. "I'm praying for all people who will believe in me. I pray that they will all work together. I pray they'll work together like you and I do, Father. You're in me, and I'm in you. So let them be in us. That way, the world can believe that you sent me.

"Father, I want my friends to be with me," said Jesus. "I want them to see the greatness you gave me because you loved me. You loved me before the world was made. The world doesn't know you. But I know you. I've told them about you. I'll keep showing you to them. That way your love for me can be in them. Then I can be in them too."

 Tuesday

The Gethsemane

A gethsemane was an olive press. After harvesting his olives, the owner of the olive grove heated the olives so the oil would come out more easily. Then he crushed the olives in a round, stone crushing-mill. After crushing the olives, he put them into round baskets, which he stacked on the bed of the press (the gethsemane). Some presses used stone weights to squeeze the oil out. Others used a screw to tighten and create the pressure. Either way, the grove-owner would press his olives three times. The best oil came out the first time. The next two pressings squeezed out oil that was not quite as good. All in all, it took about twenty-four hours to do a complete pressing. The leftover crush from the olives was used as fuel.

Next door to the olive press there might be a shop selling the oil. Making olive oil was a big business. People ate olives and olive oil. But they also used olive oil as medicine and as fuel for their lamps. They rubbed olive oil over dry skin and into their hair. Olive oil was used to anoint guests.

Jesus went to a garden that we call Gethsemane. So it must have been a place where there were olive trees and an olive press. That's where He prayed the prayer in the following story. Jesus spoke Aramaic, which was much like Hebrew. The word He uses for "Father" in His prayer is "Abba," a word a child would use to call His father "daddy."

Praying in the Garden
Matthew 26:36-46; Mark 14:32-42; Luke 22:39-46; John 18:1

Jesus and his friends crossed the valley. There was an olive garden on the other side. That's where they went. The garden was called Gethsemane.

"Sit here," said Jesus. "I'm going to go pray."

Jesus took Peter, James, and John with him. "Stay here and watch," he told them.

Jesus was beginning to feel very sad. He walked just a little way from Peter, James, and John. It was close enough to throw a stone. Jesus got down on his knees. He started praying. "Father, if you will, don't let this happen," he said. "But do whatever you think is best. I want to do what you want."

Then an angel came from heaven. He helped Jesus to be strong.

Jesus was so sad. He prayed even harder. His sweat fell on the ground in big drops.

Jesus got up. He went back to his friends. They were sleeping. They were tired because they were sad too.

"Couldn't you men watch for just one hour?" Jesus asked Peter. "Watch! Pray, so you won't think about doing wrong."

Jesus went to pray again. "Father," he said. "Do whatever you think is best. I want to do what you want."

Jesus walked back to Peter, James, and John. They were sleeping again. So he walked back to pray a third time. He told God the same thing he said before.

Then he came back to his friends. "Are you still sleeping?" he asked. "It's almost time. I'm about to be given to sinful people. Get up! Let's go! Here comes the one who is showing them where I am."

Greetings

"Peace!" was a very common greeting among the Jews in Jesus' time. It still is today: "Shalom alekh hem" (Peace be with you). The usual ancient greeting was somewhat longer: "Peace be to you, and peace be to your house, and peace be to all that you have." In any case, Jews would give this greeting only to another Jew, never to someone who was not a Jew, and not to a Samaritan either.

Greeks said simply, "Charein!" which means, "Hail!" or "Greeting!" That's the word Luke, a non-Jew, uses when he writes what the angel Gabriel said to Mary.

In our recent history (in the last few centuries), a man wearing a hat was supposed to take it off when he greeted someone, as a sign of respect. We still expect men to remove their hats in many public places. But in ancient times, they would never take off their hats or head coverings. Not even when meeting a king or other ruler. Not even in the temple or synagogue. Not even in prayer before God.

In ancient Palestine, a kiss was the way to greet a teacher who was admired and respected. This is the greeting Judas gave to Jesus. It may be that Judas truly respected and admired Jesus. Maybe he hoped that bringing guards would motivate Jesus to take action and become the warrior-king Judas hoped He would be. Or it may be that the kiss was simply meant to look like the sign of respect, while it was really just a way of showing the guards who to arrest.

Judas and the Guards
Matthew 26:47-49; Mark 14:43-46; Luke 22:47-48; John 18:2-8

Judas knew where Jesus was. Jesus and his friends often went to the olive garden. So Judas led guards and officers from the worship house to the garden. It was dark. They held lamps and sticks with fire on the end.

Judas had made a plan with the worship house leaders. He had told them, "The man I kiss will be Jesus. Have the guards take him away."

So now Judas walked up to Jesus to kiss him.

Jesus said, "Judas! Are you going to turn against me by kissing me?"

Judas said, "Teacher!" Then he kissed Jesus.

Jesus knew what was going to happen. He asked the guards, "Who are you looking for?"

"We're looking for Jesus," they said.

"I'm Jesus," he said.

Everyone stepped back. Some even fell to the ground.

"Who are you looking for?" Jesus asked again.

"We're looking for Jesus," they said.

"I told you," said Jesus. "I'm the one you're looking for. Let these other men go."

Thursday

Temple Guards

The Jews did not have an army or soldiers. And the Romans never made Jews join their troops, because a Jewish soldier would do no work on the Sabbath. So he would be of no use on a march or in a battle on the Sabbath day. But Jewish men did have swords and daggers, bows and arrows, slingshots and household knives. And there were times when they rose up and fought the foreign rulers in the hopes of becoming a free nation.

There were also temple guards who were Jewish. Their job was a mix of watching the doors and gates and serving as policemen in the temple area. These temple police were the ones who came to arrest Jesus. But they were not in the habit of carrying and using weapons, and they were not trained as soldiers. So they brought Roman soldiers with them. Since it was Passover time and Jerusalem's streets were swarming with visitors, there would have been extra Roman soldiers on patrol. The Jewish leaders probably had to ask Pilate, the ruler in charge of Jerusalem, to send the Romans to help with the arrest.

We don't know how many Roman soldiers came with the temple guards. It was probably only part of a group they called a "cohort," which was six hundred men. When Jesus says he could call for God's help and thousands of angels would come, He used the word a "legion" of angels. A legion was made of ten cohorts. That would be about 6,000. So no matter how many cohorts the Romans had on their side, Jesus had legions on His.

Swinging a Sword
Matthew 26:50-56; Mark 14:47-52; Luke 22:49-53; John 18:9-11

Then the guards took hold of Jesus.

Jesus' friends saw what was happening. They asked, "Lord, should we fight with our swords?"

Peter had a sword. He pulled it out and swung it at Malchus, the high priest's servant. Peter cut off the servant's right ear.

"Put your sword back," said Jesus. "People who fight with swords die by swords. Don't you know? I could call out to my Father. Thousands of angels would come and do whatever I asked. But this is what is supposed to happen. So no more fighting."

Then Jesus touched Malchus's ear. Malchus was well again.

Jesus talked to the officers and guards. "Am I leading people against you? You've come after me with swords and clubs. I was at the worship house every day. You didn't even touch me. Of course, you do your work after dark."

Then the guards and officers took Jesus. They also held on to a young man. He had been with Jesus. The young man was wearing just a cloth around him. But he ran away. He left his cloth behind and ran away with no clothes. All of Jesus' other friends ran away too.

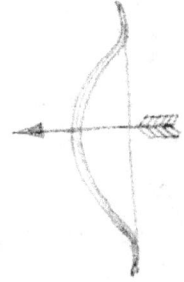

Friday

A Trial

The Jewish laws said that there had to be witnesses at a trial, especially if the person on trial was going to be given the death penalty. But instead of asking for witnesses, the high priest began asking for details from Jesus Himself. It was not considered fair for a person to condemn himself to death. That is probably why Jesus reminded the high priest that he should be asking other witnesses to answer his questions.

Before the High Priest
Matthew 26:57-63; Mark 14:53-61; Luke 22:54-57; John 18:12-23

The guards tied up Jesus. They took him to the high priest's house. Peter and John followed. John knew the high priest. So he went into a fenced yard with Jesus. Peter had to wait outside by the gate. Later, John came back. He talked to the girl who was in charge. She let him bring Peter inside the yard.

The high priest was asking Jesus questions about his followers. He asked about what Jesus taught.

"All my teaching has been done where anyone could hear," said Jesus. "I've told it to the whole world. I taught at worship places where God's people gather. I didn't teach anything in secret. So why do you ask these questions? Ask the people who heard me. They know what I said."

One of the Jewish officers was standing close to Jesus. He hit Jesus' face. "Is that how to answer the high priest?" he asked.

"Did I say something wrong?" asked Jesus. "Tell me what it was. Why did you hit me if I'm telling the truth?"

There was a fire in the middle of the big fenced yard. Peter sat down there. A servant girl saw him sitting in the fire light. She looked at him very closely. "This man was with Jesus," she said,

"I don't even know him," said Peter. He got up and went out to the gate.

The Jewish leaders were looking for something wrong that Jesus had done. They wanted a reason to kill him. But they couldn't find anything wrong. Lots of people said he had done wrong, but they were lying. They didn't agree with each other.

Then somebody stood up to talk. "Jesus said he would tear down this worship house. He said he would build another one in three days. He said it wouldn't be made by man." Even then the people couldn't agree.

The high priest turned to Jesus. "Aren't you going to answer?" he asked. "What are these people saying about you?"

Jesus was quiet. He didn't say a word.

WEEK 33

 Monday

Cockcrow

Jesus told Peter that before the cock crowed, Peter would deny three times that he knew Jesus. Some people believe that Jesus was talking about a real cock crow, a real rooster. They point out that roosters first crowed about midnight, then again about three in the morning. They say that the Roman guards depended on the sound of the rooster to signal when it was time for one set of guards to go off duty and another set of guards to take their place on patrol.

Other people say that cockcrow was what the Romans called the blast of a horn they blew when it was time for one set of guards to go home and another set of guards to watch the city. It signalled a change of shifts.

So maybe a real rooster crowed. Or maybe horns blew the cockcrow. Maybe both. At any rate, before the guards changed shifts, Peter had denied that he knew his best friend.

When we think about Jesus' pain, we usually think of the soldiers making fun of him and the physical pain of being beaten and nailed to the cross. But there was another pain Jesus felt. It's the pain you feel when people who are supposed to be your best friends betray you, leave you, and deny they know you.

The Rooster Crows
Matthew 26:63-75; Mark 14:61-72; Luke 22:58-65; John 18:25-27

"Are you the one God promised to send?" the high priest asked Jesus.

"I am," said Jesus. "Someday you'll see. I'll be sitting at God's right hand. You'll see me coming on the clouds of heaven."

"Do we need to hear any more?" asked the high priest. "You heard him. What do you think?"

Everybody said Jesus should die.

The guards around Jesus began to make fun of him. They covered his eyes. They began to beat him. Then they said, "Tell us who is hitting you." They laughed at him.

An hour passed. The people standing around Peter looked at him. "We're sure you're one of Jesus' followers!" they said. "We can tell by the way you talk."

"I don't know the man," said Peter.

One of the high priest's servants was from Malchus' family. Malchus was the man whose ear Peter had cut off. This servant looked at Peter. "Didn't I see you with Jesus in the olive garden?"

"Man, I don't know what you're talking about," said Peter.

Right then, while Peter was talking, the rooster crowed. Jesus turned and looked at Peter.

Then Peter remembered what Jesus had told him. Jesus had said, "Something will happen before the rooster crows today. You'll say you don't know me. You'll say it three times." Then Peter went outside and cried hard.

  Tuesday

Blood Money

As we have seen, the temple had several walled-in areas, courtyards with stone floors and no roofs. Picture Judas with a bag of coins in his hand, glaring straight ahead, striding through the huge outer courtyard where non-Jews could go. He marches on into the courtyard where only Jews, men and women, were allowed, and he strides straight into the courtyard where only Jewish men could go. Beyond that was the area for priests only. Judas yells for the priests. He demands that they take back the thirty silver coins. But they refuse. He throws the money at them and storms out.

The priests gathered up the coins, but they would not put the money back into the temple treasury, because Judas' coins were what they called "blood money," a payment to have someone murdered. But here they were, holding blood money. So they bought a field with it. The field was named "Akeldama," which is Aramaic, the common language, for "field of blood."

The Son of God
Matthew 27:1, 3-10; Mark 15:1; Luke 22:66-71

The sun began to rise. The leaders at the worship house had a meeting. They brought Jesus in. They said, "If you are the Promised One, then tell us."

"I could tell you," said Jesus. "But you won't believe me. From now on I'll be sitting by God's right hand."

"Then are you God's Son?" they asked.

"You're right," said Jesus.

"We don't need to have others tell about him," they said. "We've heard it now from his own mouth." Then they were sure of their plans to have Jesus killed.

Judas saw that the leaders really were going to kill Jesus. He understood what was happening, and he was sorry. He took the 30 silver coins back to the leaders at the worship house. "What I did was not right," he said. "I turned against a man who didn't do anything wrong."

"So what?" the Jewish leaders said. "That's your problem."

Judas threw the money into the worship house. He left. Then he went and killed himself. He hung himself on a tree.

The leaders picked up the money Judas had thrown down. "We can't put this back into the money box," they said. "It was money paid to kill a man." So they used the money to buy the potter's field.

The potter's field became a grave yard. Graves were made there for people from other lands. Then the field was called "Blood Field." That made Jeremiah's words come true. He had said, "They took the 30 silver coins. It was the price God's people sold him for. They used the coins to buy the potter's field."

Wednesday

Pilate

The emperor of Rome was the highest ruler of the Roman empire, but there were kings over different areas. When Jesus was born, the family of Herods had been ruling as kings in Palestine. The Herods called themselves Jews, but they were not from Palestine at all; they were from Edom. In Edom, they had married non-Jews, so their family line was not considered to be pure. Besides, their family was full of fighting and jealousy. As we saw earlier, Herod the Great had killed one of his wives and had executed three of his sons and anyone else he considered a threat to his throne. A common saying was, "It is safer to be Herod's pig than Herod's son."

By the time Jesus was grown, that Herod the Great had died. But his grandson, also named Herod, was the ruler in Galilee. The Romans no longer trusted Herod's family with the country around Jerusalem, so they sent a "procurator" to be in charge of Judea. He was called a procurator, because he was supposed to procure (get) whatever Rome needed or wanted from the land he was assigned to.

Pilate seemed to be weak. It seems that he hated the Jews. On the other hand, it appears that he was afraid of them, because they could easily write to the emperor, Caesar, and accuse Pilate of wrongdoing. So Pilate sent Jesus to Herod, obviously hoping to pass the problem of Jesus on to Herod. It didn't work.

Not Allowed to Kill
Matthew 27:2, 11-14; Mark 15:1-5; Luke 23:1-12; John 18:28-38

The Jewish leaders took Jesus to Pilate. He was the Roman leader in charge of the people in Jerusalem. It was early in the morning now. Pilate was not Jewish. So the Jewish leaders would not go into his palace. If they went in, they could not eat the Passover dinner.

So Pilate came out to them. "What did this man do wrong?" he asked.

"This man has turned against our whole nation," they said. "He tells us we should not pay taxes. He says he is the one God promised to send. He says he is a king."

"Take him yourselves," said Pilate. "Judge him by your own law."

"We are not allowed to kill anybody," the Jewish leaders said.

Pilate went back into his palace. He asked Jesus, "Are you really the King of the Jews?"

"Do you really want to know?" asked Jesus. "Or did someone else tell you to ask?"

"Am I Jewish?" Pilate asked. "Your people and leaders brought you here. I'm telling you what they told me. What have you done?"

"I have a kingdom," said Jesus. "But it's not from this world. If it were, my servants would be fighting right now. I would not have been caught by the Jewish leaders. But my kingdom is from a different place."

"Then you are a king?" asked Pilate.

"Yes," said Jesus. "That's why I was born. That's why I came to the world. I came to show the truth. Anybody who wants truth will listen to me."

"What is truth?" Pilate asked. Then he went back out to the Jews. "I see no reason to blame this man for anything," he said.

But the leaders from the worship house kept blaming Jesus.

Jesus would not say anything to answer them.

"Don't you hear what they say about you?" asked Pilate.

Jesus still said nothing. Pilate was surprised.

The leaders kept saying, "This man is fooling the people. He gets them to follow him. He started in Galilee. Now he has come all the way down here."

King Herod was the Roman leader in charge of Galilee. So Pilate thought maybe Herod should question Jesus. Herod happened to be in Jerusalem at that time.

Herod had heard about Jesus. He had wanted to see him for a long time. He hoped he could see Jesus do a wonder. So he was happy to see Jesus. He asked Jesus lots of questions. But Jesus would not answer him.

The Jewish leaders were standing there. They were telling Herod that Jesus had done wrong things. So Herod's guards made fun of Jesus. They put a king's robe on him. Then they sent Jesus back to Pilate. Herod and Pilate had been enemies. But that day, they became friends.

 Thursday

Dreams

In the ancient world, dreams were taken very seriously. Dreams were treated as if they were reality. The dreams of a common person were thought to be important only to them. But the dreams of an important person, like a king or prophet, were considered to be important for a whole people-group or nation, or even the world. When people had a big decision to make, it was not uncommon for them to go to a temple or other holy place and sleep there, hoping to have a dream that would guide them.

Some people, like the Egyptians and ancient Assyrians, wrote "dream books" in which they copied down different dream symbols and their meanings. Using these books, they would try to tell important people what their dreams meant. They thought if you ignored a dream of warning, you would face disaster.

Even sea captains made their decisions about whether to set sail or not based on dreams. If someone dreamed of an anchor, that was a bad sign. A dream about goats meant there would be high waves and a storm. If the goats in the dream were black, the waves would be tremendously huge. Dreams about bulls or boars also meant there would be storms, and if these animals attacked someone in the dream, that meant there would be a shipwreck. Owls and night birds in a dream meant there would be an attack by pirates. Danger was also signaled by the presence of gulls and other sea birds. But if you dreamed about walking on water or flying on your back, that was good news. Your journey would go well.

A Dream
Matthew 27:15-23; Mark 15:6-14; Luke 23:13-23; John 18:39-40

Now Pilate's wife sent him a message: "Don't have anything to do with Jesus. He hasn't done anything wrong. I had a dream about him, and it made me feel terrible."

So Pilate called the Jewish leaders together. He said, "You brought this man to me. Maybe he upset the people. Maybe he got people to follow him. But I talked with him. I can't find that he has done anything wrong. Herod didn't find that he had done anything wrong. Herod sent him back to us. Jesus hasn't done anything he should be killed for. So I will have some men beat him. Then I will let him go."

Every year, Pilate set someone free from jail. This person was always someone the people asked for.

"How about the King of the Jews?" asked Pilate. "Shall I let him go free?" He was talking about Jesus. He knew why the worship house leaders had brought Jesus to him. They wished people would follow them instead of Jesus.

These leaders got the crowd upset. They told the people to ask for Barabbas instead. So the crowd shouted, "No! Not Jesus! We want Barabbas! Take Jesus away! Set Barabbas free! Give Barabbas to us!"

Now Barabbas had made lots of people turn against the king. His followers had even killed people in their fights. That's why Barabbas was in jail.

"Then what should I do with Jesus?" asked Pilate.

"Kill him!" they cried.

"Why?" asked Pilate. "What has he done that's so bad?" Pilate wanted to let Jesus go.

The crowd just shouted, "Kill him! Kill him!"

Friday

A Strange Game

Ancient Roman soldiers often played games of dice. In one game, they would place a game piece, a skittle, in the center of the playing board. Then they would bet on who could "complete the ceremony" first and become "king." They would take turns throwing a four-sided dice to see how many places to move the skittle. At different positions on the board, the skittle would be "robed," then "crowned," then "sceptered." Whoever completed the ceremony first called out, "King!" and won the money the others had bet. Some people think that the soldiers played this game with Jesus as a human skittle.

The King of the Jews
Matthew 27:27-30; Mark 15:15-19; John 19:1-12

The people's yelling won. Pilate had some men beat Jesus.

Then lots of Roman guards got together. They took off Jesus' clothes and put a purple robe on him. Then they made a crown out of sharp thorns and put it on Jesus' head. The guards put a walking stick in Jesus' right hand. They bowed in front of him. "Here's the King of the Jews!" they called. They spit on him. They took the stick he held and hit him on the head with it. They hit him again and again.

Pilate went back out to talk to the Jewish leaders. "Look," said Pilate. "I'm bringing this man out to you. I don't see any reason to kill him."

Pilate brought Jesus out. He was wearing the crown of sharp thorns and the purple robe. Pilate said, "Here's your man."

As soon as the leaders saw Jesus, they shouted, "Kill him! Kill him!"

"You kill him yourselves," said Pilate. "I can't find a reason to kill him."

The Jewish leaders would not change their minds. "We have rules," they said. "Our rules say he has to die, because he said he was God's Son."

Pilate really got scared now. He went back into his palace. "Where are you from?" he asked Jesus.

Jesus didn't answer.

"You won't talk to me?" asked Pilate. "Don't you know I have power? I can set you free or kill you."

Jesus looked at Pilate. "You have power only because God gave it to you."

From then on, Pilate tried to set Jesus free. But the people kept shouting at him. "You're not the king's friend if you let Jesus go! Jesus says he is a king. So he is against our king!"

 Monday

Pilate's Downfall

Pilate was not the best governor Palestine had. He once built an aqueduct (an open pipeline that carried water) and paid for it with money he took from the temple treasury. The Jews got upset, of course, and started a riot. Pilate stopped the riot by sending Roman soldiers into the crowd dressed as Jews. They were able to attack and defeat the rioters.

What happened to Pilate after he sent Jesus to His death? Things went downhill for Pilate. Six years after Jesus died, there was a man in Samaria who claimed to be a prophet. This man said he knew where Moses' tabernacle and its holy vessels were buried. He led a crowd up a mountain called Gerazim to dig them up. When Pilate heard about it, he sent Roman soldiers to Samaria to break up the crowd. He told the soldiers to keep the people from digging on the mountain and send them back home. Instead, the soldiers killed all the people. Because of that, the emperor took Pilate out of office, brought him back to Rome, then banished him to Gaul (which is now France). In Gaul, Pilate killed himself.

On the Judge's Seat
Matthew 27:24-26; Luke 23:24-25; John 19:13-16

It was about six o'clock in the morning. It was the day for getting ready for Passover week. Pilate brought Jesus out. Then Pilate sat on the judge's seat. It was at a place called the Stone Pavement. "Here's your king," said Pilate.

"Take him away!" the people called. "Take him away and kill him!"

"You want me to kill your king?" Pilate asked.

"We have just one king. That's Caesar," they said.

Pilate could see he wasn't getting anywhere with the people. Instead, the people were getting louder and louder. So Pilate got some water. He washed his hands in front of the people. "Nobody can blame me for killing him," said Pilate. "I will have nothing to do with it. You are the ones choosing this."

"That's fine," said all the people. "We will take the blame."

So Pilate gave them what they wanted. He let Barabbas go free, and he gave Jesus to them so they could have him killed.

Tuesday

Crucifixion

For most crucifixions, the prisoner would walk through the streets surrounded by four soldiers. Another soldier went in front, carrying a sign on which the prisoner's crime was written. For Jesus, the sign said, "King of the Jews." The soldiers always led the prisoner the long way through the streets to let as many people as possible see him. It was a way to warn the people not to do whatever the prisoner had done.

When they reached the hill outside town, the soldiers laid the cross on the ground and nailed the prisoner's hands and feet to it. Then they raised it up. Sometimes the prisoner's hands were nailed to the cross beam, which was raised to a post that was already waiting there. The feet were then nailed in place. The soldiers would also nail the prisoner's sign to the cross.

The cross wasn't really very tall. But it was a terrible way to die. No one knew how long it would take to die as they tried to breathe, slowly dying of hunger and thirst as well. Many men died cursing the soldiers and other enemies. But Jesus said the most amazing thing on the cross: "Father, forgive them."

A group of women brought drugged wine to every crucifixion and offered it to every dying man. On the cross, Jesus was offered wine drugged with myrrh to help dull the pain.

Skull Hill
Matthew 27:31-34, 38; Mark 15:20-23; Luke 23:26-34; John 19:17-18

The guards made fun of Jesus. Then they took the purple robe from him. They put his own clothes back on him. They took him out to kill him on a cross. But they made him carry his own cross.

A man named Simon was walking along the road. He was on his way to Jerusalem from the country. The guards stopped Simon. They made him carry the cross for Jesus.

They took Jesus to a place called Skull Hill. Lots of people followed Jesus there. Some women were there, crying for him.

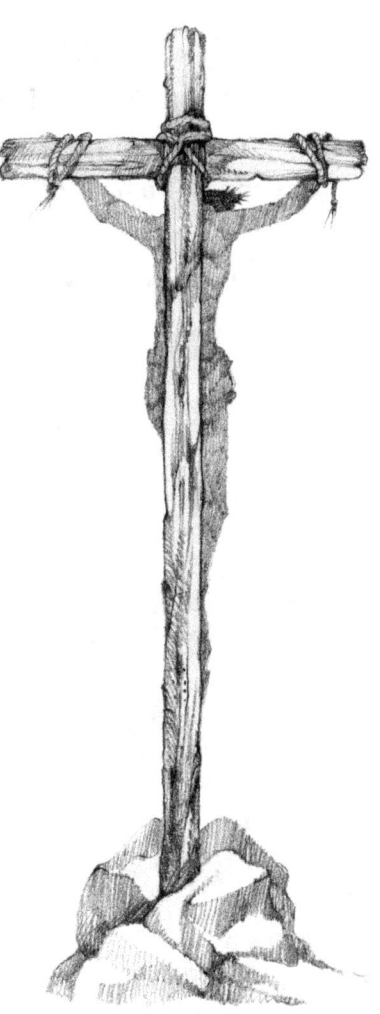

"Don't cry for me," Jesus said. "Cry for yourselves and your children. Someday you'll tell the mountains, 'Fall on us!' You'll tell the hills, 'Cover us!' If people do bad things when times are good, what will happen when times are bad?"

Two other men were going to be killed that day. They had done many wrong things. The guards took them to be killed with Jesus. They all came to Skull Hill. There they nailed Jesus and the two other men to crosses. One man was on Jesus' right side. The other man was on his left side. It was nine o'clock in the morning.

"Father, forgive the people who are doing this," said Jesus. "They don't know what they're doing."

People tried to give Jesus wine with something bitter in it. But he wouldn't drink it.

Three Languages

As we saw, Pilate ordered the sign "King of the Jews" to be written in the three main languages people read and spoke in ancient Palestine: Hebrew, Latin, and Greek. Pilate must have wanted everyone to be able to read it. The Jewish leaders had pushed Pilate into handing down the death sentence. So Pilate may have used the sign to mock the Jews and aggravate them.

A Sign in Three Languages
Matthew 27:35-37; Mark 15:24-27; Luke 23:34; John 19:19-24

Pilate told someone to make a sign and put it on Jesus' cross. The sign said, "Jesus of Nazareth. The King of the Jews." The sign was written in three languages: the Jews' language, Latin, and Greek. Many people read the sign, because Jesus was killed close to the city.

The Jewish leaders said, "Don't write 'The King of the Jews.' Write that he said he was King of the Jews."

"The sign is already written," said Pilate. "That's the way it will stay."

The four guards who killed Jesus took his clothes. Each guard got one thing. But his long shirt was left. It was all one piece of cloth, top to bottom. There was no line on the cloth because nothing had been sewn together. So the guards said, "Don't tear the shirt. Let's roll dice for it. Let's see who wins the shirt."

This made one of the psalms come true. "Each one took part of my clothes. They rolled dice for them." That's just what the guards did.

 Thursday

Crosses

We don't know what kind of wood the cross was made of. The land around Jerusalem is naturally dry, and there were not a lot of trees. Jesus, and Simon who helped him, probably carried only the horizontal "arm" beam to the hill. The upright part of the cross may have already been waiting on the hill. The upright may have been a post used over and over again for crucifixions. Or it may have been a living tree trunk.

It was hard for a crucified person to breathe properly on the cross. So it must have been hard to talk. Jesus didn't say much. When He did speak, people probably paid attention to see what this teacher would say.

Close to the Cross
Matthew 27:39-44; Mark 15:29-32; Luke 23:35-37, 39-43; John 19:25-27

People passed by the crosses. They yelled bad words at Jesus. Some of them shook their heads. "You were going to tear down the worship house," they yelled. "You said you would build it again in three days! So why don't you save yourself! Come down from the cross if you're God's Son!"

The leaders of God's people made fun of Jesus too. "He saved other people," they said. "Why can't he save himself? Is he truly the King of God's people? Then let him come down from the cross. We'll believe in him if he does. He trusts in God. Let God save him now. After all, Jesus said he is God's Son."

The guards made fun of Jesus too. They asked him if he wanted some sour wine. They said, "If you're the Jews' king, save yourself."

One of the men being killed made fun of Jesus. "Aren't you the Promised One?" he asked. "Then save yourself and us, too!"

The other man being killed got mad at the first man. "Aren't you afraid of God?" he asked. "You are going to die too! This is happening to us because we've done wrong. We're getting what was coming to us. But Jesus didn't do anything wrong. He shouldn't be killed." Then the man said, "Jesus! Remember me when you get to your kingdom."

"You will get to be with me in heaven today," said Jesus.

Jesus' mother stood close to the cross. His aunt was there too. Another Mary and Mary Magdalene were also there. Jesus looked out. He saw his mother and his friend John. "Dear woman!" Jesus said to his mother. "John will be like your son now."

"Take care of her," he told John. "Care for her like you'd care for your own mother."

After that, John let Jesus' mother stay at his house. He took care of her.

Friday

The Temple Veil

The Holy of Holies, or Most Holy Place, was the most important and honored room in the temple. In Solomon's time, it contained the ark box that held the tablets of the Ten Commandments. People said that when God visited earth, He actually lived in the Holy of Holies. In Jesus' time, the Holy of Holies was completely empty. (No one knows exactly what happened to the ark box.) But people still thought God came into that room in His power.

A double curtain (sometimes called a veil) hung over the door that led to the Holy of Holies. The room had no windows. Only the High Priest was allowed to go in. Even then, he entered only once a year on the Day of Atonement, the same day the goat was released into the desert to carry away the sins of the people.

When Jesus died, the curtains that hung over the doorway to the Holy of Holies tore in half from top to bottom. The ceiling of the Temple was about forty-five feet high, taller than seven six-foot-tall men standing on top of each other. So this curtain was not short. No one could have reached the top. No person could have torn it from top to bottom. So even as Jesus died, God gave the Jews a vivid word picture that showed He is not kept in a small room. He lives among us. Both Jesus' life and His death opened the way into the very presence of God.

Open Graves
Matthew 27:45-54; Mark 15:33-39; Luke 23:44-48; John 19:28-30

Around noon, the sky grew dark. Darkness covered the land until about three o'clock in the afternoon. Then Jesus cried out, "My God, my God, why did you leave me?"

"He is calling for Elijah!" said some of the people.

Jesus knew his time on earth was finished. "I'm thirsty," he said.

Right away, someone ran to get a cloth. He got it wet with sour wine. Then he put it on a stick. He held it up to Jesus so he could drink.

"Leave him alone," said the other people. "Let's see if Elijah will come and save him."

Jesus drank some of the sour wine. Then he said, "It's finished!" He cried out in a loud voice. He said, "Father, I give my spirit to you." Then he bowed his head. And he died.

Inside the worship house, a big, long cloth hung in front of the Most Holy Place. It kept people out of that room. But at the moment Jesus died, it tore in half. The tear started at the top. It ripped all the way down to the bottom.

The earth shook. Rocks broke. Graves came open. Dead people came back to life. These were people who had done right while they lived. Their bodies came out of the graves. They went into the city of Jerusalem. Lots of people saw them.

The guards saw the earth shake. They were scared. "He really was God's Son!" they said.

Other people felt very sad. They pounded their chests and walked away.

WEEK 35

 Monday

Preparing for Burial

Jesus' body was prepared for burial in the typical way of Jews in ancient Palestine. As we learned in the story of Lazarus' death, the usual grave was a cave or cave of rooms cut into a rocky cliff. A rich man named Joseph provided a grave for Jesus. Nicodemus, the Jewish leader who had come to see Jesus at night, helped Joseph. They probably carried Jesus' body to the grave on a stretcher. In the grave, they laid Him on a bench cut in the rock.

Nicodemus brought aloe and myrrh to use in Jesus' shroud. There are many kinds of aloe plant, all with thick leaves that contain sap. The most common aloe for us is aloe vera. But Nicodemus probably used a different kind, one that was very fragrant. He brought 75 pounds of aloe and myrrh to wrap in Jesus' grave clothes. That much spice would have been very expensive. If you had been inside the tomb when Nicodemus and Joseph placed Jesus' body in there, you would have noticed the air in the cave growing heavy with the smell of the spices.

The Grave
Matthew 27:57-61; Mark 15:42-47; Luke 23:50-56; John 19:31-42

The next day was a special worship day, and the Jews didn't want bodies left on crosses. They asked Pilate if they could break the men's legs. Then they could take them off the crosses.

The guards broke the first man's legs. Next they broke the legs of the other man with Jesus. Then they came to Jesus. But he was already dead. So they didn't break his legs. Instead, a guard put a spear into Jesus' side. Blood and water flowed out. This happened so the words of the psalm would come true. "None of his bones will be broken." It was like Zechariah said. "They will look at the one they hurt with a spear."

A man who saw this told about it. He knew the truth and told it so you can believe.

Evening came. A man named Joseph went to see Pilate. Joseph was a Jewish leader. But he was watching for God's kingdom. He was brave. He asked Pilate if he could have Jesus' body.

Pilate was surprised to hear that Jesus was already dead. He called for the man in charge of the guards. He asked if it was true. Was Jesus already dead?

The man in charge said Jesus was dead. So Pilate said Joseph could take Jesus' body.

Nicodemus went with Joseph. Nicodemus was the man who once came to see Jesus at night. He and Joseph took 75 pounds of spices with them. They took Jesus' body. They covered the body with spices. Then they put clean cloth all around the body. This was the Jewish way to get a body ready. Then they put Jesus' body in Joseph's own new grave cut out of rock in a garden. They rolled a big stone in front of the opening. Then they left.

The women who had come with Jesus from Galilee followed Joseph. They saw the grave. They saw how Jesus' body was put inside. Then the women went home. They, too, got some spices ready for Jesus' body. But then they had to rest. It was the worship day. The Law said they had to rest on the worship day.

Tuesday

Sealing Tombs

In Jesus' time, each important man had his own seal with his name or personal design on it. When you sent a letter, you rolled or folded it, placed a drip of wax across the edge to seal it closed, then stamped the soft wax with your seal. The unbroken seal showed who sent the letter as well as showing that no one had opened it.

In most ways, the grave where Jesus' body was laid was a very typical grave. In another way, it was not. Most graves were not guarded by Roman soldiers. But not only was Jesus' grave guarded, it was also sealed. That probably means a cord was stretched across the stone and attached to the rock walls on each side with clay. The clay was then stamped with some emblem of Rome. Anyone trying to move the stone and get into the tomb would have to break the seal. If someone tried to open the sealed tomb, they would be committing a crime against Rome.

Angels
Matthew 27:62–28:8; Mark 16:1-8; Luke 24:1-3; John 20:1

Some of the Jewish leaders went to talk to Pilate. "We remembered something," they said. "Before Jesus died, he said he would come back to life after three days. He was lying. But send some guards over to his grave. Tell them to make sure the grave stays closed. We don't want Jesus' friends to take his body. Then they would tell everyone he came back to life again. That would be a bigger problem for us than before."

"All right," said Pilate. "Take some guards. Make sure no one takes the body."

Guards went to the grave. They made sure the stone was in place in front of the opening to the grave. They sealed the stone so people would see that the grave had stayed closed. Then the guards stood by the grave.

The next day was the first day of the week. As the sun came up, the earth began to shake. An angel came down from heaven, went to the grave, and rolled away the stone at the opening. Then he sat on it. The angel looked like lightning. His clothes were as white as snow.

When the guards saw the angel, they were so afraid, they shook. They fell down and looked like they were dead.

Mary Magdalene, another Mary, and Salome left for the grave. They started on their way right after the sun came up. They carried spices to put on Jesus' body. But they wondered, "Who will roll the stone away from the opening of the grave for us?"

When they got to the grave, they saw the stone rolled away. So they went in.

A young man in a white robe was sitting there. The women were surprised and scared.

"Don't be afraid!" said the young man. "You're looking for Jesus, who was killed. But he is not here. He is alive again. You can see the place where he was. But don't stay here. Go tell Peter and Jesus' other friends what happened. Tell them Jesus is going to Galilee. They can see him there. Say that it's just the way Jesus told them it would be."

The women were shaking. They didn't know what to think. They left in a hurry. At first, they didn't tell anybody what had happened. They were too scared.

☐ Wednesday

Witness of a Woman

Remember that in Jesus' time, women did not normally eat with men, but stood aside and served while men ate at the table. Women sat separate from men when they gathered at the synagogue. They could not go into the inner court, the men's courtyard, at the temple, which was close to the main building. Rabbis did not have women disciples, at least no rabbi but Jesus.

So it is very interesting that the first witnesses to Jesus' missing body were women. Mary Magdalene ran to tell Peter about it. John was with Peter, and they may not have taken her word for it. After all, it was still early in the day (the word used for "early" technically meant the last watch of the night, between three and six a.m.). The grave may have been dim in early-morning shadows. So Peter and John may have thought Mary was mistaken. In any case, they ran to see for themselves.

When Peter stepped into the tomb, he saw something that didn't make sense. Jesus' shroud was lying there still folded, as if it still wrapped his body. But the body wasn't there. That's what the Greek words of this scripture mean. So it looked unlikely that anyone actually stole the body as Mary had thought. Who would have taken the time to unfold the grave clothes, take out the body, then fold them back neatly? Who would have taken the face cloth and folded it neatly and laid it aside? Anyone taking the body would have snatched it and run, with the body still wrapped.

Running to the Grave
John 20:2-18

Mary Magdalene went running to Peter and John. "Someone took Jesus' body out of the grave!" she said. "We don't know where they took it!"

Peter and John ran to the grave. John ran faster than Peter and got there first. But he didn't go in. He bent over and looked inside. He saw the cloth that had been around Jesus' body.

Then Peter got there. He went right in. He, too, saw the cloth lying there. He also saw the cloth that had been around Jesus' head. It was folded up and was lying by itself.

At last, John went inside. He saw the grave, and he believed. Peter and John still didn't understand. They had not known Jesus would come back to life. Peter and John went home.

But Mary Magdalene stayed there. She stood outside the grave. She cried. Then she bent over and looked inside. She saw two angels in white clothes. They sat where the body of Jesus had been. One angel sat where his head had been. The other angel sat where his feet had been.

"Why are you crying?" asked the angels.

"Someone took Jesus' body away," said Mary. "I don't know where they took it."

Mary turned and saw a man standing there. It was Jesus, but Mary didn't know it.

"Why are you crying?" asked Jesus. "Who are you looking for?"

Mary thought he was the gardener. "Did you take Jesus' body away?" she asked. "If you did, please tell me where you put it. I'll come and get it."

"Mary," said Jesus.

Mary looked at Jesus. "Teacher!" she cried.

"Don't try to hold on to me," said Jesus. "I haven't gone back to my Father yet. Go find my friends. Tell them I'm going to my Father and your Father, to my God and your God."

So Mary hurried to find Jesus' friends. "I've seen Jesus!" she said. And she told them what Jesus had said to her.

☐ Thursday

False Stories About the Empty Tomb

Remember that not only was the tomb guarded, but it was sealed. If someone tried to open the sealed tomb, they would have been committing a crime against Rome. But someone broke the seals and opened the tomb, and the body was gone. That meant the guards were in big trouble. They were so upset, they told the Jewish leaders about the empty tomb. The leaders told them to say Jesus' friends came and took the body away while they were sleeping.

But that excuse does not make any sense at all. You'll see why below. And you can read some other reasons people have given to explain the empty tomb over the years. Following each reason is an explanation for why that reason doesn't make sense.

1. <u>Nonsense</u>

   Jesus' friends came in the night and stole His body while the guards were asleep.

   <u>Sense</u>

   Jesus' friends had all run away. They were worried they would be arrested next. They would not want to add to their worries by committing the crime of breaking a Roman seal and stealing a body. If the Jewish leaders really thought Jesus' friends stole the body, why didn't they arrest them, question them, and punish them?

The soldiers were not likely to *all* fall asleep at the same time. The punishment for falling asleep on guard duty was death. They would not likely let themselves fall asleep at all. So if they were awake and Jesus' friends had come to steal the body, there would have been a big fight, which the well-armed Romans would most likely have won.

The grave wrappings were still in the tomb, but the body was gone. If Jesus' friends had really stolen the body, they would have been in a hurry. They would not have taken time to take the grave wrappings off and fold them neatly.

Jesus had taught His friends to be truthful and worthy of trust. If Jesus was not alive, they would have been lying to say He was. It would not be like them to lie that way. They *all* would have had to agree to lie. Most of them were later killed for their belief. Why would they have endangered their lives for a lie?

2. <u>Nonsense</u>

Jesus never really died, but just fainted on the cross. He woke up in the tomb and escaped.

<u>Sense</u>

Pilate sent soldiers to see if Jesus was really dead. They had crucified many men, and they knew a dead body when they saw one. One soldier stabbed Jesus' body in the side with a spear. Blood and water came out. That's a sign that a person has died.

Besides, if Jesus were still alive when He was buried, His body would have been very weak from the beatings and from hanging on the cross. He would not have been strong enough to live for three days in a cold tomb with no food and water. He would not have been strong enough to unbind His own grave wrappings or to push away the stone that blocked the door of the tomb. He would not have been strong enough to fight away the guards who guarded the tomb.

If Jesus had just fainted *and* had managed to escape from the tomb on His own, He would have looked very sick and weak and hungry when His friends saw Him. They would have had to nurse Him back to health.

The Guards' Story
Matthew 28:11-15

Some of the guards went back into the city. They told leaders at the worship house what happened. The leaders made a plan. They paid the guards lots of money to tell a lie.

The leaders made up a story for the guards to tell. "Say that Jesus' friends came while it was night and you were asleep. Say that Jesus' friends took his body away. If Pilate hears about it, we'll take care of Pilate. We'll make sure you stay out of trouble."

So the guards took the money. They said just what the leaders told them to say. They told their story to many of the Jewish people. And these people still tell that story, even today.

Friday

More Sense and Nonsense

Here are some more ways people have explained the empty tomb and some reasons for why their explanations don't make sense.

3. <u>Nonsense</u>
   The Jewish leaders moved Jesus' body.

<u>Sense</u>

If the Jewish leaders sealed the tomb and sent guards to keep the body from being taken, why would they then take the body?

If the Jewish leaders took Jesus' body, they could prove Jesus was dead by simply showing everyone the body. But they didn't. Because they didn't have a body to show.

4. <u>Nonsense</u>
   The Romans moved Jesus' body.

<u>Sense</u>

Pilate and the Romans wanted to keep the peace. So there's no way they would have taken the body. That would have stirred up trouble. Besides, if Pilate wanted to steal the body, it would have been a lot easier not to set guards or seal the tomb in the first place.

5. <u>Nonsense</u>
   Jesus didn't really come back to life. People just imagined they saw Him. (This is called "hallucination.")

   <u>Sense</u>
   Lots of people saw Jesus alive after He had been crucified. Paul wrote that at one point, 500 people saw Jesus at the same time (1 Corinthians 15:6). It's not likely that all of them imagined Jesus at the same time.

   People who imagine things like that (hallucinate) typically have big imaginations and are nervous people. It would be impossible that *all* the people who saw Jesus alive had that same kind of personality.

   Luke wrote that what he was telling about Jesus was what people not only saw but touched and heard, too. You can't touch an imaginary person.

6. <u>Nonsense</u>
   The women and Jesus' friends went to the wrong tomb.

   <u>Sense</u>
   The women were very close to the tomb when Joseph and Nicodemus put Jesus' body there. Why would they forget so quickly which tomb it was? Besides, the tomb was not a public cemetary that had lots of graves. It was a private tomb. So there would not have been many tombs to choose from. If Jesus' friends had gone to the wrong tomb, the Jews and the guards could have easily shown them the right tomb to prove that Jesus' tomb was not empty. Plus, Joseph and Nicodemus would have shown everyone the right tomb.

WEEK 36

 Monday

Night Travel

Most people didn't travel after dark, because robbers and wild animals were a greater threat at night. Some towns and villages had "street lights," which were torches set in stone holders here and there along the main streets. But there were probably no street lights on roads that went from city to city. If it wasn't cloudy and there was a bright moon, night travelers could see by moonlight. Otherwise, they usually carried torches, long poles with cloths wrapped around one end. The cloth end was dipped in oil and lit so it would burn. In the following story, two of Jesus' followers who lived in Emmaus walked back seven miles to Jerusalem. At least part of their trip was after sundown, although there was probably a full moon.

Two Friends on the Road
Mark 16:12-13; Luke 24:13-33

About seven miles from Jerusalem, there was a little town called Emmaus. Two of Jesus' friends were walking to Emmaus. They were talking about Jesus dying.

While they were talking, Jesus came up to them. But they were kept from knowing who he was. "What are you talking about?" asked Jesus.

The two friends stopped walking. They stood still. Their faces were very sad. One was Cleopas. "Are you the only person in Jerusalem who hasn't heard?" he asked. "Don't you know what's been happening there?"

"What?" asked Jesus.

"It's about Jesus," they said. "He was a prophet. What he said and did was powerful. But our leaders at the worship house had him killed. We hoped he would save our nation. Now two days have passed. It's the third day since this happened. Women from our group told us something surprising. Early this morning they went to the grave. But Jesus' body wasn't there. The women said they saw angels. These angels told them Jesus is alive! Then some men from our group went to the grave. It was just like the women said. Jesus was not there."

"You have a lot to learn!" said Jesus. "It takes you a while to believe what the prophets said. Didn't the Promised One have to go through these things?"

Then Jesus began telling them about Moses and the prophets. He made it all very clear. He told them what God's Word said about himself.

They came to the town where they were going. Jesus acted like he would travel on.

"Stay with us," said the two men. "The day is almost over."

So Jesus went to stay with them.

When they sat down to eat, Jesus picked up the bread. He thanked God for it. Then he started giving it to his friends. That's when they saw it was Jesus. Suddenly, he was gone.

The two men looked at each other. "Wasn't it wonderful when he talked on the road?" they said. "It was wonderful when he told us what God's Word meant."

They got up and hurried back to Jerusalem.

 Tuesday

Doubt

Often, when the leader of a group was crucified, all his followers would be rounded up and crucified as well. Jesus' followers had seen this happen before, and they were probably thinking *they* might be next. So they met in a locked room.

At this point, not many people had actually seen Jesus alive. There was a lot of doubt about what was going on. Doubt is not unbelief; it's "not being sure," not knowing whether you believe or not. How many of Jesus' friends doubted? All of them. Peter and John ran to the open tomb to see for themselves. The rest had a hard time believing until they saw Jesus. So they had no reason to feel like they were any better than Thomas.

Even though Thomas doubted that his friends were right, he did not stop meeting with them. Nor did Jesus say Thomas couldn't be His follower anymore. Jesus gave Thomas proof, a way to know that He was truly alive. The words of Jesus to Thomas in Greek mean "be not faithless but faithful." Jesus was saying, "Trust me. This is real."

In a Locked Room
Mark 16:14; Luke 24:33-44; John 20:19-29

Cleopas and the other follower from Emmaus found Jesus' followers. Jesus' closest friends were there too. They were together in a room with the doors locked. They were afraid of their own Jewish leaders.

"It's true," Jesus' friends said. "Jesus has come back to life. Peter saw him."

The two from Emmaus told what happened to them. They told how Jesus shared the bread. They said that's when they knew he was Jesus.

Everyone kept talking about this. Then, all of a sudden, there was Jesus. He was standing right there with them. "Be at peace," Jesus said.

They were scared. They thought they were seeing a ghost.

"Why are you scared?" asked Jesus. "Why do you wonder if I'm real? Look at my hands. Look at my feet. It's me! Touch me. See? A ghost doesn't have skin and bones like I have."

Jesus showed them his hands. He showed them his feet. They were surprised. They were full of joy. But they could hardly believe their eyes.

"Do you have anything to eat here?" Jesus asked.

They brought him some cooked fish. He ate it. "Remember when I was still with you?" said Jesus. "I told you all this would happen. Lots of things are written about me in God's Word. Moses wrote about me. The prophets wrote about me. The psalms are about me. Everything written about me has to come true. God the Father sent me. Now I'm sending you." Jesus breathed on them. "I'm giving you the Holy Spirit," he said.

Thomas wasn't there that night. Jesus' other friends told him, "We saw the Lord!"

Thomas said, "I don't believe it. I'm not going to believe. First I'd have to see the nail marks in his hands. I'd have to touch the places where the nails were. I'd have to put my hand on his side where the spear went in."

A week later, Jesus' friends were in the same locked house. Thomas was there too. Jesus came again. He stood with his friends. "Be at peace," he said.

Then he turned to Thomas. "Put your finger here, Thomas," he said. "Touch my side. Look at my hands. Stop thinking that this is just a story. Believe."

"My Lord and my God!" said Thomas.

"You believe because you see me," said Jesus. "Some people don't see me. They believe anyway. God will send good things to them."

Back to Fishing

Peter and Andrew, James and John probably still had lots of friends and family who were in the fishing business by Lake Galilee. Maybe Peter's family encouraged him to join the family fishing business again, since Jesus was no longer around. Or maybe Peter expected to see Jesus any day, but decided to pass the time doing something he felt comfortable with, something he knew he could do successfully, something at which he knew he could make some income. At any rate, Peter and some others were together fishing at night as it was common for them to do. For Peter, it may have felt, strangely, as if nothing had changed. He was back where he started.

One interesting thing about Lake Galilee is that it doesn't have any natural harbors. In the time of Jesus, the people built breakwaters and jetties out of large stones. Jesus may have set up His campfire on the shore near one of these jetties. He may have watched Peter's fishing boat out on the water for awhile. Then everything circled around to the beginning, to a time when Jesus fishermen friends had not known Him for very long, to a dawn when they had fished all night and caught nothing. Jesus called out, "Throw your net out on the right side of the boat. You'll find fish there."

That's when Peter knew truly that nothing had changed. But he was not back to where he started, he was back to Jesus. Jesus was telling him, "I'm still here."

Going Fishing
John 21:1-12

Peter, Thomas, Nathanael, James, John, and two other friends were together. "I think I'll go fishing," said Peter.

"We'll go with you," said the others. So off they went. They got into their boat and went fishing. But that night they didn't catch anything.

At last the sun began to come up. There was Jesus, standing on the shore. But his friends couldn't tell it was Jesus. "Don't you have any fish, my friends?" Jesus called to them.

"No," they called back.

"Throw your net into the water on the right side," said Jesus. "You'll find fish there."

So they threw their net over the boat's right side. Lots of fish got caught in the net. The net got so heavy, Jesus' friends could hardly pull it in.

"It's the Lord!" said John.

Peter heard John. Right away, he pulled his clothes around him. He had taken most of them off. Then he jumped into the water.

The other friends followed in the boat. They were only about 100 yards from the shore. They had the net full of fish with them.

When they got near the shore camp, they saw a camp fire with fish cooking on it. There was bread, too.

"Bring some of the fish you caught," said Jesus.

Peter climbed back into the boat. He pulled the net to the shore. The net was full. There were 153 big fish! But the net didn't break.

"Come have some breakfast," said Jesus.

Jesus' friends didn't dare ask him, "Who are you?" They knew he was Jesus.

Three Questions

The question Jesus asks Peter in the following story is actually, "Peter, do you love me more than *these*?" We don't really know what *these* are. It may be that Jesus is asking, "Do you love me more than you love anyone else?" Or "Do you love me more than my other friends do?" Or it could be that Jesus meant, "Do you love me more than you love fishing?" That would make a lot of sense, especially if Peter was thinking of going back to his old family business.

It's also interesting that Jesus asked the question three times. Peter probably got more uncomfortable each time. The third time, Peter was, as the Greek says, "distressed." He could hardly fail to understand what Jesus was getting at. Peter had denied that he knew Jesus three times. Jesus was giving Peter what we might call "do-overs," to erase his three denials by declaring his love three times. Not for Jesus' sake, but for Peter's sake. Then Jesus gave Peter a way to join Him. "Shepherd my sheep," said Jesus. Peter had heard Jesus teach that He was the Good Shepherd. Now he knew Jesus was including him as part of His shepherding plans.

Do You Love Me?
John 21:13-24

Jesus gave his friends bread and fish for breakfast. They ate it. Then Jesus turned to Peter. "Peter, do you love me more than anyone else?" he asked.

"Yes," said Peter. "You know I love you."

"Then feed my lambs," said Jesus.

"Peter, do you really love me?" asked Jesus.

"Yes," said Peter. "You know I love you."

"Then take care of my sheep," said Jesus.

Jesus asked again, "Peter, do you love me?"

Peter was upset. Jesus had asked three times, "Do you love me?"

"You know everything, Lord," said Peter. "You know I love you."

"Then feed my sheep," said Jesus. "You were younger once. You dressed yourself. You chose where to go, and you went. But someday you'll be old. Then you'll reach out your hands. Somebody else will dress you. They'll take you where you don't want to go." Jesus was talking about the way Peter would die. Then Jesus said to Peter, "Follow me."

Peter looked around. He saw John following them. "What about John?" Peter asked.

"What if I want him to stay alive? What if he lives until I come back?" said Jesus. "What does that have to do with you? You just follow me."

Now some of Jesus' followers began saying John wouldn't die. But Jesus didn't say John wouldn't die. He only said, "What if I want him to stay alive?"

John is the one who wrote this. He saw and heard these things. So we know that what he wrote is true.

☐ Friday

The "Whole World"

When Jesus told His friends to "go" into all the world, the only world they knew of was Europe, North Africa, some parts of Asia, and their own area, which we call the Middle East. Rome and Italy were at the center of the Roman Empire. Greece was central, too, and the area we know of as Turkey was nearby. West and north of Rome was the rest of what we call Europe, including Gaul (now France), Britain, Spain, and Germania (Germany and other lands). East was Palestine and Arabia, India, and China, which were linked to the west by caravan routes. South of Rome was North Africa, including Egypt. People had also traveled a bit inland into Africa and knew of Ethiopia and some of the other areas there, especially around the coast. But that was it.

Still, this area was large, and with slow travel by foot or donkey, wagon or ship, it took a long time to get anywhere. So it is amazing that within seventy years after Jesus died, His friends had helped spread His teachings through most of the known world.

Going into the Clouds
Matthew 28:18-20; Mark 16:15, 19; Luke 24:45-53; Acts 1:6-11

"I've been given the right to be in charge," Jesus told his closest friends. "I'm in charge of heaven and earth. So I tell you to go. Make followers for me in all nations. Baptize them in the Father's name, the Son's name, and the Holy Spirit's name.

Teach people to obey everything I've told you. I'll always be with you. Even to the very end of time."

Jesus helped his friends understand what God's Word meant. "It was all written down," said Jesus. "God's Word says the Promised One would die. It says he would come back to life. God's Word says people will teach about him in all nations. Then people will be sorry about their sins. They'll change their ways. They'll be forgiven. All this will start in Jerusalem. You've seen it all. You can tell about it. I'll send you the gift my Father has promised. But stay in Jerusalem for a while. Stay there until the Father gives you power."

Jesus led his special friends to a place close to Bethany. Then he lifted his hands up. He prayed for God to bring good to them.

"Is it time now?" asked Jesus' friends. "Will God's people be a kingdom again?"

"You can't know the times," said Jesus. "You can't know when things are going to happen. The Father has the plan. He is in charge. But you will get power when the Holy Spirit comes to you. You will tell people about me. You will teach about me in Jerusalem and Judea. You will teach about me in Samaria. In fact, you will teach about me all over the world."

Then Jesus went up off the ground. His friends watched until a cloud hid him. They peered up into the sky.

Suddenly, they saw two men standing nearby. The men were dressed all in white. "Men from Galilee!" said the two men. "Why are you just standing here? Why are you peering into the sky? Jesus has gone up into heaven. He will come back the same way you saw him go."

Jesus' friends worshiped him. Then they went back to Jerusalem. Their hearts were full of joy. They stayed at the worship house. They cheered for God there.

What Tradition Says About Jesus' Closest Friends

The Bible doesn't tell us much about what happened to Jesus' best friends after He went to sit at God's right hand. But here's what tradition tells us (that is, what people have told since ancient times about what they heard).

Peter: He traveled around Palestine and taught about Jesus. He was put in jail several times. He ended up in Rome, where he was crucified head down.

Andrew: He was Peter's brother. He went to preach in southern Russia near the Black Sea. He was killed on an X-shaped cross, which is now known as a "Saint Andrew's cross."

Philip: He is thought to be the brother of Nathanael. He preached in different parts of the world.
(Note: He is not the Philip who preached to the Ethiopian eunuch.)

Nathanael: He is probably same as Bartholomew. He is thought to be the brother of Philip. He preached in India and Armenia, where he died by being whipped and then beheaded.

Matthew: He is thought to be the half-brother of another apostle, James son of Alphaeus. He traveled to Ethiopia where he taught and was murdered there for his beliefs.

James, the son of Alphaeus: He is said to be the half-brother of Matthew. We don't have any record of what happened to him.

Thomas: Tradition says Thomas went to teach in India and was killed there for his faith.

Thaddaeus and Simon: Both went to preach in Persia; both were killed there for their faith.

John: Because he taught about Jesus, he was exiled, sent to an island called Patmos, where he had to stay for the rest of his life, forbidden to go back to his homeland.

James, brother of John: He went to teach in Spain. When he returned, he was the first to be killed for his faith. He was beheaded by Herod Agrippa (Note: He was not the writer of the book of James.)

We are not sure about any of these stories, but they are the best we know of what people say happened to Jesus' friends. Jesus said, "Follow me," and they did. They saw Jesus go up into the heavens, but He did not leave them alone to follow Him. He said He would be with them always. That's one of the mysterious and amazing things about God. He can be with each one of us every moment of every day for the rest of our lives through His Holy Spirit. And just as Jesus revealed God's life-giving love to us, so He wants us to reveal His life-giving love to all the world.

Sources

<u>A Visitor's Guide to the Ancient World</u>, Lesley Sims. London: Usborne, 2003.

<u>Daily Life at the Time of Jesus</u>, Miriam Feinberg Vamosh. Herzlia, Israel: Palphot, nd.

<u>Daily Life in Palestine at the Time of Christ</u>, Henri Daniel-Rops. London: Orion, 1961, 1979.

<u>Discovering the Biblical World</u>, Harry Thomas Frank. New York: Hammond, 1975.

<u>Eerdmans' Family Encyclopedia of the Bible</u>, Pat Alexander, ed. Grand Rapids: Eerdmans, 1978.

<u>The Gospel of Matthew</u>, vols. 1, 2; The Gospel of Mark; The Gospel of Luke; The Gospel of John, vols. 1, 2, William Barclay. Philadelphia: Westmister, 1975.

<u>Great People of the Bible and How They Lived</u>, G. Ernest Wright, ed. Pleasantville, NY: Reader's Digest, 1974.

<u>Greece and Rome: An Integrated History of the Ancient Mediterranean</u>, tape set, Robert Garland. Chantilly, VA: The Teaching Company, 2008.

<u>Growing Up in Bible Times</u>, Margaret Embry. Nashville: Thomas Nelson, 1995.

<u>Holman Bible Dictionary</u>, Trent C. Butler, ed. Nashville: Holman, 1991.

How They Lived in Bible Times, Graham Jones and Richard Deverell. Ventura, CA: Gospel Light, 1992.

The Interpreter's Dictionary of the Bible, George Arthur Buttrick, ed. New York: Abingdon, 1962.

Jesus and His Times, Kaari Ward, editor. Pleasantville, NY: Reader's Digest, 1987.

Lands of the Bible, Nigel Hepper. Nashville: Thomas Nelson, 1995.

The Life and Times of Jesus the Messiah: New Updated Edition, Alfred Edersheim. np: Hendrickson, 1993.

The New Evidence That Demands a Verdict, Josh McDowell. Nashville: Thomas Nelson, 1999.

www.ingramcontent.com/pod-product-compliance
Lightning Source LLC
Chambersburg PA
CBHW071953110526
44592CB00012B/1072